AF791457

Professionalism and Social Change

Lara Maestripieri • Andrea Bellini
Editors

Professionalism and Social Change

Processes of Differentiation Within, Between and Beyond Professions

palgrave
macmillan

Editors
Lara Maestripieri
IGOP/Department of Political Science and Public Law
Universitat Autònoma de Barcelona
Campus de la UAB, Bellaterra, Spain

Andrea Bellini
Department of Social and Economic Sciences (DiSSE)
Sapienza University of Rome
Rome, Italy

ISBN 978-3-031-31277-9 ISBN 978-3-031-31278-6 (eBook)
https://doi.org/10.1007/978-3-031-31278-6

© The Editor(s) (if applicable) and The Author(s), under exclusive licence to Springer Nature Switzerland AG 2023, corrected publication 2024
Chapters 1 and 10 licensed under the terms of the Creative Commons Attribution 4.0 International License ([+http://creativecommons.org/licenses/by/4.0/+]). For further details see license information in the chapter.
This work is subject to copyright. All rights are solely and exclusively licensed by the Publisher, whether the whole or part of the material is concerned, specifically the rights of translation, reprinting, reuse of illustrations, recitation, broadcasting, reproduction on microfilms or in any other physical way, and transmission or information storage and retrieval, electronic adaptation, computer software, or by similar or dissimilar methodology now known or hereafter developed.
The use of general descriptive names, registered names, trademarks, service marks, etc. in this publication does not imply, even in the absence of a specific statement, that such names are exempt from the relevant protective laws and regulations and therefore free for general use.
The publisher, the authors and the editors are safe to assume that the advice and information in this book are believed to be true and accurate at the date of publication. Neither the publisher nor the authors or the editors give a warranty, expressed or implied, with respect to the material contained herein or for any errors or omissions that may have been made. The publisher remains neutral with regard to jurisdictional claims in published maps and institutional affiliations.

This Palgrave Macmillan imprint is published by the registered company Springer Nature Switzerland AG.
The registered company address is: Gewerbestrasse 11, 6330 Cham, Switzerland

Acknowledgements

This book is part of a larger project that started in 2018 and included two special issues in scientific journals, a conference session, several conference papers and a few seminars. We laid the theoretical foundations of the project in a joint initiative, a special issue entitled *Varieties of Professionalism in a Globalising World: New Theoretical Perspectives and Analytical Approaches*, published on Cambio. Rivista sulle Trasformazioni Sociali (vol. 8: 16) at the end of 2018. Many colleagues participated in that special issue and many others have cited this work in their studies. Their sincere interest has pushed us in going further in this direction.

The book idea got its current shape at the Interim Meeting of the ISA RC52 Sociology of Professional Groups at the University of Florence, Italy, in 2019. A special workshop was organised the day before the conference involving more than twenty persons who worked with us—as editors—to develop the idea collectively. Most of them participated in a conference session on *Varieties of Professionalism. Exploring Heterogeneity Within and Between Professions.*

As a matter of fact, this book would not have been possible without the enthusiasm and commitment of all these people. There are simply too many to name here. But, we would like to name explicitly a few of them, to whom we are particularly indebted.

Special thanks are due to Karolina Parding, from the Luleå University of Technology, Sweden, who has been part of this project from the very beginning and has played a fundamental role in defining the book concept and translating it into a book proposal. Karolina Parding also contributed to further develop the project by organising a parallel initiative aimed to continue exploring the relationship between professionalism and social change, namely a special issue on *Heterogeneity among Professions and Professionals*, published on Professions and Professionalism. With her, we shared the pleasure of guest-editing this special issue.

We are extremely thankful to Sharla Plant, Editor at Palgrave Macmillan, who assisted us with the book proposal, and Saif Md and Sheetal Sharma, Project coordinators at Springer Nature, who supported us in the final steps towards publication. We also would like to thank Shilpa Baliga for her generous commitment as proof-reader: we spent days during the summer of 2022, reading each chapter over and over again, but we are very proud of the results of our "holidays'" efforts.

Finally, we would like to thank all the contributors for being with us since the very beginning and never giving up their trust in this project. This book is dedicated to you and to the amazing contribution that you give each day to the study of the professions.

Contents

Notes on Contributors

Tracey L. Adams is a professor at the Sociology Department at the University of Western Ontario in Canada. Her research focuses on the changing nature of professional work and professional regulation, in Canada and internationally. She is the author of the award-winning book, *Regulating Professions* (2018). She can be reached at tladams@uwo.ca.

Davide Arcidiacono is Associate Professor of Economic and Labour Sociology at the University of Catania. His research topics are the digital transition and the collaborative economy. He was a member of the Expert Group appointed by the European Parliament on the Directive on platform work. On these issues, he has recently published (with Duggan M.) *Sharing Mobilities: Questioning Our Right to the City in the Collaborative Economy* (2020); (with Pais I.) "Re-framing Community in the Platform Age: Analyzing Organization and Power in BlaBlaCar", in *Organizational Studies* 2/2021.

Pierre Bataille joined the Université Grenoble Alpes (UGA) as an Associate Professor of Education Sciences in 2019, after a PhD from the University of Lausanne and several postdocs in Switzerland and Belgium. His research covers sociology of education, sociology of work and professions, and sociology of culture and aims, and analyses the logics of production/reproduction of inequalities in the academic and artistic sectors.

Jean-Luc Bédard holds a PhD in Anthropology and teaches in the domain of adult education. His research work focuses on professional systems and the socio-professional integration of highly skilled immigrants, particularly in regulated professions. His research draws mainly from the sociology of professions and the analysis of professional systems and neo-institutionalism. He is a researcher at the Interuniversity Research Network on Globalization and Work (CRIMT), an associate researcher at the Centre for Research on Social Innovations (CRISES) and a researcher and Council member at the Jacques-Couture Institute (TÉLUQ University).

Andrea Bellini holds a PhD in Sociology from the University of Florence, Italy. He holds a position as Assistant Professor of Sociology of Economic and Labour Processes at the Sapienza University of Rome. His research interests include the analysis of the middle classes, the sociology of professions and industrial relations. From 2018 to 2021, he was the coordinator of the Florence research unit of the BreakBack Project (VS/2019/0079), on the impact of the supply of union services on union membership.

Isabel Boni-Le Goff is an associate professor in the Department of Sociology and Anthropology at the University of Paris 8 Vincennes Saint-Denis. She researches social theory with a focus on gender and gendered power relations, and the way they intersect with other inequalities and relations of power (i.e. class and race). She is interested in contemporary changes in expertise, professions and higher-level occupations, and she studies the interplay of different social processes, such as globalisation and feminisation.

Debby Bonnin is an associate professor and Head of the Department of Sociology (University of Pretoria, South Africa). She holds a PhD in Sociology from the University of Witwatersrand. Her research focuses on designers and the home textile sector in South Africa, as well as on professions, in particular the regulation of professions and questions of equity.

Natalie Browes is a research fellow at the Universitat Autònoma de Barcelona. She is conducting research as part of the international "ReformEd" project, where her work examines the adoption, development and enactment of school accountability policies in the Autonomous Dutch system. In particular, she focuses on the impact of test-based accountability policies on primary school teachers' beliefs and practices in different school settings.

Marta Choroszewicz (DSocSci, Docent in sociology) works as a university researcher at the Department of Social Sciences at the University of Eastern Finland. Her research focuses on the intersection between professional work, feminist theories and science and technology studies. In her research, she has extensively investigated social inequalities in professions, and the power dynamics at work in the development and deployment of data technologies in public organisations in Finland. More broadly, she has also engaged with the issues of building a digital welfare state and automated decision-making systems. She has also co-edited the book *Gender, Age and Inequality in the Professions*.

Joris Gjata is an economic sociologist who studies the design and implementation of new rules and forms of regulations in markets and industries, and their implications for inequality. Her research focuses on the emergence of new market institutions and their ability to persist through time. Through her work, Gjata highlights how the design and implementation of rules affects inequality and is shaped by power and culture. She is an affiliated researcher at the University of Colorado Boulder and an associate director of market research and brand strategy at C Space.

Christophe Groulx holds a Master's degree in Ancient Studies from the University of Montreal. He has worked as a research assistant on several projects concerning immigrant integration in Quebec and has contributed to the analysis of the roles of various actors in the entry of foreign-trained professionals into local professional practice.

Oihana Husson is a PhD student in Information and Communication Sciences at the University of Burgundy (Dijon, France) and member of the CIMEOS Laboratory. Her PhD thesis aims at understanding the professionalisation dynamics of health social media influencers and the ways they assert their expertise while raising awareness and building knowledge among their communities, as well as new social problems in the public sphere. This research is based on qualitative methods such as content analysis, digital ethnography and semi-directed interviews.

Valeria Insarauto is a junior lecturer at the University of Lausanne. She has specialised in the study of gender inequalities from a quantitative and cross-country comparative perspective. Her research interests and activities focus on women, work and employment, with a growing focus on occupations and careers, which she studies in the light of issues related to precariousness, the articulation between work and family life, and discriminations.

Anna Jansson holds a position as a senior lecturer at Luleå University of Technology in Sweden. She studies the organisation and governance of work, focusing on the nursing profession, with a specific interest in conditions for learning. She has published in journals such as *International Journal of Public Sector Management*, *Intensive & Critical Care Nursing* and *Professions & Professionalism.*

Nicky Le Feuvre is Full Professor of the Sociology of Work at the Université de Lausanne, where she is head of the 'Gender, mobility and vulnerabilities' (IP6) project at the LIVES Centre and Dean of the Faculty of Social and Political Sciences. She has conducted numerous comparative research projects on the feminisation of qualified professions (lawyers, doctors, academics, etc.) and is also interested in the gendered effects of ageing at work. She has published extensively on the implications of the entry of women into qualified occupations, from a comparative and life-course perspective.

Eléonore Lépinard is an Associate Professor of Gender Studies at the University of Lausanne. Her research is situated in the fields of feminist movements and theory, gender and law, intersectionality, and gender and politics. In recent years, she has published articles in *Politics, Groups & Identities*, *Gender & Society* and *Politics & Gender*. She is the author of *Feminist Trouble. Intersectional Politics in Post-secular Times* (2020) and co-editor with Elizabeth Evans of *Intersectionality in Feminist and Queer Movements. Confronting Privileges* (2020) and with Ruth Rubio Marin of *Gendered Citizenship. The Irresistible Rise of Gender Quotas in Europe* (2018).

Silvia Lucciarini (co)directed the "Mediterrapolis" Laboratory, funded by CNRS in collaboration with Sapienza University of Rome and Aix Marseille University from 2017 to 2021, where she explored socio-economic inequalities in urban contexts in southern Europe. She has been Professeur Inviteé at the University of Lyon, teaching comparative labour policies. She is a visiting scholar at the University of Nottingham's Global Public Procurement Lab, where she has been comparing procurement strategies and the (re)production of inequalities between direct and indirect employment. She is coordinating an EU-CIVIS project on co-production strategies.

Lara Maestripieri holds a PhD in Sociology and Social Research from the University of Trento (2011). She is a *"Ramon y Cajal" distinguished researcher* at the Department of Political Science at the Universitat Autònoma de Barcelona. She is also a member of the Analysis, Management and Evaluation of Public Policies (AGAPP) research group, through her affiliation to the IGOP (Institute of Government and Public Policy). She is the Secretary/Treasurer of the ISA RC52 "Sociology of Professional Groups" board. Her main research interests concern social change in post-industrial society, in particular: public policies and intersectionality, economic insecurity in Southern European countries, social innovation and emerging professions.

Grégoire Mallard is a professor in the Department of Anthropology and Sociology and Director of Research at the Graduate Institute of International and Development Studies (Geneva). He is the author of *Fallout: Nuclear Diplomacy in an Age of Global Fracture* (2014) and *Gift Exchange: The Transnational History of a Political Idea* (2019). He is also the co-editor of *Contractual Knowledge: One Hundred Years of Legal Experimentation in Global Markets* (2016) and *Global Science and National Sovereignty: Studies in Historical Sociology of Science* (2008). His other publications focus on prediction, the role of knowledge and ignorance in diplomacy, and the study of the harmonisation of legal regimes as a social process.

Marta Massana Macià holds a PhD in Anthropology and a Master's degree in Development and International Cooperation and specialises in the area of municipal action in immigration and intercultural relations. She is a founding member and project manager of the Groupe d'expertise pour le développement des cités interculturelles au Québec (GEDCIQ). She is affiliated with the Laboratoire de recherche en relations interculturelles de l'Université de Montréal (LABRRI) as a researcher and is an associate member of the Jacques-Couture Institute, affiliated with the TÉLUQ University. As a postdoctoral fellow at TÉLUQ University, she has also studied the integration of foreign-trained professionals in Quebec.

Marcel Pagès is a Margarita Salas postdoctoral researcher at the Universitat Autònoma de Barcelona, Department of Sociology. His research interests are education reform processes, school governance and inequalities in education.

Ivana Pais is Full Professor of Economic Sociology at Università Cattolica del Sacro Cuore. Her research interest focuses on the platform economy and digital labour. She is the director of TraiLab—Transformative Actions Interdisciplinary Laboratory at Università Cattolica del Sacro Cuore—and is the principal investigator of the WePlat project (Welfare systems in the age of platforms: drivers of change for users, providers and policy makers). Her recent publications include Stark, D. & Pais, I. (2020), "Algorithmic Management in the Platform Economy", in *Sociologica*, 14(3), 47–72.

Lluís Parcerisa is a lecturer at the Department of Teaching and Learning and Educational Organization at the Universitat de Barcelona (UB). His main research interests include the role of international organisations in the global governance of education, the datafication of schooling, and the enactment and effects of school autonomy and accountability reforms in the education sector.

Karolina Parding holds a position as Professor of Sociology at Luleå University of Technology in Sweden. Her main research interest is working conditions, for welfare sector professionals such as teachers including their conditions for learning. She has published in journals such as *Current Sociology*, *Professions and Professionalism* and *International Journal of Public Sector Management*.

Giorgio Piccitto is interested in the quantitative study of structural characteristics and changing trends in labour markets and migration, social stratification and inequality. On these issues, he has recently published (with Daniel Oesch) "The Polarization Myth: Occupational Upgrading in Germany, Spain, Sweden, and the UK, 1992–2015", in *Work and Occupations*, 2019, 46(4), 441–469 and (with Nazareno Panichella and Maurizio Avola) "Migration, Class Attainment and Social Mobility: An Analysis of Migrants' Socio-Economic Integration in Italy", in *European Sociological Review*, 2021, 37(6), 883–898.

Valeria Pulignano has worked at the Centre for Sociological Research (CESO) at KU Leuven University since 2005. She coordinated the CESO between 2013 and 2017, and from 2000 to 2005, she worked as a Lecturer at the Industrial Relations Research Unit (IRRU) at Warwick University (UK), where she is an associate fellow. She is a recipient of the ERC Advanced Grant for the 'Revolving Precariousness: Advancing the Theory and Measurement of Precariousness Across the Paid/Unpaid Continuum' (ResPecTMe) Research Project.

Shawhin Roudbari studies ways designers strive to address social problems with an emphasis on racial injustice. Through in-depth interviews, participant observation and analysing designs and texts, he investigates ways architects shape and organise power towards addressing social injustices. His work contributes to histories and theories of activism in the spatial professions and relies on ethnographic methods. He is Assistant Professor of Environmental Design at the University of Colorado Boulder.

Matthew S. Rowe is a cultural sociologist whose work explores the meaning of work in the contemporary creative economy. His dissertation examines the training and career experiences of graphic designers, animators and other digital media artists to show how potentially precarious workers bring order to unstable circumstances by learning to interpret their capacities and preferences in market terms, without sacrificing artistic identities. He is an affiliated researcher at the University of Colorado Boulder and Lecturer in Sociology at San Diego State University.

Marie Sautier is a PhD candidate in Sociology at the LIVES Centre, Université de Lausanne (CH), and at the Centre for the Sociology of

Organisations, Sciences Po Paris (FR). Her research focuses on recruitment practices and the internationalisation of research careers. She has published on academic mobility, gender inequalities and the intersection of mobility, gender and precariousness in academia. Her research interests also include equality policies and practices.

Paola Sedda is Lecturer in Information and Communication Sciences at the University of Lille (France) and is a member of the GERiiCO Laboratory. Her work adopts a critical and multidisciplinary approach and focuses on digital mobilisations and the reconfiguration of forms of political participation in the public sphere. Recently, she has also become interested in the dynamics of social influence and the politics of health issues. She has published several book chapters and articles and coordinated two thematic issues; one, published in 2017 in the *Variations* international journal of critical theory, deals with oppositional experiences. The other, published in 2022 in the *Études de Communication* journal of communication studies, deals with health influencers as figures in tension between political, market and professional rationales.

Antoni Verger is Professor of Sociology at the Universitat Autònoma de Barcelona and research fellow at the Catalan Institution for Research and Advanced Studies (ICREA). He has a cross-disciplinary background in sociology and education studies, and his research examines the relationship between globalisation, governance institutions and education policy.

List of Figures

List of Diagrams

List of Tables

1

Introduction: Within, Between, Beyond—A Multi-dimensional Approach to the Study of Professionalism and Social Change

Andrea Bellini and Lara Maestripieri

1 Professions in the Twenty-First Century: A Brief Introduction

Since the 1970s, professions have been subject to radical changes. The post-industrial transition initiated a new phase of capitalist development (see Touraine, 1969; Bell, 1973), stemming from its rupture from

The original version of this chapter was previously published non-open access. A correction to this chapter is available at https://doi.org/10.1007/978-3-031-31278-6_15

A. Bellini (✉)
Department of Social and Economic Sciences (DiSSE), Sapienza University of Rome, Rome, Italy
e-mail: andrea.bellini@uniroma1.it

L. Maestripieri
IGOP/Department of Political Science and Public Law, Universitat Autònoma de Barcelona Campus de la UAB, Bellaterra, Spain
e-mail: lara.maestripieri@uab.cat

© The Author(s) 2023, corrected publication 2024

L. Maestripieri, A. Bellini (eds.), *Professionalism and Social Change*,
https://doi.org/10.1007/978-3-031-31278-6_1

industrialism and the pre-eminence of the production of material goods. In this paradigm shift, knowledge became a strategic factor in production, and those who had control over it played an increasingly important role. Accordingly, the tertiarisation of the economy brought a rise in the number of expert occupations. Of these, the most significant groups were professions. This process, summed up by some authors as the rise of the knowledge society (see Machlup, 1962; Drucker, 1968; Bell, 1973), was associated with new configurations of the division of labour and increasing differences in economic and social conditions, all within the context of globalisation and technological change.

The outcome of this process is evidenced by three current trends that can be noted regarding expert labour and that have been accelerated by the recent crises: the financial crisis (2008–2014) and the COVID-19 crisis. First, the labour force has become more qualified. It can be observed that the crises primarily impacted low-skilled profiles, causing a decline in employment in manufacturing and construction, while employment in advanced business services grew, and a general upskilling of workers occurred—although how much this happened differed from one country to another (Gallie, 2013). Moreover, the crises intensified the process of outsourcing highly skilled services; these had once been provided in house by salaried workers and are now generally subcontracted out to specialised firms or independent professionals (see Leicht & Fennel, 2001). As a corollary, today, the number of people that define themselves as "professionals" is greater than ever. Second, conversely, not all expert occupations fit into typical professionalisation models, in the way that Reed describes them (2018, p. 307), which rely on "guild-like systems of occupational control and work organization ideologically anchored in autonomous regulation". Although this situation appears to fulfil Wilensky's (1964) prophecy, the upsurge in knowledge work has transformed what we mean by professionalism, challenging its very conceptualisation. Reed, again, spoke of "organisational/managerial" professions, which were the ones that adapted to these changes most successfully, versus "independent/collegiate" professions, which were challenged by the transformations produced (p. 307). Third, and more importantly, professional work no longer ensures prerogatives such as high earnings, autonomy, or job security. On the contrary, the professional labour force has become diversified in terms of occupations, income, status, and power.

In the background, long-term processes of differentiation are still ongoing. Globalisation has blurred the boundaries between professional systems, and boundaryless careers are becoming the norm for professionals in certain fields. Consequently, practitioners who have been socialised in different, country-based professional systems now perform their activities side by side, while professional groups struggle to establish or restore the mechanisms of social closure that had once been ensured by national laws. The disruptive power of digital technologies has made the knowledge that had been previously possessed by professionals available to everyone, profoundly changing how this knowledge is produced, managed, and shared in society. Besides, it has created new cleavages among professionals, with its impact going beyond the issue of how professionals do their jobs and build relationships of trust—both with clients and society at large.

In brief, we are dealing with a puzzle which is composed of many pieces. In the attempt to put it together, however, the sociology of professions still seems to be dealing with its (theoretical) frame while struggling to identify (interpretive) patterns to link the (empirical) pieces to each other. Furthermore, the academic debate revolves around theories and concepts that were developed in the twentieth century, which can partly explain the above trends. As a matter of fact, the increasing complexity of social reality makes it necessary to seek out a systematic understanding of professions by considering the processes of professional, institutional, and social change as being interconnected. Despite the fact that categories such as "social closure", "professional project", "jurisdiction", and "professional logic" continue to exert an essential heuristic function, they seem to suffer from the absence of a comprehensive framework that is capable of combining different perspectives and guiding the analysis of professionalism within the new historical circumstances created by post-industrial society.

The processes of differentiation that are occurring and their outcomes in terms of heterogeneity can be used to decipher what is currently happening in the context of professional work with regard to individual professionals, the work settings in which they are situated, and professions overall. Differentiation and heterogeneity are straightforward terms which imply a growing division of labour among professions and professionals (Bellini & Maestripieri, 2018; Parding et al., 2021). *Heterogeneity* involves professionals being increasingly diversified in terms of age, gender, social origins (class, ethnicity, migrant background), employment contract, type of organisation, and workplace, as well as their degree of professionalisation and the model of professionalism in question (established versus emerging professions). It has to do with the changing social bases of professions and with emerging patterns of professional practice and work organisation. *Differentiation* refers to two interconnected phenomena: *labour* differentiation, understood in the Durkheimian terms of the functional specialisation of occupations and individuals, in the Weberian terms of hierarchical stratification based on the unequal distribution of power between professional groups, or in the Marxian terms of renewed relations of exploitation; and *social* differentiation, understood in the Simmelian terms of growing individualisation and inequality among professionals. As such, it encompasses substantial divergences in structural positions, which call for novel ways to conceptualise, analyse, and interpret professional work.

The aim of this book is, first and foremost, to provide new conceptual tools to understand the changes occurring in professions and their interactions with society. The main contribution of this introduction lies in building an analytical framework by identifying three dimensions along which differentiation may be developed—*within*, *between*, and *beyond*—also referred to as the WBB model (Chap. 14). The edited collection of chapters proves its explanatory capacity by presenting notable research on various professional groups, in different countries, with distinct focuses and approaches, organised within a coherent three-pronged framework. This variety is the result of a deliberate choice that is aimed at highlighting similarities and differences across countries, professions, and issues—all englobed within the sociology of professions.

To sum up, the book's argument is that professions are becoming differentiated along multiple dimensions, all of which are worth exploring, possibly within a unitary framework. That said, the reader must be made aware that the three dimensions mentioned above are theoretical constructs which refer to social phenomena that are artificially separated—as a conscious strategy—despite actually being interrelated.

Before presenting the analytical framework, it is nevertheless good practice to define the object of our study: professionalism in its interaction with social change. The following section thus introduces the fundamental concepts—profession and professionalism—and the main theoretical implications of their recent evolution. The subsequent section identifies the critical processes of change at play in contemporary societies, highlighting their impact on professionalism.

2 Professions and Professionalism: (Re)defining the Concepts

The theoretical background of this book consists of a relatively small set of fundamental concepts. However, their meanings and uses have changed and diversified over time, making it essential to describe how they have evolved and provide a proper definition of them. The reference here is primarily the notion of "professionalism", its significance, and its analytical uses. Scholars largely agree on the heuristic capacity of this concept, so much so that it has gained prominence over "profession" (see Torstendahl, 2005; Evetts, 2011). This shift of focus is not only a matter of conceptualisation; it is, at the same time, the cause and effect of a change of perspective within the sociology of professions due to a substantial transformation of society, in which *expert labour* and *profession* have become increasingly separated—with the latter understood in a Weberian sense as a historical construct of norms and rules.

The initial contributions to the discipline tended to see professions as distinct groups in the division of labour. The approach was the one labelled by Saks (2010, 2012) as "taxonomic": aimed at identifying and listing, with great care and diligence, the intrinsic and unique characteristics that distinguished professions from other occupations. In this sense, the work of Carr-Saunders and Wilson (1933) was pioneering. The emphasis was given to two specific traits: the possession of specialist competencies and the inclination to altruism (Greenwood, 1957; Wilensky,

1964), which allowed professionals to play a "positive" role in society. This approach found theoretical support in functionalism. From that perspective, exerting a "function" of great significance for society guaranteed practitioners appropriate rewards in terms of income and social prestige, thus allowing professions to attract the best talents (Goode, 1957; Barber, 1963).

At the heart of this approach was the implicit conception of professionalism as a "normative value system" (Evetts, 2003), which had its roots in Durkheim's (1890–1900) representation of professional groups as "moral communities", and promoted the idea of professionalism as a force for stability and freedom (Carr-Saunders & Wilson, 1933; Marshall, 1939). In Parsons (1951), this idea was formulated rather comprehensively. In his view, professions were forces that contributed to maintaining social order in capitalist societies.

At the end of the 1950s, this approach became subject to increasing criticism, which would soon lead to it being abandoned, despite its continuing, implicit influence over the following decades. Hughes' (1958, 1963) argument was of particular significance since it was inherent to conceptualising professions. In his view, depicting professions as the only occupations to rely on competencies and ethics was misleading. Later, several works inspired by Marxist theory brought about a shift in viewpoint. With them, the approach to the study of professions entered a processual dimension, turning its attention to long-term trends, despite offering different understandings of change. Ehrenreich and Ehrenreich (1977), for instance, posited that the members of the "professional-managerial class" were playing the role of agents of the capitalist class, to whom the latter had transferred the tasks of expropriating production skills and controlling labour processes, putting them in opposition to the working class. An alternative view was that of Oppenheimer (1973), who maintained that the integration of professional workers into bureaucratic organisations necessarily implied the "proletarianisation" of their employment status and working conditions, as well as the rise of problems related to low-income levels and exposure to the risk of unemployment (see also McKinlay & Arches, 1985). From a less radical position, Navarro (1988) argued that it would be more appropriate to speak of a loss of professional autonomy. A further thesis was developed by Haug (1972, 1975) concerning a supposed process of "de-professionalisation", indicating the loss of the distinctive qualities of professions, such as a monopoly of expert knowledge, unconditional trust in their service ethos and, again, professional autonomy.

The emergence of a neo-Weberian approach marked a paradigm shift. Saks (2010, 2016) outlined its distinguishing features and defined professions as institutionalised forms of closure, understood as "exclusionary" closure, a term borrowed from Parkin (1979). From this perspective, professionalisation is seen as a strategy to control the labour supply in a given occupational field, safeguarding its market value. The rise of neo-Weberianism also designated the assumption of a "negative" conception of professionalism as "ideology", indicating a hegemonic value system which relied on mechanisms of social control (Evetts, 2003). Among the most influential contributions that can be ascribed to this approach is the concept of "professional project", coined by Sarfatti Larson (1977) to describe the process by which an occupational group obtains monopolistic control of the labour market and, in so doing, achieves a project promoting social mobility. Abbott (1986) added an important point, drawing attention to conflicts over a "jurisdiction" in order to legitimise the monopoly of practice in a professional field. Along these interpretive lines, Freidson (2001) then developed the idea of professionalism as a "third logic" of organising the labour market, in contrast to (and preferable to) the market and bureaucracy; however, this third logic needs market closure to guarantee high-quality performance.

Neo-Weberian scholars transformed the notion of professionalism, already in use at the origins of the discipline, although with a generic, undetermined meaning, making it into a theoretical tool for social critique. In this sense, their contribution was extremely valuable. Thanks to them, professionalism and the other categories mentioned above permanently entered the conceptual toolbox of the sociologists of professions. That said, neo-Weberianism has shown its limits when called upon to explain the *processes* of differentiation that affect professions and their *outcomes* in terms of the increasing heterogeneity among professionals. These limits have revealed themselves to be intrinsic to the neo-Weberian approach, in that they are derived from the definition of a profession as an "institution" and place much emphasis on exclusionary practices, as well as permanence instead of change. They make it necessary to begin any discussion by defining what a profession is and by determining who is included and who is excluded, in a kind of Sisyphean task.

In the second half of the 1990s, a need to codify the changes occurring in professional work pushed scholars to rethink professionalism. The changes in question can be inscribed within an overall process of "rationalisation" related to the promotion of an organisational-managerialist culture, which first affected the UK and North America (see Fournier, 1999; and, again, Evetts, 2003). In this regard, Hanlon (1996, 1998) reported the emergence of a new model, labelling it "commercialised" professionalism, which implies that professionals are increasingly dependent on the ability to generate profit for their clients; in so doing, he indicated a further shift of focus towards aspects such as responsibility and performance, and emphasised how it was increasingly important for professionals to possess entrepreneurial and managerial skills.

Academics have paid growing attention to the role of organisations—that is, large corporations and professional service firms—as employers of professionals. Evetts (2006) coined the expression "organisational" professionalism, in opposition to the traditional concept of "occupational" professionalism. Moreover, she redefined the notion of professionalism, arguing that both forms of professionalism can be better understood in terms of "discourse" (see Fournier, 1999). What has been called organisational professionalism has been conceptualised as a discourse developed in work organisations (rather than occupational groups), which incorporates the principle of hierarchy (rather than collegiate authority), involves the standardisation of work processes and the exercise of managerialist control (rather than relationships of trust with the employers/clients), and relies on externalised forms of regulation and accountability measures (rather than self-regulation).

Some further remarks should be made concerning the role of organisations. They have been indicated as the "fifth actor" in the regulation of professions (Muzio et al., 2011), in addition to professionals, clients, states, and universities (the actors formerly identified by Burrage & Torstendahl, 1990). A thesis that a new paradigm was emerging gained currency, one that went beyond the conception of professionalism as a third logic. Among its promoters was Noordegraaf (2007), who devised the concept of "hybrid" professionalism, aiming to reinforce the idea of professionalism in changeable organisational contexts. According to this author, this is a reaction to an attack on classic professions that can be described by the expression "professionalism under pressure". In relation to this, the idea of a threat of de-professionalisation emerged once more, to which professions reacted by searching for new sources of identity within organisations (see Dent & Whitehead, 2002). This change involved the reorganisation, restratification, and relocation of professional work within occupational fields that were increasingly heterogeneous and fragmented (Noordegraaf, 2016). Others have referred to a thesis of hybridisation. Among them, Faulconbridge and Muzio (2007) offered a different way of understanding the phenomenon, arguing that going back to the hypothesis of de-professionalisation could lead to the depiction of professions as "passive victims", and could undervalue their capacity to reach leading positions within organisations. In this sense, we are faced with a new model of organisational professionalism, which implies that even collegiate professions use organisational structures and principles to promote their professional projects and to gain control of the strategic resources of large private companies (Evetts, 2006).

We will return to this point in the next paragraph. What is worth noting here is that the redirecting of attention from professions to professionalism and the reconceptualisation of the notion of professionalism as discourse have given the discipline new life, allowing the changing social reality to be interpreted more effectively. Evetts (2006), again, made a decisive contribution to developing this conception. In her words, the *discourse of professionalism* refers to "the ways in which occupational and professional workers themselves are accepting, incorporating and accommodating the idea of 'profession' and particularly 'professionalism' in their work" (p. 139). As such, it is used both as a "disciplinary" mechanism aimed at controlling professional practice within organisations and as a mechanism for controlling work within occupational groups. In this way, it can be seen as a fully-fledged means of social control.

Other authors have proposed variations on the theme, depending on the level and focus of the analysis. The most radical position was that of Watson (2002), who suggested considering the possibility of abandoning the concepts of profession and professionalism, instead using occupation as an analytical category and looking at "professional talk" as a topic. In his view, the notion of profession is ambiguous since it relies on the assumption of being "special" compared to other occupations. Furthermore, he sees professionalism as a "bandwagon" idea, namely a vehicle used by members of occupations to further or defend their interests. Both terms are conceptualised as "discursive resources" that are strongly connected to "occupational mobilisation". The author clarified that professional talk is one of several discourses that are typical of contemporary culture and that we can draw upon several different discourses of professionalism. He also offered a definition of *discourse* as a set of "interconnected concepts, expressions, and statements that constitute a way of talking and writing about an aspect of the world, thereby framing and influencing how people understand and act with regard to that aspect of the world" (p. 100)—that is, resources that social actors use to pursue their purposes rather than analytical tools in the hands of social scientists. This approach is nevertheless more attuned to a macro level of analysis, centred on the role that social actors play in the construction of reality.

Here, it is helpful to make a distinction between "discourse" and "rhetoric" to gain a clear view of the problem and consider the possible implications for research. As Suddaby and Viale (2011, p. 434) pointed out, "rhetoric is distinct from, but dependent upon, discourse". The latter, the authors explained, operates at the macro level, reflecting positions of power within society and not associated with the agency of individuals, whereas the former operates at the lower levels and is more "agentic" (see also Suddaby, 2010). Indeed, at the micro level, different agent-based approaches have been developed that draw attention to the use of rhetorical devices as means of influence. Neo-institutionalism has provided a theoretical basis for this line of research, with the focus being on the strategic use of rhetoric "to influence the direction and pace of [institutional] change, but also to legitimate or delegitimate the acceptance of a particular programme of change" (Suddaby & Viale, 2011, p. 434). As such, rhetoric is an active element in the transformative process called *institutional work*, namely "the creation, maintenance and transformation of institutions" (p. 424). Professionals are "institutional agents" (see Scott, 2008; and, more recently, Muzio et al., 2013). In the words of

Suddaby and Viale (2011, p. 435), again, "language is a crucial weapon [...] and professionals are skilled rhetoricians".

Another stream of literature, starting from different theoretical premises, was inspired by Abbott's work, then concentrated on discursive strategies and practices as the underlying mechanisms of the *boundary work* at the basis of jurisdictional conflicts (see, for instance, Bucher et al., 2016; for a broader overview, see Heusinkveld et al., 2018). Here, the aim was to explain how discursive resources contribute to redefining occupational jurisdictions and inter-occupational relationships, above all in the cases of "emerging" professions. With this term, we mean "those professional activities that are in the process of professionalization but are yet to be recognized as professional by public regulation, although their practitioners lay claim to professionalism" (Maestripieri & Cucca, 2018, p. 365).

Generally, we agree with Evetts (2006, p. 141) that focusing on the discourse of professionalism "offers some new directions and areas of interest for sociologists of professional groups". A point to make here is that *discourse,* in the strict sense, refers to boundary work, a type of cognitive work that affects the relationships between either professions or professional groups, thus producing its direct effects at the macro level. Instead, *rhetoric* refers to types of "self-reflective" cognitive work conducted individually by professionals and that produce their effects at the micro level, although they are likely to also influence the macro level. The latter is linked to identity work, which occurs in the context of subjectivity, although it is reconducted to a coherent epistemic framework; hence, it contributes to consolidating or even giving rise to a professional project. It also involves institutional work carried out by professionals in organisational contexts and produces institutional change (Muzio et al., 2013).

Despite conceptual specificities, however, the two perspectives are not mutually exclusive. On the contrary, rhetoric can always be traced to a general discourse of professionalism. What is more, all these types of cognitive work are interrelated with processes of change occurring at different levels. Indeed, they generate change at the *professional, institutional,* and *societal* levels. In turn, they are influenced by broader processes of change, which should induce us to go beyond the conception of macro-phenomena as being "micro-founded" (see Powell & Colyvas, 2008), and to focus on the "interactions" between macro-phenomena and micro-processes (on this idea, see Wright, 1997).

In conclusion, we agree that the conception of professionalism as a discursive practice is a more functional way of studying professions in the context of social change, which implies the differentiation of professions themselves and, as an outcome, increasing heterogeneity among professionals. In particular, it seems more effective in explaining the redefinition of professional boundaries in light of the emergence of new forms of professionalism. The conceptualisation work we have conducted has nevertheless revealed the existence of notional variants of the idea of discourse. This book adopts an open approach, pragmatically trying to take advantage of the shades of meaning and their analytical uses. This is coherent with the aim of investigating differentiation from multiple angles while adopting a "micro-macro" approach.

3 Critical Processes of Change

In an increasingly complex social reality, the research agenda of the sociology of professions has shifted its focus onto three large-scale processes of change—the *post-industrial transition*, *globalisation*, and *digitalisation*—that are deemed critical due to their impact on professionalism. These processes have a pervasive and bivalent nature, and present various opportunities and challenges. Here follows a discussion of their empirical implications.

3.1 The Post-Industrial Transition

This concept has gained ground in the social sciences to explain the progressive change in the composition of the labour force that began in advanced capitalist economies in the early 1970s. From then onwards, employment in manufacturing began to gradually lose ground in favour of services, owing to a combination of the outsourcing of business activities, the delocalisation of production, and a substantial change in the types of goods produced (from material to immaterial). This process was endogenous to the productive sphere, but its effects permeated society. Tertiarisation gave a central role to those capable of producing and managing knowledge. Professionals belonging to this category rapidly increased in number.

An important consequence was that women—who benefitted the most from the democratisation of education—entered the post-industrial labour markets massively, obtaining positions that required relational and knowledge skills instead of the physical strength needed for producing material goods. By virtue of their educational performance, they began to compete successfully to access professions. An increasing number of female professionals entered male-dominated professional groups, although this process occurred at the cost of their marginalisation in subaltern positions or niches considered suitable for feminine skills (e.g., paediatrics or divorce law). The greater accessibility of education also allowed more working-class people to acquire the knowledge and skills required to perform expert labour.

A further consequence was the erosion of salaried employment. Services, contrary to manufacturing, rely on target-oriented workflows, which do not necessarily require the standardisation of working schedules. The need for service labour began to change on the basis of demand from clients in a way that was far less predictable than in the past. Employers thus asked for more flexible organisation of work. Since the 1980s, governments have pursued deregulation in employment contracts in almost all capitalist countries. The outcome has been a progressive loss of the pre-eminence of "standard", that is, permanent, full-time dependent employment, in favour of "non-standard" jobs. Fixed-term, part-time contracts and self-employment started becoming the norm among professionals.

The feminisation of labour markets and the de-standardisation of employment augmented the heterogeneity of the professional labour force. These days, professionals are more diverse: they include people that belong to different social groups (more women and people from the working classes); in addition, different professionals might perform the same job in the same organisation but under different employment statuses.

3.2 Globalisation

With this term, social scientists refer to the growing integration of economic, social, and cultural systems across the globe. In the context of our argument, a few points should be stressed. First, globalisation affects all dimensions of social life, which are closely intertwined. Second, the economic dimension is central but must be seen in the light of its interconnections with all the other dimensions. Third, businesses are key global players, proactively fostering processes of "transnationalisation", which, for instance, implies the exercise of pressure to obtain changes in state legal regulations. As such, globalisation has called into question the heuristic capacity of monolithic, "Western-centric" theories of professionalism.

Broadly speaking, globalisation has facilitated the mobility of products, services, and workers across countries in different regions around the world. On the other hand, it has implied an international division of labour between advanced capitalist countries, which mainly produce knowledge, and recently industrialised countries, where the production of material goods has been delocalised. Besides, it has caused the competition among companies and workers to move to the global scale and has intensified it. Specifically, the growing number of professionals and the new ways of embodying professionalism in developing countries are leading to a new division of labour between the Global North and the Global South. The composition of the labour force and the size of professional service firms are also changing rapidly (Dent et al., 2016; Saks & Muzio, 2018). Furthermore, it is easier for professionals to travel outside their countries of origin to provide professional services: not only because services are supplied by multinational corporations that dominate the markets at home and abroad (Muzio & Kirkpatrick, 2011), but also because individual careers are becoming boundaryless and globally mobile (Cohen & Mallon, 1999). Accordingly, it is common for practitioners from different countries to work side by side within the same global professional service firm. In this situation, professional practice is carried out under different combinations of state regulations and socio-cultural norms. New "local" ways of interpreting professionalism are also emerging;

indeed, regulative inputs can have different outcomes when transferred from one country to another. Moreover, there is more demand for professionals to work internationally, and some have more possibilities than others to move in other countries, depending on their (economic, cultural, and social) capital: their family circumstances, language skills, and, not least, whether they are women, which makes them less able to move or commute long distance.

3.3 Digitalisation

Technological change involving how knowledge is produced, managed, and stored has been summed up under the term digitalisation. The adoption of information technology and the diffusion of the Internet are pervasive phenomena that affect professionals and clients, without exception and regardless of whether they want it or are conscious of it. This has occurred in two ways. On the one hand, digitalisation has created new channels to express the demand for professional services. On the other hand, it has offered professionals new instruments to respond to this demand for professional services in a prompt and economical manner; in turn, this demand has become more sophisticated and sensitive to price variations. Digital technologies have also changed how expert knowledge is produced and conveyed, impacting the capacity of professional groups to control labour markets (a critical aspect already stressed by Sarfatti Larson, 1977) and altering the power balances between professionals and clients (as described by Forsyth & Danisiewicz, 1985). In this sense, they have made esoteric knowledge more easily accessible.

Digitalisation exposes professional workers to a process of polarisation between "good" and "bad" jobs, with the consequence of putting them, or some of them at least, in precarious work situations. As a matter of fact, the topic of how technological change interacts with socio-professional stratification principles is unexplored. Digital technologies may reproduce or even increase the inequalities between those who have the resources to invest in innovation or have the capacity to keep up with technological advancements and those who do not. Then again, they offer professionals "at the margins" (see Butler et al., 2012) new opportunities to promote their businesses or directly sell services and, therefore, to reach a wider audience in an economical way. This aspect reveals the ambivalence of digitalisation in that it brings about the "know-how" allowing experts to reassert their "dominance" over clients as well as over marginal professionals and, at the same time, it opens up the field for new occupational figures. As such, it provides fertile ground for social conflict and offers new instruments in the fight for social rights in a sector that is typically impervious to collective action.

Among "disruptive" technologies (Christensen, 1997)—that is, innovative technologies that make it possible to offer low-cost services and activate a latent demand for services—*online work platforms* take the outsourcing trend to the extreme. Clients can now hire experts for one-off, simple tasks without even knowing who they are. Platforms, as Farrell and Greig (2016, p. 2) note, "have created a new marketplace for work by unbundling a job into discrete tasks and directly connecting individual sellers with consumers". As these authors have further explained, "these flexible, highly accessible opportunities to work have the potential to help people buffer against income and expense shocks"; on the other hand, they offer "fewer worker protections than traditional work arrangements" (p. 2). These organisations are primarily multinational companies operating on a global scale.

3.4 Professions and Society

The above processes have combined to bring about the breach of the "social contract" between professions and society, something which had implied high rewards in terms of income and prestige in exchange for the monopolistic exercise of functions that had great importance for society itself. They have operated by bypassing state-centred professional systems and by penetrating professional groups to produce their most significant effects on professionals themselves. Their most visible expression is the proliferation of what actually fits into the category of professions and, among them, the differentiation of professional groups and figures. At present, professions can hardly be considered to form homogeneous and cohesive groups, something which calls into question the feasibility of pursuing solid professional projects. As a direct consequence, professionals are affected by growing inequalities. These phenomena affect both traditional and emerging professions. They contribute to the loss of professional power of the former, while, in the case of the latter, the dominance of the market logic and the increasing competition to which professionals are exposed have given rise to processes of marginalisation (Butler et al., 2012). Overall, these processes of differentiation have produced increasing heterogeneity.

As already stated, we argue that the heterogeneity of professions derives from multiple processes of differentiation and can be better understood by using a multi-dimensional analytical framework. The following paragraph gives operative definitions of the dimensions along which differentiation develops.

4 A Three-Pronged Analytical Framework

Given the above theoretical premises, three dimensions can be identified that delineate the loci of the differentiation of professions and professional groups and account for the increasing heterogeneity that is occurring among professionals, brought about by large-scale processes of change. The three dimensions through which we study differentiation—within, between, and beyond—have a great capacity to organise thoughts and ideas along—metaphorically—spatial lines. Indeed, they refer to the distance between the constitutive components of a profession (*within*), the distance that separates different and sometimes competing professional groups (*between*), and the distance that divides professionals and society at large (*beyond*). In this framework, the term "distance" has a dual meaning, both "relational" and "processual", as it implies the existence of connections of variable lengths between two or more elements: the idea it recalls is that the greater the distance, the more different individuals are from each other, and the less homogeneous, cohesive, and influential the groups. Defined in this way, distance may refer to professions, professional groups, or professionals. Its "unit of measurement" identifies the analytical perspective; for instance, it may focus on job stability and security, earned income, social prestige, or political power, depending on the particular situation, which might be influenced by objective factors, such as gender, class, ethnic origins or migrant background, and age.

The spatial metaphor gives us an idea of the ambiguity of the relationship between professionals and society. On the one hand, the more distant professionals are from society—in the sense that they are bearers of esoteric, inaccessible knowledge, which is indispensable for the functioning of society itself—the more likely they are to be appropriately rewarded for their work. On the other hand, the more distant they are in terms of their participation in social life, the less likely they are to have a significant impact on social change.

Although the three dimensions are irreducible, they can be analytically distinguished in order to present them to the reader.

4.1 The Within Dimension

The first dimension of analysis has to do with the processes that contribute to differentiating professionals *within* a given profession. The rise of post-industrial society has brought about higher skill levels in the labour force as well as increased diversity and mobility. Barriers to entry into the professions, in many cases, have ceased to exist or are less rigid than before. People from disadvantaged groups, such as women or people from working-class backgrounds, have entered the professions in great numbers, modifying their social structure. Furthermore, technological change, in the form of digitalisation, has led to a further opening up of professional labour markets: nowadays, practitioners only need a personal computer and easy-to-use software to compete on the market. However, openness does not necessarily imply equal opportunities. That is, access does not guarantee favourable employment terms and working conditions.

On the contrary, there is a rising heterogeneity in how professional work is contracted out, which increases the degree of insecurity of expert labour (Murgia et al., 2016). Being on the market, per se, is not sufficient to ensure adequate income levels or access to welfare (Maestripieri & Cucca, 2018). And not all practitioners within a profession—not even when it is an established one, such as law (see Alacevich et al., 2017)—have equal status in their community of peers. What is more, deregulation has eroded the capacity of professional groups to secure their status. Professions are no longer immune to social inequalities or power struggles (Butler et al., 2012).

"Differentiation within", it should be noted, can occur over time when regulation intervenes to loosen the boundaries of a professional field or to modify the terms through which social closure is put into practice. In this sense, institutional change can be seen as a form of change which shapes professionalism *from within*.

4.2 The Between Dimension

A critical feature that scholars have taken into consideration when distinguishing professions from occupations is the capacity of specific occupational groups to obtain social recognition and control membership to their associations (Johnson, 1972; Freidson, 1994); this guarantees their members stable and remunerative jobs by limiting the number of acknowledged practitioners and, in so doing, keeps internal competition at bay. This takes us to the second dimension, which is linked to the relationships *between* professions and other occupations and *between* professional groups themselves. The latter are characterised by enjoying different degrees of protection against market risks; this depends on public regulation but also on the capacity of professionals to organise collectively and exert control or influence over a specific area of expertise (Butler et al., 2012).

This is a typical neo-Weberian analytical perspective, focusing on the dynamics of professional power (Johnson, 1972) and the mechanisms of exclusionary closure (Parkin, 1979; Macdonald, 1995), which operate against the backdrop of interactive relationships between contiguous occupational jurisdictions (Abbott, 1988) and determine the success or failure of a professional project (Sarfatti Larson, 1977). From this viewpoint, professions are depicted as hierarchically differentiated groups, and the analysis is centred on the inequalities between professional groups (Saks, 2015).

If we assume that professional groups are situated both historically and locally—either enabled or constrained by country-based professional systems and embedded in institutional and socio-cultural contexts—it seems convenient to extend the discourse on "differentiation between" to include the rising inequalities between professionals who belong to the same professional group but to different professional systems, which have been put under pressure by globalisation. As already noticed, globalisation has manifested itself in professionals becoming increasingly mobile and in the rise of boundaryless careers, but also—and more importantly—in the growing role of global professional service firms supplying services in different countries, across the borders that exist between country-based professional systems, hence putting national regulations and cultures to the test. At the same time, due to the rising number of professionals in developing countries, locally specific ways of embodying professionalism are emerging that increase the differentiation of professional standards.

4.3 The Beyond Dimension

The third dimension is concerned with what lies *beyond* professionalism. The term "beyond", it is worth noting, does not mean denying the value of professionalism as a heuristic category, nor does it indicate a transition to any form of post-professional society. On the contrary, it implies assuming the persisting significance of professionalism as a conceptual tool that can be used to analyse and interpret social change. Furthermore, it shifts the focus of the academic discourse from professionalism in the strict sense to the relationship between expert labour and society: namely, to examine how social change influences professionalism and, from the opposing point of view, the implications of professional change for society.

This aspect relates to the forms of social control that have already been enumerated by Goode (1957), particularly the "indirect" control exerted by society on professionals through clients' choices. The same phenomenon can be observed from a different perspective, as an element of power in the "social exchange" between professionals and clients, understood as the autonomy of the former from the latter (Forsyth & Danisiewicz, 1985). In this case, the focus is on the changing relationship between professionals and clients, the related effects on relationships of trust, and the dynamics of social recognition. Indeed, so far, the academic debate has not been able to fully consider the extent to which professionalism has changed because of the decline in public recognition of the—economic and social—value of professional work.

An alternative approach to the problem is to look at the role played by professionals in society, beyond the boundaries of their ordinary activity, by focusing on their—actual or potential—contributions to the processes of change (see Bellini, 2014).

In this regard, Scott (2010) called attention to the critical role played by professionals in legitimising new institutional arrangements. The author referred to Berger and Luckmann (1966) to argue that "institutionalisation", as a growing set of new organisational forms or practices, is a gradual process, one that implies the production of meanings and their integration into existing beliefs and values in a given field. He affirmed that, as the process evolves, innovators lose control and professional actors appear that are specialised in the construction and management of cultural, normative, and regulatory frameworks. In the words of Scott (2008, p. 220), professionals are the "lords of the dance", namely "choreographers" of the "dances of individuals and organizations", defining, interpreting, and applying beliefs, norms, and rules, thus giving meaning and stability to social life.

The focus mentioned above is on the role played by individual actors as "institutional agents" in influencing the life of complex organisations from the inside and the outside (see also Muzio et al., 2013). A further field of analysis should be examined to assess the role of professionals and professions in civil society. This could be done in two ways: by looking at professionals' "civic engagement" and "political activism" in the context of their multiple roles while concentrating on their *individual* contributions to social change (Flam, 2019); or by relating to the issue of "participation", which is more properly linked to *collective* action. As argued elsewhere (see Bellini & Maestripieri, 2018), research on the sociology of professions generally focuses on the *within* or the *between* dimensions; not many contributions take the dynamics occurring *beyond* professions as their focal point of analysis, although this dimension is often latently present since it is inherent to the discourse of professionalism. The latter tends to emphasise the impact of professionalism on society as a basis for claiming public recognition and adequate rewards in the social exchange with society itself.

That said, the beyond dimension may be the domain in which a meta-reflection is taking place on the very nature of professionalism. Noordegraaf's (2020, p. 209) idea of "connective" professionalism has added new fuel to this debate (for a critical appraisal of this concept, see Adams et al., 2020a, 2020b; Alvehus et al., 2021; Faulconbridge et al., 2021; Noordegraaf & Brock, 2021). With it, the author calls for "a move *beyond hybridity*". In his words, "apart from 'organizing' aspects, within organizational settings, professional acts can be related to the outside world, including external influences and pressures" (p. 210). Therefore, "professionalism becomes meaningful in relation to clients, stakeholders, and actors, in wider service systems and societal settings" (p. 210). As Noordegraaf himself argues, "professionalism is not residing 'in' professionals but happens in-between professional action [...] and the outside world" (p. 218).

4.4 The WBB Model

Each of the three dimensions maintains its specific heuristic capacity. At the same time, taken together, the dimensions allow us to frame the processes and outcomes of change that affect professions and society as a whole, providing a vivid representation of current social reality. In the conclusions of the book (Chap. 14), we will show how the three dimensions taken together could offer new inputs to the study of professionalism in contemporary society.

5 Differentiation in Action: An Overview

5.1 The Scope of the Book

The collection of chapters in this book aims to provide evidence that the analytical framework presented above is capable of reading the changes to professions that are being brought about by processes of differentiation. The studies contained here apply this framework across different geographical contexts, examining different professional groups, and inspired by different approaches and traditions in the study of professions and professionalism.

We consider the three dimensions (within-between-beyond) as "irreducible", meaning that their influence and effects are mutually interrelated; we have separated them for analytical clarity alone, following Beckert's (2010) model. For this reason, we asked the book contributors to pick one of the three dimensions as their central analytical axis while leaving the other two in the background. The table of contents is in line with this purpose: indeed, the chapters are not grouped together on the basis of the countries or professions studied but on the analytical dimension applied.

The outcome of this exercise is a detailed picture of the ongoing research that is taking place worldwide in the field of professions, with each contribution focusing on an issue related to the processes of change described previously.

5.2 An Outline of the Chapters

Part I collects the contributions that explore the processes of differentiation *within* professions. This group of chapters presents empirical cases and shows how an increasing differentiation of professionals is taking place in relation to employment situations, working conditions, opportunities for career development, and, more generally, socio-professional status, thematised in terms of job instability, unequal opportunities, and gendered segmentation. Extensive research has been dedicated to investigating corporate professionalism, while less attention has been given to precarious forms of employment, including those related to self-employment and platform work. The latter are growing fast, especially among the weakest members of professional groups: women, people from working-class backgrounds, and migrant professionals.

In detail, Chap. 2, by Pierre Bataille, Nicky Le Feuvre, and Marie Sautier, focuses on the influence exerted by employment frameworks on the definition of professionalism. The authors adopt an employment-based approach to studying the differentiation occurring within academia in Switzerland. Specifically, three ideal types of academics are identified: the "researcher", the "teacher", and the "manager". This typology is employed to explain the different individual orientations towards the process of managerialisation within universities and the related increasingly precarious nature of academic labour.

Chapter 3, by Debby Bonnin, assesses the consequences of globalisation and the disruptive effects of the use of Computer-Aided Design (CAD) technologies on the textile design profession. In South Africa, where the study is based, textile designers have never developed "pure" professionalism. Good jobs and "situated" professionalism, as defined by Noordegraaf (2007), had characterised the sector until the 1990s, when most textile designers were employed in large companies as salaried workers. Since then, the combined effect of the integration of the textile industry into the global economy, market deregulation, and the introduction of new technologies has resulted in the rise in internal competition among designers, implying a deterioration in employment and working conditions, increasingly characterised by freelancing, contract work, and, generally speaking, a loss of professional autonomy.

Chapter 4, by Valeria Insarauto, Isabel Boni-Le Goff, Grégoire Mallard, Eléonore Lépinard, and Nicky Le Feuvre, examines how the restructuring of firms and new organisational forms in the legal professions pressure women to conform to male working patterns and career profiles. The authors posit that new transnational patterns of professional work based on global professional standards favour organisational logics, practices, and strategies, reinforcing the established male-centred model of professionalism. However, while most studies related to the gendered segmentation of the legal professions have focused on the macro-processes of work organisation, this chapter concentrates on the micro level, investigating individual work experiences of early-career lawyers in two countries, France and Switzerland.

Chapter 5, by Davide Arcidiacono, Ivana Pais, and Giorgio Piccitto, analyses how digital platforms shape professionalism in four regulated fields in Italy: law, journalism, psychology, and architecture. Technologies are simultaneously a mirror of and a mechanism for reinforcing the existing logics of division and organisation of labour. The authors show that the expansion of work platforms has been made possible by the erosion of the privileged position of professionals in the labour market. They also show how platforms might be appropriate marketplaces for weaker professionals who have been marginalised or excluded from the primary professional labour market, since they aim to respond promptly and economically to the demand for simple and repetitive tasks.

Chapter 6, by Karolina Parding and Anna Jansson, discusses how the current regulation of professional work impacts professionals' learning conditions. To do so, it focuses on the cases of nurses and teachers in Sweden: the former as temporary agency workers; the latter as being divided between various public and non-public realms. The two cases reveal the emergence of different employment patterns for professionals working in private and public environments, often side by side in the same workplace. The research findings show how policy reforms, solely or partially addressed to the public sector, amplify the differentiation of welfare-sector professionals' learning conditions. The authors argue that these changes are driving a differentiation within professions, resulting in unequal opportunities for learning and career development.

Part II focuses on the processes of differentiation *between* professional groups, which belong either to different professions within the same professional system or even to the same profession but in different professional systems. The following chapters address very different cases, which nevertheless develop against a common background marked by marketisation and globalisation. Professions rely increasingly on the market and organisations as the loci of professional dominance: hybridisation is key to this and is subject to a fierce debate in the field. In addition, the mobility of professionals has increased: multinational corporations, transnational projects, and boundaryless careers challenge state regulation, giving rise to the need for further regulation efforts across different localities. A contradiction emerges between *country-based* systems of professions and *globalised* markets of professional services. This contradiction calls into question professional power and the related capacity to pressure regulatory systems that had once been presided by professional bodies.

Chapter 7, by Jean-Luc Bédard, Marta Massana, and Christophe Groulx, explores the movements of foreign-trained professionals across country borders and professional jurisdictions. The authors take the cases of doctors and engineers moving to Canada to compare a profession governed by public institutions (medicine) with one dominated by private organisations (engineering). The public-private distinction creates different spaces for socio-professional integration within and around these regulated professions. The analysis draws on Abbott's (1988) theory of professions, particularly regarding jurisdictional conflicts within and between professional groups.

Chapter 8, by Marta Choroszewicz, gives evidence of how lawyers in Finland, French Canada, and Poland use knowledge as a resource in the struggle for status and power in the market, where institutional mechanisms are less powerful in creating shelters for professionals. The author borrows Freidson's (1986, 2001) definition of professionalism as a mode of organisation of the labour market based on the recognition of professionals' knowledge and expertise and argues that, even though professionals are losing autonomy and influence as a collective, they strategically use different forms of professionalism in their everyday micro-practices to renegotiate their status. Her work employs a comparative perspective across countries by giving evidence on a single profession—law—in different institutional contexts.

Chapter 9, by Lluís Parcerisa, Antoni Verger, Marcel Pagès, and Natalie Browes, analyses the consequences of the encroachment of private-sector values (such as managerialism and performance orientation) into the public domain of education. In particular, by conducting a systematic literature review, the authors aim to evaluate the impact of test-based accountability on teacher professionalism. For this purpose, they compare two different institutional settings: "high-stakes" systems, in which students' test results are often tied to rewards and sanctions for the school, the head teacher, and/or teachers; and "low-stakes" systems, where there are no administrative consequences, but there exists a strong perception that the schools' and/or teachers' reputations are at risk. The focus on the institutional context helps delineate the impact that different models of external evaluation have on teachers' performance and their capacity to sustain coherent professionalism across different environments.

Chapter 10, by Silvia Lucciarini and Valeria Pulignano, focuses on how contemporary creative professional work challenges traditional models of professionalism. The professionalism that creative workers claim to embody, in fact, is neither legally recognised nor formally certified; as such, it leaves them at the mercy of the market, with no chance of gaining a monopoly of the labour market. The chapter analyses emerging forms of professional closure in Italy, concentrating on the *boundary work* performed by multi-professional, mutual aid cooperatives of creative workers such as photographers, video makers, and lighting and sound technicians.

Part III discusses the changing role of professionals in society, hence going *beyond* professions. Here, a significant, cross-cutting theoretical perspective is applied to the discourse on marketisation, which makes professionals dependent on clients' choices. Two supplemental perspectives are used to look at professionals as actors of change: the perspective emphasising their role as *institutional agents*, who influence the life of complex organisations either from the inside or from the outside, and another perspective—less diffused among scholars in the sociology of professions—which identifies them as key players in political and social movements. The contributions selected deal with these topics from different, innovative perspectives, which include, for instance, looking at how client organisations influence the professionalisation of emerging professions. An original insight is also provided into the relationship between professions and society, focusing on professionals' activism.

Chapter 11, by Tracey Adams, investigates the forces challenging, altering, or even undermining professional self-regulation in two Canadian provinces. Taking on a theoretical perspective derived from Abbott (1988, 2005), the author considers professions and states as *linked ecologies* and, therefore, attempts to understand how different institutions combine to shape regulatory outcomes. The chapter is also informed by

Weber's theories of social action and the state, and identifies stakeholders' concerns and explains how their values, interests, and actions influence regulatory trends over time.

Chapter 12, by Joris Gjata, Matthew Rowe, and Shawhin Roudbari, calls attention to the work professionals perform when they engage beyond their fields of practice, such as through humanitarian or other kinds of social justice projects. The authors refer to two major streams of research in the sociology of professions: once again, Abbott's (2005) *linked ecology* perspective; and also the neo-institutional approach, which sees professionals as agents of institutional change. Their theoretical framework draws upon Abbott's concepts of "hinge" and "avatar" to theorise the practices through which professionals extend their expertise into new social domains. The analysis then focuses on the actions of a group of professionals of the built environment in the United States—architects—who engage in activism, advocacy, and social justice efforts, with specific attention paid to the relationship of this work with their formal professional organisations. The findings show that professional movements may lead to a new type of hybrid professionalism and a new actor, the "activist professional".

Chapter 13, by Paola Sedda and Oihana Husson, deals with social media influencers, a case of *hybrid professionalism* in which quantitative performance criteria prescribed by platforms are combined with creative logic and collective action. The chapter analyses how influencers participate in redefining professionalism and professional practices in the marketing and communication fields, despite not necessarily engaging in actual processes of institutionalisation. Indeed, the influence they exert in their communities mainly derives from their differentiation from institutional actors. The authors thus examine professionals as actors of change who are constantly reframing their discourse on "professionalism" on the basis of public demands and the emergence of new political and societal issues.

The conclusions (Chap. 14) aim to put the pieces of the puzzle together by identifying theoretical links and isolating empirical regularities and specificities within the various contributions along the lines of the three-pronged analytical framework. This approach draws inspiration from Merton's (1949) teachings about *middle-range theories*. Professions are heterogeneous, multifaceted, and variable, and depend on historical and contextual contingencies. As such, they can be studied effectively by referring to theories that "deal with delimited aspects of social phenomena", based on "minor" hypotheses which can be verified through limited empirical observations and, in so doing, they can contribute to the development of a "unified theory" (pp. 39–40).

6 Taking Up the Challenge

Professions are changing radically because the society in which professionals live and work has undergone a profound transformation. The current phase in which capitalist societies find themselves lends a new centrality to expert knowledge. Professionals are at the heart of this change because of their privileged role in the production and management of knowledge. Their renewed importance is associated with changes in the nature of professions. At the same time, they are becoming increasingly differentiated, so much so that the concept of professionalism itself, in the way it is understood in the academic debate, is being called into question. For this reason, we need to find new conceptual lenses through which we look at professions, as this allows us to effectively understand the changing social reality in which professionals and professional groups are embedded.

Heterogeneity is the outcome of multiple processes of differentiation, which have been described in this introduction. These processes of differentiation are not neutral in defining the puzzle we are dealing with when confronting the current reality of professionalism.

We have identified three analytical dimensions to accomplish this complex and challenging task: within, between, and beyond. We have combined these "irreducible" dimensions to form a flexible analytical framework, allowing us to create order in an ambiguous reality, which involves, at the same time, diversity and inequality, local and global, tradition and innovation. The authors of the 12 chapters that follow have accepted this challenge. They have applied the three lenses to read their cases across various countries around the globe, examining both established and emerging professions, focusing on the growing heterogeneity—and inequalities—among professionals and the processes of differentiation that engender them.

References

Abbott, A. (1986). Jurisdictional conflicts: A new approach to the development of the legal professions. *American Bar Foundation Research Journal, 11*(2), 187–224.

Abbott, A. (1988). *The system of professions: An essay on the division of expert labour*. University of Chicago Press.

Abbott, A. (2005). Linked ecologies: States and universities as environments for professions. *Sociological Theory, 23*(3), 245–274. https://doi.org/10.1111/j.0735-2751.2005.00253.x

Adams, T. L., Clegg, S., Eyal, G., Reed, M., & Saks, M. (2020a). Connective professionalism: Towards (yet another) ideal type. *Journal of Professions and Organization, 7*(2), 224–233. https://doi.org/10.1093/jpo/joaa013

Adams, T. L., Kirkpatrick, I., Tolbert, P. S., & Waring, J. (2020b). From protective to connective professionalism: Quo Vadis professional exclusivity? *Journal of Professions and Organization, 7*(2), 234–245. https://doi.org/10.1093/jpo/joaa014

Alacevich, F., Bellini, A., & Tonarelli, A. (2017). *Una professione plurale. Il caso dell'avvocatura fiorentina*. Firenze University Press.

Alvehus, J., Avnoon, N., & Oliver, A. L. (2021). "It's complicated": Professional opacity, duality, and ambiguity—A response to Noordegraaf (2020). *Journal of Professions and Organization, 8*(2), 200–213. https://doi.org/10.1093/jpo/joab006

Barber, B. (1963). Some problems in the sociology of the professions. *Daedalus, 92*(4), 669–688.

Beckert, J. (2010). How do fields change? The interrelations of institutions, networks, and cognition in the dynamics of markets. *Organization Studies, 31*(5), 605–627. https://doi.org/10.1177/0170840610372184

Bell, D. (1973). *The coming of the post-industrial society: A venture in social forecasting*. Basic Books.

Bellini, A. (2014). *Il puzzle dei ceti medi*. Firenze University Press.

Bellini, A., & Maestripieri, L. (2018). Professions Within, Between and Beyond. Varieties of Professionalism in a Globalising World. *CAMBIO, 16*(8), 5–14. https://doi.org/10.13128/cam-bio-24947

Berger, P. L., & Luckmann, T. (1966). *The social construction of reality: A treatise in the sociology of knowledge*. Doubleday.

Bucher, S. V., Chreim, S., Langley, A., & Reay, T. (2016). Contestation about collaboration: Discursive boundary work among professionals. *Organization Studies, 37*(4), 497–522. https://doi.org/10.1177/0170840615622067

Burrage, M. C., & Torstendahl, R. (Eds.). (1990). *Professions in theory and history: Rethinking the study of the professions*. Sage.

Butler, N., Chillas, S., & Muhr, S. L. (2012). Professions at the Margins. *Ephemera, 12*(3), 259–272.

Carr-Saunders, A. M., & Wilson, P. A. (1933). *The professions*. Clarendon Press.

Christensen, C. M. (1997). *The Innovator's Dilemma: When New Technologies Cause Great Firms to Fail*. Harvard Business Review Press.

Cohen, L., & Mallon, M. (1999). The transition from organisational employment to portfolio working: Perceptions of "boundarylessness". *Work, Employment and Society, 13*(2), 329–352. https://doi.org/10.1177/09500179922117962

Dent, M., & Whitehead, S. (2002). *Managing professional identities: Knowledge, performativity and the 'new' professionalism*. Routledge.

Dent, M., Bourgeault, I. L., Denis, J.-L., & Kuhlmann, E. (Eds.). (2016). *The Routledge companion to the professions and professionalism*. Routledge.

Drucker, P. F. (1968). *The age of discontinuity: guidelines to our changing society*. Heinemann.

Durkheim, É. (1890–1900). *Leçons de sociologie: physique des mœurs et du droit*. Presses Universitaires de France 1950.

Ehrenreich, B., & Ehrenreich, J. (1977). The professional-managerial class. *Radical America, 11*(2), 7–13.

Evetts, J. (2003). The sociological analysis of professionalism. Occupational change in the modern world. *International Sociology, 18*(2), 395–415. https://doi.org/10.1177/0268580903018002005

Evetts, J. (2006). Short note: The sociology of professional groups: New directions. *Current Sociology, 54*(1), 133–143. https://doi.org/10.1177/0011392106057161

Evetts, J. (2011). A new professionalism? Challenges and opportunities. *Current Sociology, 59*(4), 406–422. https://doi.org/10.1177/0011392111402585

Farrell, D., & Greig, F. (2016). *Paychecks, paydays, and the online platform economy: Big data on income volatility*. JPMorgan Chase & Institute.

Faulconbridge, J. R., Henriksen, L. F., & Seabrooke, L. (2021). How professional actions connect and protect. *Journal of Professions and Organization, 8*(2), 214–227. https://doi.org/10.1093/jpo/joab008

Faulconbridge, J. R., & Muzio, D. (2007). Reinserting the professional into the study of globalizing professional service firms: the case of law. *Global Networks, 7*(3), 249–270. https://doi.org/10.1111/j.1471-0374.2007.00168.x

Flam, H. (2019). Civil society and professions: US civic and politicized lawyering. *Professions and Professionalism, 9*(1), e3221. https://doi.org/10.7577/pp.3221

Forsyth, P. B., & Danisiewicz, T. J. (1985). Toward a theory of professionalization. *Work and Occupations, 12*(1), 59–76. https://doi.org/10.1177/0730888485012001004

Fournier, V. (1999). The appeal to "professionalism" as a disciplinary mechanism. *Social Review, 47*(2), 280–307. https://doi.org/10.1111/1467-954X.00173

Freidson, E. (1986). *Professional powers. A study of the institutionalization of formal knowledge*. University of Chicago Press.

Freidson, E. (1994). *Professionalism reborn: Theory, prophecy and policy*. University of Chicago Press.

Freidson, E. (2001). *Professionalism, the third logic: On the practice of knowledge*. Polity.

Gallie, D. (Ed.). (2013). *Economic crisis, quality of work and social integration*. Oxford University Press.

Goode, W. J. (1957). Community within a community—the professions. *American Sociological Review, 22*(2), 194–200. https://doi.org/10.2307/2088857

Greenwood, E. (1957). Attributes of a profession. *Social Work, 2*(3), 45–55. https://doi.org/10.1093/sw/2.3.45

Hanlon, G. (1996). "Casino capitalism" and the rise of the "commercialised" service class—An examination of the accountant. *Critical Perspectives on Accounting, 7*(3), 339–363. https://doi.org/10.1006/cpac.1996.0038

Hanlon, G. (1998). Professionalism as enterprise: Service class politics and the redefinition of professionalism. *Sociology, 32*(1), 43–63. https://doi.org/10.1177/0038038598032001004

Haug, M. R. (1972). Deprofessionalization: An alternate hypothesis for the future. *The Sociological Review, 20*(S1), 195–211. https://doi.org/10.1111/j.1467-954X.1972.tb03217.x

Haug, M. R. (1975). The deprofessionalization of everyone? *Sociological Focus, 8*(3), 197–213. https://doi.org/10.1080/00380237.1975.10570899

Heusinkveld, S., Gabbioneta, C., Werr, A., & Sturdy, A. (2018). Professions and (new) management occupations as a contested terrain: Redefining jurisdictional claims. *Journal of Professions and Organization, 5*(3), 248–261. https://doi.org/10.1093/jpo/joy015

Hughes, E. C. (1958). *Men and their work*. Free Press.

Hughes, E. C. (1963). Professions. *Daedalus, 92*(4), 655–668.
Johnson, T. J. (1972). *Professions and power*. Macmillan.
Leicht, K. T., & Fennel, M. L. (2001). *Professional work: A sociological approach*. Blackwell.
Macdonald, K. (1995). *The sociology of the professions*. Sage.
Machlup, F. (1962). *The production and distribution of knowledge in United States*. Princeton University Press.
Maestripieri, L., & Cucca, R. (2018). Small is beautiful? Emerging organizational strategies among Italian professionals. *Canadian Review of Sociology, 55*(3), 362–384. https://doi.org/10.1111/cars.12208
Marshall, T. H. (1939). The recent history of professionalism in relation to social structure and social policy. *Canadian Journal of Economics and Political Science, 5*(3), 325–340. https://doi.org/10.2307/137036
Merton, R. K. (1949). *Social theory and social structure*. Free Press.
McKinlay, J. B., & Arches, J. (1985). Towards the proletarianization of physicians. *International Journal of Health and Services, 15*(2), 161–195. https://doi.org/10.2190/JBMN-C0W6-9WFQ-Q5A6
Murgia, A., Maestripieri, L., & Armano, E. (2016). The precariousness of knowledge workers (part 1): Hybridisation, self-employment and subjectification. *Work Organisation, Labour and Globalisation, 10*(2), 1–8. https://doi.org/10.13169/WORKORGALABOGLOB.10.2.0001
Muzio, D., Brock, D. M., & Suddaby, R. (2013). Professions and Institutional Change: Towards an Institutionalist Sociology of the Professions. *Journal of Management Studies, 50*(5), 699–721. https://doi.org/10.1111/joms.12030
Muzio, D., & Kirkpatrick, I. (2011). Introduction: Professions and organizations—a conceptual framework. *Current Sociology, 59*(4), 389–405. https://doi.org/10.1177/0011392111402584
Muzio, D., Kirkpatrick, I., & Kipping, M. (2011). Professions, organizations and the state: Applying the sociology of the professions to the case of management consultancy. *Current Sociology, 59*(6), 805–824. https://doi.org/10.1177/0011392111419750
Navarro, V. (1988). Professional dominance or proletarianization? Neither. *Milbank Quarterly, 66*(S2), 57–75. https://doi.org/10.2307/3349915
Noordegraaf, M. (2007). From "pure" to "hybrid" professionalism. Present-day professionalism in ambiguous public domains. *Administration and Society, 39*(6), 761–781. https://doi.org/10.1177/0095399707304434
Noordegraaf, M. (2016). Reconfiguring professional work: Changing forms of professionalism in public services. *Administration and Society, 48*(7), 783–810. https://doi.org/10.1177/0095399713509242

Noordegraaf, M. (2020). Protective or connective professionalism? How connected professionals can (still) act as autonomous and authoritative experts. *Journal of Professions and Organization, 7*(2), 205–223. https://doi.org/10.1093/jpo/joaa011

Noordegraaf, M., & Brock, D. M. (2021). Protective and connective professionalism: What we have learned and what we still would like to learn. *Journal of Professions and Organization, 8*(2), 228–236. https://doi.org/10.1093/jpo/joab009

Oppenheimer, M. (1973). The proletarianization of the professional. *The Sociological Review Monograph, 20*(S1), 213–227. https://doi.org/10.1111/j.1467-954X.1972.tb03218.x

Parding, K., Bellini, A., & Maestripieri, L. (2021). Heterogeneity among professions and professionals. *Professions and Professionalism, 11*(1), e4398. https://doi.org/10.7577/pp.4398

Parkin, F. (1979). *Marxism and class theory: A bourgeois critique*. Tavistock.

Parsons, T. (1951). *The social system*. Free Press.

Powell, W. W., & Colyvas, J. A. (2008). Microfoundations of institutional theory. In R. Greenwood, C. Oliver, R. Suddaby, & K. Sahlin (Eds.), *The Sage handbook of organizational institutionalism* (pp. 276–298). Sage.

Reed, M. I. (2018). Elites, professions, and the neoliberal state: Critical points of intersection and contention. *Journal of Professions and Organization, 5*(3), 297–312. https://doi.org/10.1093/jpo/joy010

Saks, M. (2010). Analyzing the professions: The case for the neo-Weberian approach. *Comparative Sociology, 9*(6), 887–915. https://doi.org/10.1163/156913310X522624

Saks, M. (2012). Defining a profession: The role of knowledge and expertise. *Professions and Professionalism, 2*(1), 1–10. https://doi.org/10.7577/pp.v2i1.151

Saks, M. (2015). Inequalities, marginality and the professions. *Current Sociology, 63*(6), 850–868. https://doi.org/10.1177/0011392115587332

Saks, M. (2016). A review of theories of professions, organizations and society: The case for neo-Weberianism, neo-institutionalism and eclecticism. *Journal of Professions and Organization, 3*(2), 170–187. https://doi.org/10.1093/jpo/jow005

Saks, M., & Muzio, D. (Eds.). (2018). *Professions and professional service firms: Private and public sector enterprises in the global economy*. Routledge.

Sarfatti Larson, M. (1977). *The rise of professionalism: A sociological analysis*. University of California Press.

Scott, W. R. (2008). Lords of the dance: Professionals as institutional agents. *Organization Studies, 29*(2), 219–238. https://doi.org/10.1177/0170840607088151

Scott, W. R. (2010). Entrepreneurs and professionals: The mediating role of institutions. *Research in the Sociology of Work, 21*, 27–49. https://doi.org/10.1108/S0277-2833(2010)0000021006

Suddaby, R. (2010). Challenges to institutional theory. *Journal of Management Inquiry, 19*(1), 14–20. https://doi.org/10.1177/1056492609347564

Suddaby, R., & Viale, T. (2011). Professionals and field-level change: Institutional work and the professional project. *Current Sociology, 59*(4), 423–442. https://doi.org/10.1177/0011392111402586

Torstendahl, R. (2005). The need for a definition of "profession". *Current Sociology, 53*(6), 947–951. https://doi.org/10.1177/0011392105058029

Touraine, A. (1969). *La société post-industrielle*. Denoël-Gonthier.

Watson, T. (2002). Professions and professionalism—should we jump off the bandwagon, better to study where it is going? *International Studies of Management and Organization, 32*(2), 93–105. https://doi.org/10.1080/00208825.2002.11043660

Wilensky, H. L. (1964). The professionalization of everyone? *American Journal of Sociology, 70*(2), 137–158. https://doi.org/10.1086/223790

Wright, E. O. (1997). *Class counts. Comparative studies in class analysis*. Cambridge University Press.

Open Access This chapter is licensed under the terms of the Creative Commons Attribution 4.0 International License (http://creativecommons.org/licenses/by/4.0/), which permits use, sharing, adaptation, distribution and reproduction in any medium or format, as long as you give appropriate credit to the original author(s) and the source, provide a link to the Creative Commons license and indicate if changes were made.

The images or other third party material in this chapter are included in the chapter's Creative Commons license, unless indicated otherwise in a credit line to the material. If material is not included in the chapter's Creative Commons license and your intended use is not permitted by statutory regulation or exceeds the permitted use, you will need to obtain permission directly from the copyright holder.

Part I

Within

2

When Employment Status Shapes Professionalism. The Case of the Academic Labour Market in Switzerland

Pierre Bataille, Nicky Le Feuvre, and Marie Sautier

1 Introduction

According to the classical sociology of professions (Hughes, 1971; Parsons, 1939), "professionalism" is understood as a process through which a particular group of workers achieves "monopolistic control"

P. Bataille (✉)
LaRAC, Université Grenoble Alpes, Grenoble, France
e-mail: pierre.bataille@univ-grenoble-alpes.fr

N. Le Feuvre
LACCUS – ISS, NCCR LIVES, Université de Lausanne, Lausanne, Switzerland
e-mail: nicky.lefeuvre@unil.ch

M. Sautier
LACCUS – ISS, NCCR LIVES, Université de Lausanne, Lausanne, Switzerland

Centre for the Sociology of Organisations, Sciences Po, CNRS, Paris, France
e-mail: marie.sautier@unil.ch

© The Author(s), under exclusive license to Springer Nature Switzerland AG 2023

L. Maestripieri, A. Bellini (eds.), *Professionalism and Social Change*,
https://doi.org/10.1007/978-3-031-31278-6_2

(Forsyth & Danisielwicz, 1985, p. 62) over a set of tasks or services. Achieving such a monopoly is the result of a range of actions (Bajard, 2015), including the progressive specialisation of workers (Strauss, 1992), the relegation of certain activities to other—usually subordinate—occupations (Arborio, 1995), the combination of previously distinct activities (Abbott, 1988), competition with other occupations for an expertise-based jurisdiction over a specific issue or the claim to a jurisdiction that has temporarily been left vacant (idem.). As Julia Evetts has stressed, professionalism may thus occur either "from within", through the "successful manipulation of the market by a given occupation", or "from above", as a consequence of "forces external to the occupation" (Evetts, 2018, p. 45). Independently of the process involved, professionalisation is most commonly defined as "the activity by which the rules governing the exchange of goods and services are made and implemented" (Moran & Wood, 1993, p. 17). The sociology of professionalisation and professionalism appears therefore to be mainly *task-based*, exploring how professional groups mobilise "knowledge and expertise" to stake claims with regard to clients, competing professions and the State (Evetts, 2008; Saks, 2012, 2016). From this perspective, the defining quality of a profession is often reduced to "[its] ability to solve important problems for a clientele that is willing to pay for [...] solutions" (Fogarty, 2014, p. 52).

Perhaps because the sociology of professions emerged in North America, where the State does not play a central role in the regulation of professional activities (Demazière & Gadéa, 2010; Sapiro, 2006), the influence of employment status on determining the boundaries of a "professional jurisdiction" (Abbott, 1988) or on the monopoly a profession may exercise over a given "bundle of tasks" (Hughes, 1971) has rarely been addressed.

This relative lack of research interest in the role of employment status may also be due to the fact that these constitute aspects of "ordinary" work, whereas the sociology of professions tradition in the United States focused primarily on elite occupations (Evetts, 2008). Furthermore, since the sociology of professions usually studies a particular occupation within a given societal context (*i.e.* what Julia Evetts (2008, p. 525) calls "within-State theorizing"), cross-national variations in the employment conditions of a given occupation have rarely been taken into consideration.

In this chapter, we argue that more attention needs to be paid to how day-to-day services are rewarded, and to the social and legal structures that frame these rewards. In a context where professionals no longer represent an "elite minority" that condenses power and prestige (Haug, 1975, p. 201), there has been increasing interest in this aspect of professionalism. Also, in line with the theoretical perspectives that underpin this book, we argue that by focusing on employment status, rather than on tasks alone, we can enhance our understanding of the differentiation processes that occur *within* and not only *between* professional groups (see Chap. 1 in this volume).

We therefore advocate stepping away from a task-based approach to professionalism, in order to explore the influence of employment status on professionalism and professional identity. We focus on the higher education (HE) sector in Switzerland. Academics are traditionally seen as archetypal professionals: they have a monopoly over a well-established "bundle of tasks", they are relatively autonomous in the way they manage their own "jurisdiction" and their legitimacy is based on their expertise and scientific knowledge rather than on tradition. We nevertheless argue that it is difficult to understand what "being an academic" means today without recognising the transformations in the employment conditions currently taking place in the HE sector in most Western countries. Here, we analyse in some depth the challenges faced by academics in the early stages of their careers and consider the implications of the expansion of this "precarious" category of knowledge workers for the "professionalism" of the academic occupation as a whole. Our analysis is based on the results gleaned from an online survey and interview data with postdocs previously or currently working in a single Swiss university.[1] By analysing how these aspiring professionals see their academic careers, we identify some of the challenges they face and analyse the implications of their experiences for understanding contemporary academic professionalism.

[1] Data were collected during the *Gendering Academy and Research: Combating Inequalities and Asymmetries* (GARCIA) research project, funded under the EU 7th Framework Programme (Grant agreement n° 611737), with additional funding from the Swiss Centre of Expertise in Life-Course Research – LIVES (https://www.centre-lives.ch/fr). The authors are grateful to the European Commission and to the Swiss National Science Foundation for their support.

2 Linking Micro-Level Practices and Macro-Level Regulations: For an *Employment-Based* Approach to Professionalism

Promoting an *employment-based* approach to professionalism, thereby challenging the traditional *task-based* approach, offers an interesting opportunity to renew and reframe the way that professions and occupations are analysed.

Adopting an *employment-based* approach to professionalism requires us to consider the contractual arrangements under which professionals carry out their activities and determine the "material rewards" they obtain for their work and any associated social protection measures or benefits (Kelloway et al., 2004, p. 109). In other words, we need to explore the contractual arrangements that distinguish individuals who otherwise share a similar "bundle of tasks". For example, medical doctors may either work in a salaried or self-employed capacity, in a hospital, clinic or medical practice, and they are likely to receive different levels of pay, recognition and social benefits according to their employment status.

When exploring the idea that employment status has a significant impact on academic professionalism, we argue that studying the conditions of a particular occupation enables us to link the micro, meso, and macro levels of the analysis. By paying attention to both the legal framework within which professionals offer their services and the compensation they receive for these services, it is possible to develop a sociologically embedded understanding of professional careers and of professionalism. Furthermore, this approach seems to be particularly effective for studying the professionals located at the bottom of the career ladder, who may not have enough power to negotiate the rules that frame professional interactions and the internal division of labour.

As Mike Saks (2016) has stressed, several macro-level studies have already explored the links between "professions and the organizational context in which they operate", providing a "theoretical examination of the nature and role of professions in the wider society" (p. 174). Saks argues that these contributions have often been "underpinned by an abstracted teleological view", rather than by "rigorous evidence-base discussion" or empirical data (idem. p. 174). In this chapter, we look at the case of the academic profession in Switzerland in order to highlight how adopting an *employment-based* approach offers an interesting opportunity to empirically implement our approach to professionalism.

3 Three Task-Based Profiles of Academics: The Researcher, the Teacher and the Manager

Most research about the academic profession has adopted a *task-based* approach. Thus, in most cases, a "bundle of academic tasks" is used to describe the three constitutive activities of the academic profession: teaching, research and administration. The relative weight of each of these tasks, especially that of research and teaching, varies according to socio-historical and economic contexts (Charle & Verger, 2012; Gingras, 2003). However, since the end of the twentieth century in most European and North American countries, academic work has almost always involved a combination of these "bundles of tasks" (Capelleras, 2005; Losego, 2004; Musselin, 2009; Oshagbemi, 2000; Bodin et al., 2018).

When comparing academic recruitment processes in France, the United States and Germany, Christine Musselin distinguishes between two ideal-types through which academics judge their prospective colleagues: the "research active academic" and the "good citizen academic" (Musselin, 2009, pp. 136–139). The first ideal-type profile is defined by an outstanding capacity and ability for research-related tasks. The second profile is defined by commitment to the smooth running of the institution, notably through teaching and supervision.

As an alternative to this binary model, other authors have suggested that administrative and managerial tasks have recently become more central aspects of academic professionalism. Some authors have argued that the "academic manager" is becoming an increasingly important ideal-type in a number of countries (Harley et al., 2004; Henkel, 2000), implying a potential conflict with the traditional values of "academic autonomy and collective ideals" (Winter, 2009, p. 123). The emergence of this third ideal-type profile of academic professionalism reflects the rise of "accountability" within academic institutions, and results from attempts by appropriately qualified individuals to improve their career prospects (Paye, 2015), to maintain their leadership over a research team (Louvel, 2010) or to find a "niche" for themselves when research funding opportunities become rare (Gabrysiak, 2020).

The relative value attributed to these three profiles varies according to the national and historical context (Kwiek, 2015) and the academic discipline (Bodin et al., 2018). However, "research tasks" are usually valued more by the academic community, while "service tasks" (teaching, administration, etc.) are often seen as less desirable (Bamber et al., 2021), sometimes to the point of being regarded as a form of "academic housework" (Misra et al., 2012; Heijstra et al., 2016). The way academics navigate between these three types of tasks also depends on the institutional and national contexts. Moreover, the career paths leading to these three ways of "being an academic" are profoundly shaped by gender, race and other forms of cultural and social capital (O'Meara et al., 2017; Gabrysiak, 2020). However, it is presumed that the internal fragmentation and segmentation of the academic profession is adequately described by referring to these three ideal-type profiles, each based on a specific contribution to the overall "bundle of tasks" of academic work. Individuals who correspond to one or another of these three profiles are assumed to benefit from similar (stable) employment status.

This unified vision of the academic profession becomes rather more difficult to sustain in a historical context where increasing numbers of academic staff no longer have permanent positions (Bosanquet et al., 2017, p. 890). It would therefore seem legitimate to question to what extent structural changes to employment conditions in HE institutions might have an impact on professional identities and practices.

4 The Rise of Fixed-Term Contracts within Academic Institutions

Historical accounts of the professionalisation of academic work have suggested that between the end of the nineteenth century and the end of the twentieth century, academic careers were mostly based on a two-stage process (Enders & Musselin, 2008, p. 134), usually beginning with a period of "academic apprenticeship", characterised by fixed-term positions that provided the basis for selection into the tenured professorships (or their equivalents) that made up the core of the academic profession. Although the relative chances of moving up from a fixed-term to a tenured position vary considerably across countries and disciplines, as did the time required to make this transition, the overall pattern of an academic career was similar in many countries around the world.

However, in the wake of the extensive adoption of new public management strategies in academic systems in most Western countries (Enders, 2001; Ferlie et al., 2008), more diverse recruitment and selection processes have emerged (Enders & Musselin, 2008, p. 134). Over the last three decades, the relative share of permanent positions in the academic labour market has dropped, sometimes quite spectacularly. Although the increase in fixed-term positions varies from country to country, the trend has been widely observed (Murgia & Poggio, 2019). In the United States, for instance, the share of the academic workforce hired on non-tenured contracts rose from 43% in 1975 to 64% in 2003 (Ehrenberg, 2006). Likewise, in France, where a relatively short transition phase towards the first level of tenure used to be the norm, the share of permanent positions has sharply decreased since 2004 (Quéré, 2012, pp. 312–313). Between 30% and 40% of the academic staff in French universities are now employed on temporary contracts (MESRI 2021). This generalised restructuring of the academic career path can be partly explained by the rise of a "managerial culture" within HE institutions (Enders & Musselin, 2008, p. 135). From this perspective, academic tenure is represented as a risk, since it can: "entrench highly specialized staff whose domains of competence may quickly become irrelevant owing to the rapid transformation of science" (Enders & Musselin, 2008, p. 135). In such conditions, "contingent (i.e. non-tenured) positions tend to develop as alternative career tracks, less secure, distinct from the traditional two-stage tracks and with few bridges from one to another" (idem.). Non-tenured academics tend to be excluded from the core of the occupation and may hold a "probationary" status for many years (Le Feuvre et al., 2020). Indeed, fixed-term teaching and research contracts are becoming an increasingly common alternative to tenured positions for many academics in the early (and not so early) stages of their careers.

5 Mapping the Experiences of Early-Career Stage Academics in the Swiss Context

In the following section, we base our analysis on the case of Switzerland, a country where the proportion of fixed-term academic positions has risen sharply over the past twenty years (Bataille et al., 2017; Leemann et al., 2010). We argue that this has changed the ways in which academics view their work, but also their experience of belonging to an HE institution and the way they carry out their work.

A vast body of literature has documented the process of academic "proletarisation" (Dearlove, 1997; Ellis et al., 2014; Wilson, 1991) or of academic deprofessionalisation (Raina, 2019; Roberts & Donahue, 2000). In line with Marxist critiques of contemporary capitalism (Braverman, 1974), these studies have focused on the changes that have occurred in a number of countries since the end of the 1980s, leading to diminished prestige and professional autonomy for academics in general. These structural changes may involve, among other things: "less trust and discretion"; "a strong division of labour", "stronger hierarchies of management control", "greater conflict"; "growing routinisation", "bureaucratisation", "worse conditions and facilities" and a "steep decline in relative pay" for many academics (Wilson, 1991, p. 251).

Our line of reasoning differs from this deprofessionalisation perspective. We argue that the rise of destandardised academic employment conditions has created new fault lines within the academic occupation as a whole. On the one hand, there is still a widespread belief that academics benefit from relatively stable resources and recognition, occupying tenured positions and navigating between the ideal-type profiles of the academic "researcher", "teacher" or "manager" (Musselin, 2009). On the other hand, we observe a large number of academics in the early stages of their careers who are employed on fixed-term contracts. Interestingly, in order to maintain their employability over time, these precarious academic workers are unable to specialise in a particular form of academic professionalism, and thus appear to perform a "bundle of tasks" that is quite distinct from those of their tenured counterparts. In other words, job security appears to largely determine the ability of academics to specialise in a specific set of academic tasks over time. In contrast, choosing to specialise in a specific type of academic task appears to be too risky for academics who have yet failed to secure a stable position, since this form of specialisation could significantly limit their future employment opportunities.

5.1 A Diverse "Bundle of Tasks"

Our analyses are based on data gathered during the GARCIA European research project (2014–2018). This project studied gendered career asymmetries in the early stages of academic careers. Research teams from six countries (Austria, Belgium, Iceland, Italy, Slovenia and Switzerland) gathered qualitative and quantitative data on the working routines and work-life balance strategies of men and women currently in the so-called postdoc phase of their careers (*i.e.* employed in research and/or teaching and/or project management capacities, following the successful completion of a PhD). For this chapter, we used the quantitative and qualitative data collected in Switzerland. Our target population included all the men and women who had been hired as postdocs in a single Swiss university between 2010 and 2013 (N = 406). In 2015, all of them were invited to complete an online survey. About a third of the target group filled out our questionnaire (n = 138, resp. rate = 34%). This response rate compares favourably with other online surveys in the same field (Shih & Fan, 2009). Furthermore, a comparison of the socio-economic characteristics of our respondents with the human ressources data of our case-study university revealed no selection bias. The respondents' characteristics broadly mirror those of the target population, at least in terms of age, gender and disciplinary field.

Our respondents described a variety of employment status. In 2015, 75% were employed on fixed-term academic (postdoc) contracts, 15% had moved on to permanent academic positions, 8% had left academia altogether, and 2% were unemployed. Since this chapter deals with professionalism in academia, we will focus our analyses on the respondents who had remained in academic employment (n = 121). In terms of work experience, 50% of the respondents had defended their theses fewer than six years earlier, and 25% seven or more years earlier. About 60% of our respondents were female, 73% were from a science (STEM) background, and 37% from a social sciences and humanities (SSH) background. Finally, only 17% of the respondents held permanent or tenured positions.

We asked these postdocs and former postdocs about what their current jobs entailed, and we invited them to use a 5-point scale (from 1 = "Never" to 5 = "Mostly") to rank the relative importance of different tasks: ("theoretical work", "empirical work", "cooperation with external private sector partners", "project management", "administration", "teaching" and "other"), in their daily routines. Since their answers were self-reported, the scale allowed us to capture the subjective perception our respondents had of what they did in their work. We were also able to assess the interrelation between "work" and "self" for our respondents and to explore how their work shaped "value and prestige judgments" about themselves and others (Hughes, 1971, p. 339).

The main purpose of our study was to analyse whether or not their employment status had any bearing on the degree to which our respondents reported particular configurations of task specialisation. To this end, we used a model that we had previously used in a study of artistic occupations (Perrenoud & Bataille, 2017). We ran a Principal Component Analysis (PCA) on the self-estimated weight of each of the above-mentioned daily tasks (Fig. 2.1). Then we visualised where each individual was located on the PCA factorial plan according to different variables: their discipline (STEM or SSH); their employment contract (fixed-term or permanent); their "academic age" (*i.e.* the number of years since defending their PhD) and their gender (Fig. 2.2).

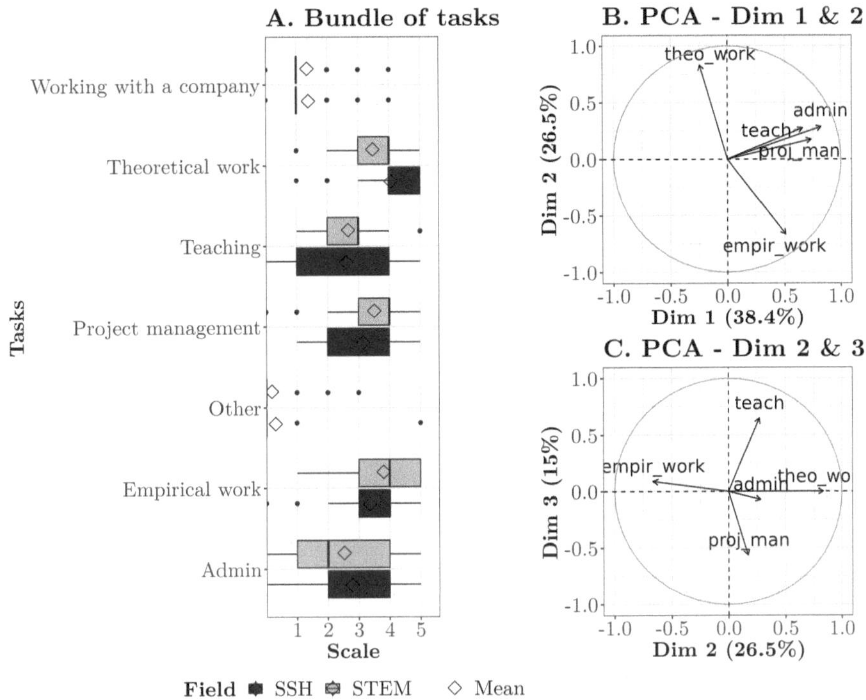

Fig. 2.1 The "bundle of tasks" carried out by early-career stage academics working in a Swiss University **(A)** Bundle of tasks **(B)** PCA – Dim 1 & 2

Figure 2.1 shows the average "bundle of tasks" (A) observed among our respondents. We also plotted the result of our PCA (B). The more frequently two tasks were mentioned together, the closer the two arrows are on the graph. Here, we only account for the three main dimensions of the PCA, which make up 79.9% of the variance observed.

Figure 2.1A shows that the tasks that feature in the daily work routines of postdocs in Switzerland are similar to those observed elsewhere (Capelleras, 2005; Oshagbemi, 2000; Bodin et al., 2018). On average, research-related tasks ("theoretical work" and "empirical work") are seen as daily core tasks, followed by administrative duties ("project management" and "administration"), all well ahead of teaching. Other kinds of tasks ("working with industry", etc.) are not central to the daily activities

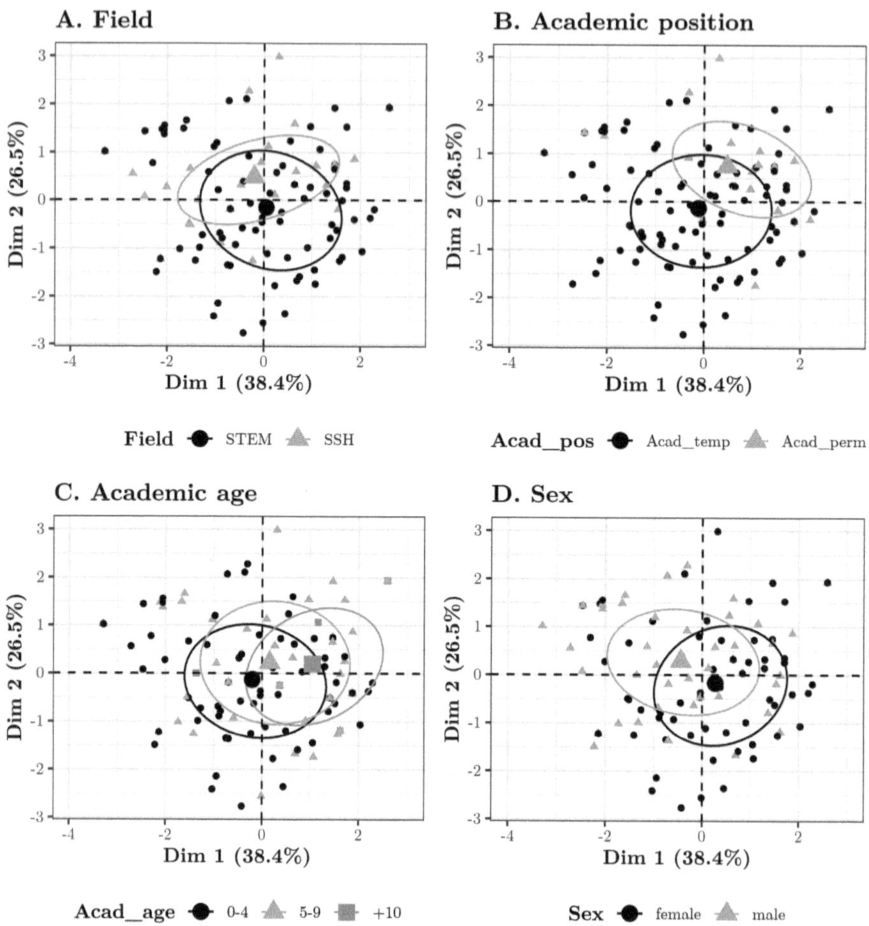

Fig. 2.2 Scatterplot and clouds of early-career stage academics working in a Swiss University **(A)** Field **(B)** Academic position **(C)** Academic age **(D)** Sex. (Source GARCIA Web survey)

of our respondents. The differences in the task distribution for postdocs in the STEM and SSH fields are relatively small.

According to our PCA (Fig. 2.1B), the main difference among our respondents (Dim 1) is between those who claim that their work routine corresponds to the traditional distribution between the three types of tasks performed by academics (i.e. research, teaching and management), and those who do not feel specialised at all. Thus, on the PCA factorial plan plotted in Fig. 2.1B, the left part of the diagram is almost entirely blank. The second dimension (Dim 2) divides our respondents according to two research-related tasks: those who state that their time is mostly invested in empirical work and those who feel more focused on theoretical work. Figure 2.1C shows that the third dimension (Dim 3) opposes a "teaching" profile to a more "administrative" one. Overall, the three ideal-typical academic profiles (*i.e.* research, teaching and management) can be traced with the second and third dimensions of our PCA.

5.2 The Importance of Employment Status

Figure 2.2 represents the individuals on the first (horizontal axis) and second (vertical axis) dimensions of our PCA. The median ellipses represent the areas where at least 50% of the individuals presenting one of the characteristics are located. For instance, our SSH respondents tend to be located near the "empirical research" pole less frequently than their STEM counterparts (Fig. 2.2A), since the SSH ellipse (in grey) is located towards the top of the graph. The STEM specialists (in black) are more evenly spread across the whole surface. Figure 2.2D shows that women (in black) are also slightly more likely to be located near the "empirical research" pole than men. However, gender is not as important as we had expected for the distribution of our respondents between the different types of tasks. For example, we did not identify a clear specialisation of women in the traditionally undervalued teaching activities. At this early stage in academic careers, gender differences only appear important when other factors, such as parental status, are taken into consideration (Le Feuvre et al., 2018).

Regarding the postdocs' level of investment in one or several specific tasks (*i.e.* the position on the first axis), academic age is clearly a relevant variable (Fig. 2.2C): a higher declared involvement in specific types of academic tasks is more common among respondents who had defended their PhD over ten years previously (dark grey). Our (academically) younger respondents (i.e. those who had defended their PhD fewer than nine years earlier and in particular, fewer than five years earlier) did not identify any particular set of tasks that are central to their daily routines. They are thus more often located on the left-hand side of the axis, with other respondents who do not feel specialised in any way. Nevertheless, the ellipses do overlap to a large extent. It is the nature of the academic position occupied (fixed-term or permanent) that appears to determine the localisation of our respondents, rather than academic age per se (Fig. 2.2B). Those who have a tenured academic position (in grey) are all located on the right-hand side of the graph. Respondents who were still in fixed-term positions at the time of the survey are more evenly spread across the whole of the surface.

These results suggest that self-identification with a specific bundle of academic tasks is linked with occupying a stable academic position. The majority of our respondents who had stable academic positions identified a particular group of core tasks, whereas those on fixed-term contracts did not identify a similar set of core tasks. This can be interpreted in two ways. On the one hand, it could be that although postdocs have specific job descriptions (managing new research projects, supervising graduate students, etc.), they often end up doing additional tasks. Since they are obviously at pains to remain on good terms with their supervisors on whom they depend to renew their employment contracts (Le Feuvre et al., 2020), refusing to do the extra work is not an option. On the other hand, and perhaps on a more subjective level, non-tenured academics often experience a fragmented workload (Bataille, 2016). This feeling is compounded by the need to enhance their publication record and develop their networks in order to maintain or improve their future chances of employment (*i.e.* employability), in addition to fulfilling their current contractual obligations.

In both cases, the impression of having a fragmented workload often led our respondents to question the meaning of their work and the high price they felt they were required to pay in order to simply "stay in the system". It thus appears that the lack of self-identification with a specific set of tasks and the inability to cultivate a profile in line with one of the historical forms of academic professionalism is a direct consequence of the precarious employment conditions of our respondents.

6 Conclusion

Our results suggest that changes in employment conditions have eroded the prevalence and significance of the traditional ideal-type task-based profiles for academics currently in the early stages of their careers, leading to the emergence of new fault lines within the profession. Indeed, there appears to be a clear distinction between those who can identify with a particular "bundle of tasks" and those who are required to "fill the gaps" in order to remain in the academic labour market.

As we show here and elsewhere (Le Feuvre et al., 2020), recent structural changes to employment conditions within HE institutions raise serious questions about academic professional boundaries and about academic professionalism as a whole. An oversimplified use of categories such as "early career researcher" or even "postdoc" when speaking about non-tenured academics can lead to the erroneous idea that people employed on fixed-term contracts are only temporarily located on the margins of the occupational group and that in due time they will be admitted to more central and permanent positions. In reality, the growth of fixed-term positions and the fact that a large number of core academic tasks are being permanently handled by a succession of highly qualified people employed on a temporary basis suggest the need to revisit some of the broadly held views about the academic profession and academic professionalism as a whole. In short, the time has perhaps come to question whether permanent or tenured academic positions should still be considered as the norm and as the basis of academic professionalism. We suggest that fixed-term positions now represent an alternative academic career path, rather than merely representing an "early stage" in academic careers, through which individuals are destined to transition before eventually specialising in research, teaching or management. Considering non-permanent academics as professionals to much the same extent as their tenured colleagues would require the development of innovative analytical tools that could monitor emergent forms of fragmentation and internal segmentation *within* the academic labour market.

The *employment-based* analysis developed here provides an innovative way to study the differentiation processes occurring *within* professions

(Bellini and Maestripieri, 2018). Firstly, shifting the approach towards employment status enables us to move beyond the study of "boundary work" and to focus on diverse forms of occupational segregation and segmentation. Secondly, understanding how "being a professional" is framed jointly by contractual arrangements and by employment conditions allows us to focus on the interaction between processes at work at the macro, meso and micro levels of society. Far from invalidating traditional analyses of professionalism, we suggest that this approach could foster more productive and insightful dialogue between different branches of the academic literature on employment, work, organisations and professionalism that are still too often considered separately rather than in combination.

References

Abbott, A. (1988). *The system of professions: An essay on the division of expert labor.* University of Chicago Press.

Arborio, A.-M. (1995). Quand le "sale boulot" fait le métier: Les aides-soignantes dans le monde professionnalisé de l'hôpital. *Sciences sociales et santé, 13*(3), 93–126. https://doi.org/10.3406/sosan.1995.1338

Bajard, F. (2015). L'invention de la céramique d'art. Contribution à la sociologie de la construction des groupes professionnels. *Sociologie du travail, 57*(3), 299–321.

Bamber, M., McCormack, J., & Lyons, B. J. (2021). Conceptualising 'within-group stigmatisation' among high-status workers. *Work, Employment and Society*, 095001702110412. https://doi.org/10.1177/09500170211041287

Bataille, P. (2016). Qualitative report on the leaky pipeline in Switzerland. In B. Fusulier & F. Dubois-Shaik (Eds.), *GARCIA Deliverable D6.2* (pp. 190–221). Trento University.

Bataille, P., Le Feuvre, N., & Kradolfer Morales, S. (2017). Should I stay or should I go? The effects of precariousness on the gendered career aspirations of postdocs in Switzerland. *European Educational Research Journal, 16*(2–3), 313–331.

Bellini, A., & Maestripieri, L. (2018). Professions within, between and beyond. Varieties of professionalism in a Globalising world. *Cambio, 8*(16), 5–14. http://www.fupress.net/index.php/cambio/article/view/24947

Bodin, R., Millet, M., & Saunier, É. (2018). Entre triple contrainte et ancrage disciplinaire. Pratiques et conditions d'enseignement à l'Université. *Cahiers de la recherche sur l'éducation et les savoirs, 17*, 143–167.

Bosanquet, A., Mailey, A., Matthews, K. E., & Lodge, J. M. (2017). Redefining 'early career' in academia: A collective narrative approach. *Higher Education Research & Development, 36*(5), 890–902. https://doi.org/10.1080/07294360.2016.1263934

Braverman, H. (1974). *Labor and monopoly capital: The degradation of work in the twentieth century* (Vol. 26, p. 1). Monthly Review Press.

Capelleras, J.-L. (2005). Attitudes of academic staff towards their job and organisation: An empirical assessment. *Tertiary Education and Management, 11*, 147–166.

Charle, C., & Verger, J. (2012). Histoire des universités. XIIème-XXIème siècle. Presses universitaires de France.

Dearlove, J. (1997). The academic labour process: From collegiality and professionalism to managerialism and proletarianisation? *Higher Education Review, 30*(1), 56–75.

Demazière, D., & Gadéa, C. (2010). *Sociologie des groupes professionnels*. La Découverte.

Ehrenberg, R. G. (2006). The changing nature of the faculty and faculty employment practices. In R. Clark & M. d'Ambrosio (Eds.), *The new balancing act in the business of higher education* (pp. 103–117). Edward Elgar.

Ellis, V., McNicholl, J., Blake, A., & McNally, J. (2014). Academic work and proletarianisation: A study of higher education-based teacher educators. *Teaching and Teacher Education, 40*, 33–43. https://doi.org/10.1016/j.tate.2014.01.008

Enders, J. (2001). *Academic staff in Europe: Changing contexts and conditions*. Greenwood.

Enders, J., & Musselin, C. (2008). Back to the future? The academic professions in the 21st century. Paris: OECD Publications Higher Education to 2030, 1, 125–150. https://doi.org/10.1787/9789264040663-en.

Evetts, J. (2008). Introduction: Professional work in Europe. *European Societies, 10*(4), 525–544. https://doi.org/10.1080/14616690701871696

Evetts, J. (2018). Professions in turbulent times: Changes, challenges and opportunities. *Sociologia, Problemas e Práticas, 88*, 43–59. http://journals.openedition.org/spp/4955.

Ferlie, E., Musselin, C., & Andresani, G. (2008). The steering of higher education systems: A public management perspective. *Higher Education, 56*, 325–348.

Fogarty, T. J. (2014). The bloom is off the rose: Deprofessionalization in public accounting. In S. Mintz (Ed.), *Accounting for the public interest: Perspectives on accountability, professionalism and role in society* (pp. 51–72). Springer. https://doi.org/10.1007/978-94-007-7082-9_3

Forsyth, P. B., & Danisielwicz, T. J. (1985). Toward a theory of professionalization. *Work and Occupations, 12*(1), 59–76. https://doi.org/10.1177/0730888485012001004

Gabrysiak, L. (2020). Publish or what? *Zilsel, n°, 7*(2), 128–159.

Gingras, Y. (2003). Idées d'universités. *Actes de la recherche en sciences sociales, 148*(3), 3–7.

Harley, S., Muller-Camen, M., & Collin, A. (2004). From academic communities to managed organisations: The implications for academic careers in UK and German universities. *Journal of Vocational Behavior, 64*(2), 329–345. https://doi.org/10.1016/j.jvb.2002.09.003

Haug, M. R. (1975). The Deprofessionalization of everyone? *Sociological Focus, 7–213.* https://doi.org/10.1080/00380237.1975.10570899

Heijstra, T. M., Steinthorsdóttir, Finnborg Salome & Einarsdóttir, Thorgerdur (2016): Academic career making and the double-edged role of academic housework, Gender and Education: http://dx.doi.org/https://doi.org/10.1080/09540253.2016.1171825, 29, 764

Henkel, M. (2000). *Academic identities and policy change in higher education.* Jessica Kingsley Publishers.

Hughes, E. (1971). *The sociological eye: Selected papers.* Routledge.

Kelloway, E. K., Gallagher, D. G., Barling, J., & Kaufmann, B. E. (2004). Work, employment, and the individual. In B. E. Kaufmann (Ed.), *Theoretical perspectives on work and the employment relationship* (pp. 105–131). Labor and Employment Research Association.

Kwiek, M. (2015). Academic generations and academic work: Patterns of attitudes, behaviors, and research productivity of Polish academics after 1989. *Studies in Higher Education, 40*(8), 1354–1376.

Le Feuvre, N., Bataille, P., del Río Carral, M., Kradolfer Morales, S., & Sautier, M. (2018). The gendered diversification of academic career paths in comparative perspective. In A. Murgia & B. Poggio (Eds.), *The Precarisation of research careers: A comparative gender analysis* (pp. 50–80). Routledge.

Le Feuvre, N., Bataille, P., & Sautier, M. (2020). Probationary or second-class citizens? Postdoctoral experiences in the Swiss context. In S. Sümer (Ed.), *Gendered academic citizenship: Issues and experiences* (pp. 65–101). Palgrave Macmillan.

Leemann, R. J., Dubach, P., & Boes, S. (2010). The leaky pipeline in the Swiss university system: Identifying gender barriers in postgraduate education and networks using longitudinal data. *Revue Suisse de Sociologie, 36*(2), 299–323.

Losego, P. (2004). Le travail invisible à l'Université: Le cas des antennes universitaires. *Sociologie du travail, 46*(2), 187–204.

Louvel, S. (2010). Changing authority relations within French academic research units since the 1960s. In R. Whitley, J. Gläser, & L. Engwall (Eds.), *Reconfiguring knowledge production* (pp. 184–210). Oxford University Press. https://doi.org/10.1093/acprof:oso/9780199590193.001.0001

Misra, J., Lundquist, J. H., & Templer, A. (2012). Gender, work time, and care responsibilities among faculty. *Sociological Forum, 27*(2), 300–323. https://doi.org/10.1111/j.1573-7861.2012.01319.x

MESRI. (2021). Bilan social 2019-2020 des personnels de l'enseignement supérieur. Paris: Ministère de l'Enseignement supérieur, de la Recherche et de l'Innovation.

Moran, M., & Wood, B. (1993). *States, regulation, and the medical profession.* Open University Press.

Murgia, A., & Poggio, B. (Eds.). (2019). *The precarisation of research careers: A comparative gender analysis.* Routledge.

Musselin, C. (2009). *The market for academics.* Routledge.

O'Meara, K., Kuvaeva, A., Nyunt, G., Waugaman, C., & Jackson, R. (2017). Asked more often: Gender differences in faculty workload in research universities and the work interactions that shape them. *American Educational Research Journal, 54*(6), 1154–1186.

Oshagbemi, T. (2000). How satisfied are academics with their primary tasks of teaching, research and administration and management? *International Journal of Sustainability in Higher Education, 1*, 124–136.

Parsons, T. (1939). The professions and social structure. *Social Forces, 17*(4), 457–467. https://doi.org/10.2307/2570695

Paye, S. (2015). Temporaires, permanents,'vedettes': La tripartition du salariat académique au Royaume-Uni. Sociologie du Travail, 57(2), 175–199.

Perrenoud, M., & Bataille, P. (2017). Artist, Craftsman, Teacher: "Being a musician" in France and Switzerland. *Popular Music and Society, 40*(5), 592–604.

Quéré, M. (2012). Repères et références statistiques sur les enseignements, la formation et la recherche. Ministère de l'enseignement supérieur et de la recherche.

Raina, S. (2019). Academic Deprofessionalization: A case study of the effects of privatization on academic profession in private Indian universities. *International Journal of Sociology, 49*(5–6), 370–388. https://doi.org/10.1080/00207659.2019.1677354

Roberts, K. A., & Donahue, K. A. (2000). Professing professionalism: Bureaucratization and Deprofessionalization in the academy. *Sociological Focus, 33*(4), 365–383. https://doi.org/10.1080/00380237.2000.10571175

Saks, M. (2012). Defining a profession: The role of knowledge and expertise. *Professions and Professionalism, 2*(1). https://doi.org/10.7577/pp.v2i1.151

Saks, M. (2016). A review of theories of professions, organizations and society: The case for neo-Weberianism, neo-institutionalism and eclecticism. *Journal of Professions and Organization, 3*(2), 170–187. https://doi.org/10.1093/jpo/jow005

Sapiro, G. (2006). Les professions intellectuelles entre l'État, l'entrepreneuriat et l'industrie. *Le Mouvement Social, 214*, 3–18.

Shih, T.-H., & Fan, X. (2009). Comparing response rates in E-mail and paper surveys: A meta-analysis. *Educational Research Review, 4*(1), 26–40. https://doi.org/10.1016/j.edurev.2008.01.003

Strauss, A. L. (1992). La trame de la négociation: Sociologie qualitative et interactionnisme. L'Harmattan.

Wilson, T. (1991). The proletarianisation of academic labour. *Industrial Relations Journal, 22*(4), 250–262. https://doi.org/10.1111/j.1468-2338.1991.tb00642.x

Winter, R. (2009). Academic manager or managed academic? Academic identity schisms in higher education. *Journal of Higher Education Policy and Management, 31*(2), 121–131. https://doi.org/10.1080/13600800902825835

3

Processes of Differentiation and Fragmentation within: South African Textile Designers

Debby Bonnin

In their introduction to this book (Chap. 1), the editors point to increasing differentiation both *within* and *between* professions. They argue this process of differentiation goes *beyond* the professions and affects society as a whole, and that to understand the changes in the professional project, it is necessary to locate them within the broader processes of institutional and societal change.

This chapter contributes to the discussion of the increasing heterogeneity and differentiation occurring within professions, sketching the processes of *differentiation within* the expert occupation of textile designers in South Africa. Drawing on the results of a qualitative research study, the chapter analyses the differentiation processes that have led to increasing heterogeneity. It casts light on how technological change, a relatively unexplored area (Bellini & Maestripieri, 2018, 7), joined by economic and labour market challenges exacerbated by globalisation, has been an important element that has contributed to the change in the professional

D. Bonnin (✉)
University of Pretoria, Pretoria, South Africa
e-mail: debby.bonnin@up.ac.za

© The Author(s), under exclusive license to Springer Nature Switzerland AG 2023

L. Maestripieri, A. Bellini (eds.), *Professionalism and Social Change*,
https://doi.org/10.1007/978-3-031-31278-6_3

status of textile designers. As the research demonstrates, these two aspects have fragmented the profession, extending the boundaries of professional expertise and contributing to growing inequality, poorer employment opportunities and more precarious working conditions.

South African designers have had little control over how the industry has changed—to survive, they have had to adapt to the new situations as best they can. The chapter identifies four differentiated "segments" (Noordegraaf, 2016) that have emerged from these changes. First, those who stayed within the ever-shifting textile industry even when it became more difficult to maintain their professional autonomy. Second come those who used their professional knowledge and status to create new jobs for themselves within organisations. Third, those who left organisations and launched themselves as independent professionals. And fourth are the "newcomers", the "self-employed" who never had the possibility of working in an organisation, since they entered the labour market when very few large mills were still in operation.

1 Methods

The chapter is based on a qualitative research study. In-depth interviews were conducted using a non-probability sample. I identified several cohorts which are key to the broader home textiles supply and production chain. These cohorts are textile designers, stylists, retail buyers, manufacturers, suppliers of home textile products, convertors/wholesalers, importers of home textile products and educators of textile designers. Key informants were identified within these different cohorts, and snowball sampling was used thereafter.

A total of fifty-six in-depth interviews were completed using a semi-structured interview guide. Thirty were with textile designers located in the three major industrial centres (Durban, Cape Town and Gauteng). A further fifteen interviewees worked within the broader supply chain—chief executive officers of textile mills, suppliers, importers, convertors and retail buyers. Some respondents fitted into more than one cohort, such as textile designers who became stylists or importers. Ethical clearance for the research was obtained, with informants giving informed consent to be interviewed. Interviews were recorded and transcribed, and pseudonyms were used to protect the identity of the informants.

Within each interview, a work narrative was identified; this was situated in time and space and contextualised within the broader social, economic and political frame. Points of transition or change were identified and a comparison established across the work narratives of all the designers.

2 Professions and Professionalism

Chapter 1 highlights the discussions within the "professions" literature around the concepts of *professions* and *professionalism*. The term *professionalism* has become increasingly prominent in the literature, as Bellini, Maestripieri and Parding argue, not only because scholars have agreed on its heuristic usefulness, but also because societal transformations have pointed to the need to distinguish conceptually between "expert labour" and "profession" (Chap. 1).

Initially, the literature demarcated professions through the "taxonomic" approach (Saks, 2012). However, over time the neo-Weberian paradigm, which defines professions "in terms of exclusionary social closure in the marketplace sanctioned by the state" (Saks, 2012, 4), became dominant. The primary focus was on the traditional professions, such as doctors, lawyers and accountants. Nevertheless, there was increasing recognition that perhaps the difference between the traditional professions and other kinds of expert occupations were "differences of degree rather than kind" (Evetts, 2006, 134).

From the mid-1990s, shifts in the broader economy and society, particularly the tertiarisation of the economy and employment, have seen organisations becoming more significant as employers of professionals. This in turn has stimulated new debates within the literature, focusing on professionals within organisations and conceptualising professionalism in this context, as academics have sought to understand what these shifts meant for "the professions".

Evetts (2006, 140) suggested that the term *organisational professionalism* (in contrast to *occupational professionalism*) can be used to describe "discourses of control" used by managers within organisations. The concept of *hybrid professionalism* to describe professionalism in different organisational situations was introduced by Noordegraaf (2007). The development of these ideas and the accompanying debates are outlined in Chapter 1. However, the concept of *situated professionalism* (Noordegraaf, 2007, 772–773) is not discussed. Noordegraaf suggests that situated professionalism illustrates situations where professionals can exert professional control while embedded within organisations and subjected to organisational control. This reinforces the point made by Evetts (cited in Noordegraaf, 2007, 774) that "the meaning of professionalism is not fixed": as changes occur in the broader economy and society, so professionalism changes to accommodate these new situations. It is necessary to explore the broader "societal forces on professional work" (Noordegraaf, 2016, 790) to wholly understand the impact of these and other changes on the professional field.

This in-depth analysis of the expert occupation of textile designer sheds some light on these discussions. Through tracing the impact of broader societal changes (in this specific example, the challenges associated with globalisation and digitalisation), it demonstrates empirically the challenges faced by situated professionals and illustrates the way in which these occupations have become fragmented by processes of differentiation.

3 South African Textile Designers, Professionalism, Professional Values and Disruption

Textile designers are people who design (creatively conceive) the fabric used to produce apparel, furnishings or even industrial textiles. Across these industrial sub-sectors, there are some common skills and knowledge required; but there is also great diversity related to technologies, products and markets. All textile designers should be able to interpret a brief from a customer or manager and translate their creative concept (response) into a marketable product, using the design and production technologies available.

In South Africa, textile design was widely acknowledged as an "expert occupation" (see Dent et al., 2016, 1). Until the early twenty-first century, textile mills were dominant in the labour market and were the primary employers of textile designers (Bonnin, 2013). Most employed designers had graduated as textile designers (National Diploma in Textile Design, a three-year tertiary qualification), but some had other qualifications: in commercial art, fine art or graphic design. Graduates quickly found full-time employment in South Africa's thriving textile industry. These were secure jobs with good pay and conditions.

> In the year that I graduated [1984], it was common that the best three students got taken up by David Whiteheads, who was the most prestigious textile mill in those days, the next three by Frame, and maybe the next three by Da Gama. [...] Every single year, industry used to take them in. (Interview, Gil Anderson).

Management accepted that designers were "different" from other employees. As creatives, they needed to be nurtured in an artistic environment—a more "genteel" environment, separate from the factory. Most integrated textile mills had large design studios staffed by twenty to thirty designers headed by a studio manager. Designers were not "controlled" and monitored like the workers employed in other labour processes. The designers managed themselves—both their working schedules and their work processes. Designs and the different colourways were hand-painted. A designer could take two months to produce a design. They did not have to "clock in", and could leave the workplace to find inspiration, research and "feed" the creative process.

> Then we had the flexibility. We could just tell Dave [the studio manager] or one of the designers, I'm just going out to the bookshop. [...] We would go there and look at the books, then we could take them [on account]. We used to buy a lot of books from Adams [Bookshop]. (Interview, Paul Nair)

The studio manager was less of a "manager" and more of a facilitator or bridge between the "factory" (sales and production) and the "studio". At some mills, the person heading the design studio had the job title Head of Design or Creative Director, suggesting their role was creative rather than managerial. The more junior or less skilled designers were given a "tight brief" by the studio or product manager. The more experienced designers were furnished with a "concept", and had the freedom to interpret the brief as they wished. Creative freedom was embedded in the organisational culture of mills supplying the higher-end market.

> The Creative Director used to brief us because he went overseas and he used to know what the trend was and come back and have this whole big thing [presentation] with us. And then he used to sit with our senior designers, and he would give you the brief and say, this is what I am looking for, and this is the type of thing that I have seen. So you went away, and you did that. (Interview, Serena Pillay)

Unlike other expert occupations (see Muzio et al., 2011), South African textile designers did not strive for professionalisation—that is, to create a formal association, to vet membership and to develop a code of conduct. Perhaps this was because most textiles designers were women, and, as Butler, Chillas and Muhr (2012) argue, occupations that are overwhelmingly dominated by women are less likely to be professionalised in the "pure" sense (Noordegraaf, 2007, 765–768). Nevertheless, South African textile designers based their claim to being professionals on their qualifications, skills, expertise, competence and autonomy in the workplace. Their place of work was an important component of their professional identity—according to the type of work produced by a particular mill, its status was higher (or lower), as was the status of the designers who worked there. The "high-end" mills were known for outstanding, original designs and the designers working there were held in similar esteem by their colleagues. There was a strong sense of professional community and a close network existed among designers. Many had trained at the same institutions, and the number of workplaces was limited; thus, they all knew the designers who worked in other studios and recognised their "handwriting" (design style).

In turn, the designers' expertise was acknowledged by their peers and by industry that employed them, with the "best" designers developing a professional reputation based on their individual expertise. Thus, while textile designers were subject to the organisational discipline of the company that employed them, they were still able to exercise their professional discretion and control, described by Noordegraaf (2007) as situated professionalism.

Over the two decades from the mid-1980s onwards, dramatic changes in the industry disrupted the professional status and reputation of South African textile designers and turned the labour market upside down. At the heart of these changes were two underlying forces: first, the introduction of new technologies that significantly changed how designers did their work; second, economic change within the South African economy and the effects of globalisation, which severely impacted the South African textile industry.

4 Changing "Societal Forces" Transforming the Professional Work Environment

As the work environment described above began to change, it became less leisured and autonomous and a lot more pressurised and controlled. At first, the transformations came slowly, but from the mid-1990s, they began to have a significant impact on designers. From the 2000s, developments accelerated, and the textile industry and designers' work environment changed completely. Two dynamics were significant: technological advancements in the industry and a shifting economic-political environment post-liberation.

New technologies, ranging from photostat machines to scanners and Computer-Aided Design (CAD), as well as developments in printing technology (initially inkjet printers and later digital printers), altered the work environment. In combination, these technologies facilitated the "speeding up" of the labour process of design. It allowed the product manager (or studio manager) to request designers to "play around with some ideas" which could then be used to obtain strike offs (printed fabric samples) almost immediately without having to set up the printing machines, a process that would previously have taken one to two weeks (Interview, Robyn Silver).

CAD technologies allowed for the separation of a design on computer (that is, the separation of the design into layers by colour). This eliminated one of the product development steps (thus making the process faster), but also made the job of the separator obsolete.

> When you are working on the design on the CAD, you work in separations anyway, so it's just a matter of then taking those, cleaning them, sending them off, and they can work with them immediately. [...] Whereas before we would have to actually paint each separation by hand, scan it, work with it, put it on to the laser and then the laser would engrave the screens. (Interview, Susan Robbins)

Technological developments allowed managers to require designers to produce their work faster, enabling the organisation to be more competitive and profitable. These demands changed the work environment, and it became more pressurised.

Furthermore, the new technologies impacted the designers' skills and knowledge and "broke" their control over their expertise. CAD, in particular, undermined the expertise, skills and autonomy of some textile designers. Some interviewees reflected on this transition:

> There were a couple of girls sitting and working, but on computers, and it was actually so sad. They scan a thing from a magazine and then sort of place it, your ability to draw and things fall away. [...] We belong to the older school: we had no computer background. And everything that we did [was] with hand drawing. (Interview, Serena Pillay)

While CAD required a different set of skills to those of a designer who drew and painted designs by hand, most of the people interviewed, from designers to mill managers, refer to a loss of skill. They agree that the most basic skill required by a designer is the ability to draw, and many people who now work as designers are no longer able to draw.

The technological developments, particularly CAD, undermined the occupation's boundaries—it was no longer necessary for a designer to receive a formal qualification to work as a designer. It became possible for those with "creative ability" but little technical knowledge of textile design to be employed as textile designers.

> I started [...] doing communications and visual merchandising. Obviously I know the programmes that are used for design, and then I wanted to move into a more creative role, and they moved me across to design. [...] Because I haven't studied as a textile designer, I don't, can't, paint like Steph. [...] But what I can do is, I can take Steph's art work and step it up, clean it up, manipulate it, change colour, do all that kind of thing on computer. [...] I can also create designs and patterns on computer. I can draw things and manipulate them, do pattern repeats. (Interview, Cathy Baines)

The second force that dramatically changed the industry occurred in the wake of political liberation and the end of sanctions: after 1994, the South African economy was integrated into the global economy. Macroeconomic policy moved from import-substitution to export-orientated policies; in accordance with WTO directives, tariffs were dropped and industries deregulated, particularly in the textile sector (Roberts & Thoburn, 2003). Ultimately, some imported products became cheaper than those manufactured in South Africa (Roberts & Thoburn, 2004, 129), resulting in an overall increase in imports that provided robust competition for South African mills. Alongside this came significant changes in the market. The end of the decade saw a mushrooming of mass-market retail stores focused on the home furnishings sector, not only forcing a change in the mills' main product—from "fabric-on-the-roll" to "ready-mades" (mostly bedding and curtaining)—but also facilitating a shift from a production-led supply chain to a retail-led supply chain. Over ten to fifteen years, a major restructuring of the textile sector took place as it attempted to respond to these changes. Several mills downsized, closed sections and/or focused on one aspect of the production process; ultimately, many mills closed their doors permanently. From a scenario of many large, vertically integrated firms employing thousands of people, there emerged a landscape of fewer, smaller, more specialised companies (Bonnin, 2011).

As the economic circumstances of the industry changed and mills downsized, they cut back their design studios.

> Basically, as a designer left, they were not replaced, and that is kind of how it went. (Interview, Susan Robbins)

When a mill closed, so did its design studio. Subsequently, the employment and labour market for textile designers changed significantly. Many designers lost their jobs. They were forced to rethink what it meant to be a textile designer and how they could continue their careers.

The consequences were increasing differentiation and fragmentation within the occupation. To cite Noordegraaf (2016, 793), "'differentiated' segments [...] appeared" within the labour market. There was a temporality to the "appearance" of this differentiation in response to changes in the industry and the economy. Furthermore, as Noordegraaf (2016, 794) has argued, the tendencies towards fragmentation were not neutral; not only were some of the segments viewed as more prestigious than others, but they offered better conditions and more secure employment.

5 Staying within the Organisation

Several designers attempted to continue working within the textile industry. They adapted as the industry changed its technologies, markets and products. They learnt new skills, took on new responsibilities and moved from company to company, endeavouring to stay ahead of retrenchments and closures. Within this group, two different segments were formed.

5.1 Intensifying Managerial and Technological Control

In the first segment were the designers who remained employed despite the downsizing and restructuring of the sector.

> I started working in 1981. I walked straight into a job at Frame Fabrics, [...] that is when we had like 30 designers, and over the years, it dwindled down to like two left. Number one was, computers took over, [...] and, gradually, people were just retrenched, one after the other. And CAD took over from textile designer. (Interview, Candice Brown)

As a result of digitisation and restructuring, jobs were scarcer, and, simultaneously, competition increased as those with other qualifications (graphic designers, illustrators) entered the sector. The changing market meant that mills did not need many designers to "feed" production. They employed one or two designers, offering a design facility to their customers (primarily large South African retail chains).

The designers that remained within the sector saw their working conditions change considerably. There was less opportunity to create original design work. Their task was to carry out the customers' instructions and ensure the designs supplied were ready for production.

> You are briefed by the customer as to, you know, what they want; because they are looking for a specific thing, or they have got a specific look. You know, like [Company X], they have an artist who does their work, and then all I do is interpret that on the computer so that we are able to print it. [...] Most of the time, it's not in a repeat, so then we have to put it into the correct repeat. (Interview, Ingrid Smith)

> The customer sourced this pillowcase, where there are bits and pieces of design, and so I've had to draw it and fill in the missing bits. So we draw on our old design expertise from that stage, but we don't sit and endlessly create like we used to. (Interview, Melanie Thompson).

These designers worked under intensifying managerial and technological control—their work became increasingly standardised and their autonomy and status was greatly diminished.

> Even though we have jobs, and we are working in the industry, it's not you being creative, you know. [...] Some of them try to play designer and tell you, no, put that texture on or that colour [...] or you get told, here is your fabric. [...] It's a piece of fabric or a picture of a piece of fabric that they couldn't get. (Interview, Salt River Designers)

The chief executive of one of the few remaining print mills explained:

> We have a different calibre of designer today who doesn't have to be the interpreter, the originator, innovator. They really have to copy what they are told or given to make. (Interview, Solly Brand, cited in Bonnin, 2013, 126)

While these designers were still embedded within an organisation, they were now subject to strict organisational and market-driven controls, and it was increasingly difficult for them to maintain their professional autonomy. They retained their skills and their expert knowledge, albeit different from those of textiles designers of an earlier period, but institutional closure (in the Weberian sense) no longer held any purchase. I suggest that for this segment of designers, the organisational context eradicated professional control (Noordegraaf, 2007, 772).

5.2 Taking on Managerial Roles within Organisations

The second segment of designers also remained employed by the large textile mills (for as long as possible). However, some moved to new organisations and found employment with convertors or in retail. They managed the changing conditions by using their professional knowledge to create new roles (jobs) for themselves (Kirkpatrick, 2016; Muzio et al., 2011; Noordegraaf, 2007). They took on managerial roles within these organisations—their new jobs as stylists or product managers were grounded in their professional knowledge as designers. One of the designers who left designing to enter these new spaces explained:

> I wouldn't have had a job otherwise. [...] I learnt to flex and change, and I think I am still surrounded by people that I have known in the industry that can't do it; [...] they land up with no job, basically. Whereas I always have, I have looked at the thing; I have said okay, that era is finished. [...] What can I do now. [...] I thought to myself, okay, in a few years' time there isn't going to be a mill left in this country. Do I want to carry on working in manufacturing until there isn't a mill left to go to, earning less and less and less because they can't afford to pay me, or do I look at what is working, which is "ready-mades" and retail and [...] try and make a living out of that? And if you can't do that in this industry, well, then you will find yourself waitressing. (Interview, Gil Anderson)

This segment comprises designers who were considered to be (more) talented and, most importantly, aware of the market. Jobs as stylists or product managers required professional design knowledge plus technical knowledge of the design and production process. Using these skills and this expertise, stylists liaised with customers, briefed designers (either freelance or employed by the company), conceptualised ranges and oversaw processes at the mill.

The work story of Andrea Campbell illustrates this trajectory. Andrea trained as a textile designer, graduating in the mid-1980s. After two years working in one of the largest mill studios, she asked to move into a production-linked position. Here, she learnt about production, oversaw the development of products and liaised with customers.

> [I] worked in the mill on the creative side, colouration, getting involved with projects and designs, and coming to present them to [wholesalers and convertors]. (Interview, Andrea Campbell).

As the industry began to change and became more retail driven, stylists like Andrea left the mills and were employed by convertors (convertors "convert" base cloth or greige into printed fabric), who had themselves set up design capacity.

> Obviously, I had a background in design: I could style, I could colour. So we started to create our own collections and try to not be as dependant on [the mills]. [...] Basically, the business just, you know, changed, and I took on more and more responsibility. So, today I look after designer marketing. (Interview, Andrea Campbell)

The question is: can people who are in this segment still be considered professionals? In their positions, they draw on their professional reputations and use their professional knowledge. They are in management positions but are also recognised within their peer group as being very successful professionals, not only in terms of their craft but also as having escaped being crushed by a collapsing industry. They wield professional power and, in the "new" world of design, serve as "points of entry" into the labour market.

6 Operating Outside Organisations

When mills closed or downsized, many designers lost their jobs. Since the sector had contracted, these designers and other, newly-qualified ones found it difficult to (re-)enter the labour market. They either had to leave the profession altogether or to find alternatives. This group also formed two segments, each with a slightly different relationship with their clients.

6.1 Freelancers

As a result of retrenchments or lack of formal employment opportunities, some designers moved into freelancing and contract work. They used their existing networks to find business, often with organisations where they had previously been employed. Their ability to secure contracts was dependent on their reputations for excellence and on their existing networks, as well as the broader business environment. "New organisations" that opened up in the sector provided opportunities for freelance work. These included recently established cut-make-and-trim firms and retail (some large retailers like Mr. Price Home or Sheet Street started developing their own design capacity). Freelance work was hard to obtain, and many designers found life increasingly precarious.

One freelance designer explained that after she left her job at a design studio, she contacted retail store buyers. One of them offered her work, and she expanded her network over time. Soon she became quite busy, but as the industry changed and retail stores developed in-house design capacity, freelance work opportunities diminished (Interview, Sally Oliver). Other freelance designers described similar experiences:

> In the beginning, we did very well, and then as time went and this whole recession thing hit, and that is what happened. Like nobody wants print. (Interview, Devi Perumal)

> We had a bit of a problem when the bottom fell out of the market, and people weren't doing anything. (Interview, Fey Clarke)

Freelancers were also dependent on the vagaries of their customers, who pressurised them for design changes but refused to pay for the additional work.

> It would sit for weeks, and it had to go through, I don't know, another four or five selections before they decided, yes, I want this. And then [...] they would send it back to you and say, no, I would like this thing to change because I don't want a circle there, I want an oval there. And after that, no, I don't think the oval works; put it back into a circle. [...] Eventually, like, you get fed up, and they don't know what they told you to do, and it has to sit again in the pile to get back through that whole selection process and then eventually they will take it. (Interview, Devi Perumal)

> I had enough, [...] enough of all the buyers just changing stuff because they could [...], and young buyers had come in. And often [they] didn't know what they wanted, so they would brief you, but didn't really give you a good solid brief because they didn't really know what they wanted, and so they would constantly make changes. (Interview, Sally Oliver)

Income levels varied, and most designers found freelance work precarious and insecure.

> When we did freelance, we were not well paid. Because they feel that you are doing it in your spare time. They forget all the stuff involved, and yet art work is so expensive. (Interview, Devi Perumal)

As stated by Maestripieri and Cucca (cited in Bellini & Maestripieri, 2018, 7), "being on the market, however, is not always sufficient to ensure adequate income levels".

Some freelance designers were more successful and managed to build a secure relationship with one or more organisations. They enjoyed the "freedom" of freelance work. However, despite this, their creative autonomy was diminished, their professional power diminished and they had to abide by the logic of the market (see Bellini & Maestripieri, 2018).

6.2 The Post-Crisis Designers

Many designers in this segment completed their training and entered the field as the industry went into decline post-2000. Some had studied textile design, but many had obtained qualifications in related fields—for example, fine art, illustration, graphic design and printmaking. They had never worked as designers in the mills and had never designed commercially or produced long-runs in textile mills.

Upon qualifying, many of them were not employed as textile designers. Some began their careers in other areas; for example, Monica Church worked in sales for various convertors and fabric houses before starting her own small design business. Others, like Andi Burger, designed and printed fabrics at home to produce craft-like items, such as tea towels or cushion covers, to sell at local markets.

The designers who set up small businesses were unknown; however, they were able to build their professional reputation and expertise through the internet and e-commerce. Many of them created blogs, enabling them to showcase their talent, thus creating a professional network and establishing an international reputation.

> [I] started blogging at the very beginning […], and that's how a lot of the shops have found me. (Interview, Sharon Spence)

By presenting themselves in the online space, they came to the attention of larger retail companies searching the web for new talent and products. Their next step was to create online stores, securing clients and building up their reputation. Initially, they used services like Etsy (which started in Brooklyn, New York), which provided an (international) online platform to sell unique, home-crafted items. Later, they set up online stores tailored to South African customers. These strategies allowed their businesses to grow, and brought them to the attention of the media, which developed their reputation further.

All these designers resisted establishing relationships with large organisations, whether as permanent and secure "collaborations" or as temporary relationships. They argued that such relationships compromised their independence and autonomy; they would not have been able to set the conditions of a contract, which would always have been on the larger organisation's terms (Interview, Monica Church). They preferred to make their own way, slowly building up and controlling their own businesses and reputations.

Some designers in this segment became extremely successful, eventually opening small businesses. An element in their success has been the organisational strategy of creating networks and sharing resources with other professionals in similar positions (see also Maestripieri & Cucca, 2018), enabling them to mediate market pressures. Overall, these were informal networks made up of people who held a similar position in the market who felt that they would all benefit by sharing information and resources.

> Sometime last year, I thought it might be nice if all the local independent fabric designers and producers got to meet each other. Part of the reason was that a large cotton mill in Cape Town had closed all of a sudden, and most of us found ourselves floundering a little and in need of some support and advice. So we met, and immediately there was a generosity of spirit. [...] We all shared our contacts, advice, experience, and enjoyed echoing each other's moans about our problems with printers/CMTs/etc. Soon enough, we were meeting more often, and the Threadcount Collective was born: a loosely woven group of independent textile designers and producers who meet to help and support one another. (Skinny la Minx, 2010)

The Collective is seen as a source of support:

> It's been great to have support – somebody you could call. I mean, we all are kind of similar in our experience, which I realised. We are all doing pretty much the same thing, [...] you may be struggling too, instead of feeling like odds and competing with each other as it were, helping to support and grow the industry. (Interview Sharon Spence)

> Besides meetings, there have also been collective projects – for example, sharing space at the Cape Town Design Indaba and pop-up shops in their early days. Ten years later, the collaboration was still active. (Skinny la Minx, 2019)

Although organised with a different purpose, a similar informal network existed in Durban. When the mill they worked at closed, a group of designers pooled their resources and set up a design "collective". One of the members who had experience as a designer and stylist took on the role of liaising with customers.

> So I said to them, why don't we all go freelance. [...] I will be a consultant and you get paid consultancy fees, and in order to provide a service to my customers, I will sell your artwork and pay you for it. (Interview, Gil Anderson)

The designers in this segment have found spaces within the new economy and have successfully adapted their ways of working. They have deliberately avoided being incorporated into large organisations; ironically, in time many of them have become (successful) organisations themselves. While their success is subject to having "mastered" the market, they can still exercise their professional discipline and retain control.

7 Conclusions

The chapter demonstrates the process of differentiation that has taken place over the last forty years within the expert occupation of textile designer, resulting in great heterogeneity. It shows how transformations in the broader economy and society disturbed the status quo and sparked a series of disruptions that undermined and fragmented the profession, creating differentiated segments with higher or lower status. Existing forms of closure were eradicated by digitalisation and social and economic changes in the sector. The outcome was significant changes to the labour market, locations and employment conditions of textile designers.

As a result, four different segments formed—some retained their professional status with good, secure jobs, while others were left in marginal and precarious situations. Two segments of designers remained employed within organisations: the first became subject to increasing organisational and market-driven controls and consequentially diminished professional control; the designers in the second segment were able to use their professional knowledge to transcend professional boundaries and create new jobs for themselves within organisations—these were jobs that used their professional expertise but were outside the boundaries of the profession strictly speaking. The third and fourth segments exist outside the traditional labour market. Many freelancers, the third segment, are in precarious positions, with their professional power reduced by the market. Designers in the fourth segment have found spaces within the new digital economy and have been able to exercise professional discipline and control despite the powerful logic of the market.

This discussion highlights several issues for the broader literature. The chapter has argued that situated professionalism best describes the position of textile designers: they are embedded within organisations but still able to exert professional control. However, for most South African textile designers, this status has changed due to social and economic changes and digitalisation. While digitisation has played a key role in disrupting the position and status of textile designers, taking over some of their work and undermining the skills that used to confer them their status, it has been significant in allowing the "post-crisis designers" to establish themselves as "new professionals" and build up their reputations. This suggests that professionals located within organisations might be particularly vulnerable to processes of change: while some (e.g. segment two) were able to use their positions to promote their professional projects, many others were forced to capitulate to the market logic and surrender their professional autonomy.

Segmentation within the textile designer occupation provides insights into the debates around changing notions of professionalism and, in particular, the role of organisations. While some of these outcomes might be interpreted as resulting in deprofessionalisation, this ignores the agency of textile designers (in all segments) in attempting to position themselves to promote their professional projects. Designers accept the "discourse of professionalism"; but while it might be a means of social control, as Evetts suggests (see Chap. 1), it has also been used by designers as a means of positioning themselves in the face of digitisation and a shifting labour market. We can see how designers (particularly those in segment two and four) have played an active part in creating a "rhetoric" to protect their professional positions. Organisational collaboration has been central to creating both the discourses of professionalism and this new rhetoric.

Acknowledgements Thanks to the University of KwaZulu-Natal Competitive Research Fund, the College of Humanities Competitive Research Fund (University of KwaZulu-Natal) and the National Research Foundation (Grant No 80395) for grants that have enabled the research in this study to be undertaken.

Annex: List of Interviews

Pseudonym	Profession	Place and date of interview
Anderson, Gil	Textile designer, colourist, stylist, supplier	Durban, February 2009 and March 2009
Baines, Cathy	Graphic artist/textile designer	Durban, 9 June 2011
Boyd, Tricia	Textile designer	Durban, 15 March 2011
Brand, Solly	CEO in a division of a large textile mill	Cape Town, 23 August 2011
Brown, Candice	Textile designer	Durban, 14 July 2011
Burger, Andi	Fine artist, illustrator, designer	Cape Town, 25 August 2011
Campbell, Andrea	Textile designer, colourist, stylist, convertor	Johannesburg, 17 October 2011
Clarke, Fey	Textile designer	Durban, 16 February 2011
Church, Monica	Textile designer, sales, convertor	Cape Town, 22 August 2011
Nair, Paul	Textile designer	Durban, 1 March 2011
Oliver, Sally	Textile designer	Durban, 31 May 2011
Perumal, Devi	Textile designer	Durban, 18 June 2011
Pillay, Serena	Textile designer	Durban, 18 February 2011
Robbins, Susan	Textile designer and product manager	Durban, 26 May 2011
Salt River Designers	A group of young textile designers working at a manufacturer	Cape Town, 13 June 2012
Silver, Robyn	Textile designer, product manager	Durban, 5 March 2011
Smith, Ingrid	Textile designer	Cape Town, 23 August 2011
Spence, Sharon	Teacher, illustrator, textile designer	Cape Town, 24 August 2011
Thompson, Melanie	Textile designer	Durban. 14 March 2011

References

Bellini, A., & Maestripieri, L. (2018). Professions within, between and beyond: Varieties of professionalism in a globalising world. *Cambio. Rivista sulle trasformazioni sociali, 8*(16), 5–14.

Bonnin, D. (2011). Changing work in the context of globalisation working life stories of textile designers in South Africa. *Loyola Journal of Social Sciences, 25*(2), 191–215.

Bonnin, D. (2013). Global integration, new technologies and the work of South African textile designers. *South African Review of Sociology, 44*(2), 112–130.

Butler, N., Chillas, S., & Muhr, S. L. (2012). Professions at the margins. *Ephemera, 12*(3), 259–272.

Dent, M., Bourgeault, I. L., Denis, J.-L., & Kuhlmann, E. (2016). The changing world of professions and professionalism. In M. Dent, I. L. Bourgeault, J.-L. Denis, & E. Kuhlman (Eds.), *The Routledge companion to the professions and professionalism* (pp. 1–10). Routledge.

Evetts, J. (2006). Short note: The sociology of professional groups. *Current Sociology, 54*(1), 133–134.

Kirkpatrick, I. (2016). Hybrid managers and professional leadership. In M. Dent, I. L. Bourgeault, J.-L. Denis, & E. Kuhlman (Eds.), *The Routledge companion to the professions and professionalism* (pp. 175–187). Routledge.

Maestripieri, L., & Cucca, R. (2018). Small is beautiful? Emerging organizational strategies among Italian professionals. *Canadian Review of Sociology, 55*(3), 362–384.

Muzio, D., Hodgson, D., Faulconbridge, J., Beaverstock, J., & Hall, S. (2011). Towards corporate professionalization: The case of project management, management consultancy and executive search. *Current Sociology, 59*(4), 443–464.

Noordegraaf, M. (2007). From "pure" to "hybrid" professionalism: Present-day professionalism in ambiguous public domains. *Administration and Society, 39*(6), 761–785.

Noordegraaf, M. (2016). Reconfiguring professional work: Changing forms of professionalism in public services. *Administration and Society, 48*(7), 783–810.

Roberts, S., & Thoburn, J. (2003). Adjusting to trade liberalisation: The case of firms in the South African textile sector. *Journal of African Economies, 12*(1), 74–103.

Roberts, S., & Thoburn, J. (2004). Globalisation and the South African textiles industry: Impacts on firms and workers. *Journal of International Development, 16*, 125–113.

Saks, M. (2012). Defining a profession: The role of knowledge and expertise. *Professions & Professionalism, 2*(1), 1–10.

Skinny la Minx. (2010). Meet Threadcount. Skinny la Minx, 10 February 2010. Retrieved August 5, 2011, from https://skinnylaminx.com/2010/02/10/meet-threadcount/

Skinny la Minx. (2019). Threadcount collective reunite. Skinny la Minx, 26 April 2019. Retrieved May 25, 2019, from https://skinnylaminx.com/tag/threadcount-collective/

4

Models of Professionalism and Perceptions of Gender Discrimination in the Legal Profession

Valeria Insarauto, Isabel Boni-Le Goff, Grégoire Mallard, Eléonore Lépinard, and Nicky Le Feuvre

1 Introduction

The rapid, large-scale entry of women into the practice of law in recent decades has begun to challenge customs, standards and patterns of behaviour within the legal profession (Macerollo, 2008; Bolton & Muzio, 2008; Sommerlad, 2016). However, the feminisation of occupations often coexists with widespread gender discrimination based on entrenched masculinist practices and gender stereotypes that maintain male privilege in a profession (Sommerlad, 2002; Bolton & Muzio, 2008; Acker, 2009; Tomlinson et al., 2013). This is also the case within the legal profession,

V. Insarauto (✉) • E. Lépinard
Institute of Social Sciences, University of Lausanne, Lausanne, Switzerland
e-mail: valeria.insarauto@unil.ch; eleonore.lepinard@unil.ch

I. B.-L. Goff
Department of Sociology and Anthropology, University of Paris 8, Vincennes, France
e-mail: isabel.boni-le-goff@univ-paris8.fr

© The Author(s), under exclusive license to Springer Nature Switzerland AG 2023
L. Maestripieri, A. Bellini (eds.), *Professionalism and Social Change*,
https://doi.org/10.1007/978-3-031-31278-6_4

where globalisation, structural reorganisation and demographic shifts have fuelled mechanisms that have consolidated existing gender inequalities (Faulconbridge & Muzio, 2008; Ashley & Empson, 2017). This process has been achieved through the implementation of organisational principles and practices that assume the paradigmatic professional to be male, hence excluding women—alongside other minorities—from full access to legal knowledge and power (Macerollo, 2008; Tomlinson et al., 2013) as a result of prescribed routes to professional acceptance and recognised forms of professionalism. We refer to professionalism as a discursive strategy and rhetorical resource (see Chap. 1 in this volume) that has the power to socialise, motivate and control practitioners, particularly by realigning their individual professional identities, practices and procedures with organisational principles and corporate priorities that benefit the ruling elites within a profession (Evetts, 2003; Muzio & Tomlinson, 2012). In law, the discourse of professionalism remains predicated on a masculine ideology, stamped with the image of the paradigmatic professional as a white, class-privileged, career-oriented and unencumbered male (Muzio & Tomlinson, 2012; Tomlinson et al., 2013; Sommerlad, 2016). The commitment to this male-centred model of professionalism has been reinforced by recent developments within the legal profession (Sommerlad, 2016; Santos, 2018), which have implications for female lawyers, who are increasingly expected to conform to this model and are heavily penalised when they fail to do so, notably by being denied professional recognition, career rewards and advancement (Muzio & Tomlinson, 2012; Tomlinson et al., 2013).

In this chapter, we explore the extent to which women are able to challenge the male-centred model of professionalism, particularly though

G. Mallard
Department of Anthropology and Sociology, Graduate Institute of International and Development Studies, Geneva, Switzerland
e-mail: gregoire.mallard@graduateinstitute.ch

N. Le Feuvre
LACCUS – ISS, NCCR LIVES, Université de Lausanne, Lausanne, Switzerland
e-mail: nicky.lefeuvre@unil.ch

their awareness of gender inequalities. We inquire into the potential emergence of alternative, gendered, models of professionalism, and we emphasise the importance of women's perceptions of gender discrimination, particularly in relation to the organisational structure and culture of law firms that shape the contours of professionalism for lawyers (Wallace & Kay, 2008). The pillars of the male-centred model of professionalism, such as the culture of long working hours and a linear progression to rise to senior ranks, are major sources of gender discrimination based on the stereotypical opposition between professionalism and care responsibilities, with the later generally ascribed to women (Macerollo, 2008; Sommerlad, 2016). When aware of this, women's perceptions of discrimination may lead them to comply differently with the male-centred model of professionalism and to react by developing alternative models of professionalism, helping to diversify professional models and to reduce gender hierarchies within the legal profession.

Drawing on the analysis of the quantitative data collected during a comparative study on lawyers in France and Switzerland, we investigate to what extent the early stages of a legal career are characterised by competing models of professionalism, and how these alternative models relate to perceptions of gender discrimination. Our focus on lawyers in the early stages of their careers is particularly interesting, since it enables us to show that the male-centred model of professionalism continues to attract aspiring lawyers, and to discipline them once in practice (Sommerlad, 2016; Santos, 2018). Our aim is not to engage in a debate on whether female lawyers can be considered as professional as their male counterparts, but rather to study whether they endorse different models of professionalism, and to explore whether or not these differences have any relation to perceptions of gender discrimination. Our ultimate aim is to explore whether having an awareness of gender inequalities may potentially serve as leverage for contestation and change. Although the male-oriented model of professionalism dominates within the legal profession, this paradigm does not necessarily provide a fixed, coherent vision of what constitutes appropriate behaviour for a lawyer: it consists of multiple visions that reflect the different arenas in which they are produced (Wallace & Kay, 2008). In fact, our results reveal four models of professionalism, characterised and distributed differently among men and women in the two countries, that are related to perceptions of gender discrimination only in the case of women. This chapter contributes to the analytical framework of this book by approaching professionalism as a discourse and looking at the different ways men and women incorporate and accommodate it in their work, exposing the redefinition of professional barriers *within* an established profession. It shows how, against a background of occupational feminisation, stereotypically masculine professional standards serve as an internal form of social closure that maintains gender inequalities in the legal profession.

2 Professionalism and Gender Inequalities in the Legal Profession

Over the last two decades, new transnational patterns of professional work based on global professional standards have favoured the mutually reinforcing links between professional values and organisational structures, with professionalism becoming increasingly centred on organisational logics, practices and strategies (Noordegraaf, 2007; Faulconbridge & Muzio, 2008; Evetts, 2011). In the legal profession, the restructuring of organisational and business models has marked a shift from individual professionals as the primary units of professionalism, to the law firm as the main locus of socialisation and control (Faulconbridge & Muzio, 2008). The rise of mega law firms has triggered the rebuilding of legal work around a hypercompetitive organisational model, characterised by an increasingly intensive working ethos, more competition for clients and even longer working hours (Sommerlad, 2016).

All these aspects, which are widely reflected in the profession's male-dominated culture, have reinforced the lack of flexibility and the resistance to diversity in law practices, further penalising aspiring and established female lawyers. Tasks, responsibilities and rewards are based on the established male-centred work pattern, favouring the assignment of women to the least rewarding areas of work and career tracks (Sandefur, 2007; Sommerlad, 2016), especially in the early phases of their careers, where formal criteria for the evaluation of individuals' professional merit and ability are based on their capacity to 'fit in' (Rivera, 2012). Likewise, the linear career model continues to serve as the guide for career advancement and represents the traditional norm for professional success, for men and women alike (Macerollo, 2008; Tomlinson et al., 2013). Law firms continue to view deviations from this model as disruptive to the practice, leading to the marginalisation of women, and sometimes pushing them to leave legal practice altogether (Reichman & Sterling, 2004; Sommerlad, 2016; Kay et al., 2016). Against this background, it is possible to see how professionalism emerges as a normative discourse imbued with symbolic and disciplinary power. It is employed to retain and reproduce a gender order in professional work and also acts as a normalising career device that legitimises the limited career prospects and professional recognition of female lawyers (Suddaby & Viale, 2011; Saks, 2012; Sommerlad, 2016).

Stereotyping, reinforced by social hierarchies, structures how this discourse generates disadvantages for female lawyers, contributing to widespread gender discrimination in the legal profession (Sommerlad, 2002; Le Feuvre & Lapeyre, 2005; Nelson et al., 2019) and to a hegemonic, masculine-oriented definition of professionalism (Reichman & Sterling, 2004). The combination of stereotypes regarding gender and the primarily family-oriented role ascribed to women plays a crucial part in producing and reproducing biases against women lawyers (Benard & Correll, 2010; Byron & Roscigno, 2014). The rhetoric of the incompatibility of law practice with caring responsibilities and the discourse of female domesticity continues to reinforce the construction of women as 'natural carers', as opposed to men, who are perceived as 'natural professionals' (Sommerlad, 2016). Female lawyers are hence seen as largely incapable of serving the organisational priorities of law firms. Through the further naturalisation of the synergy between masculinity and professional identity, organisational professionalism imposes a male-centred pattern of work, increasing the fragility of women's professionalism and the diversification of professionalism (Sommerlad, 2016).

Research in social psychology contends that women are more aware of workplace discrimination and that they are more likely to recognise collective disadvantage, especially when these are related to gender-based mistreatment, owing to their membership of a discriminated group (Gutek et al., 1996; McCord et al., 2018). Socio-legal studies confirm that female lawyers are more likely than their male counterparts to perceive discrimination in the workplace (Collins et al., 2017; Nelson et al., 2019). They are also likely to react more vigorously to it (Kay & Gorman, 2008). For example, even when work-life balance policies are available, women often refuse to avail themselves of these measures (Sommerlad, 2002; Muzio & Tomlinson, 2012), due to the potentially detrimental impact that options like flexible working time arrangements may have on their career prospects. Perceived gender discrimination hence represents an important element to consider, as it is rooted in the stereotypes and biases that contribute to the conflicts and obstacles that female lawyers experience when attempting to achieve professional recognition (Macerollo, 2008). The empirical analysis that follows explores how women are endorsing alternatives to the dominant male-centred professional model and the role that perceptions of gender discrimination play in this regard.

3 Methodology

3.1 Comparative Perspective

The current analysis draws on the quantitative data collected through an online survey that was administrated in the context of an international comparative research project studying the early careers and life-course trajectories of lawyers who entered the legal profession after 1998 in France and in the French-speaking part of Switzerland.[1] In our study, France and Switzerland were selected because they offer different societal gender regimes, enabling us to better contrast and highlight the dynamics under study. The term gender regime refers to the various social structures and normative expectations that shape gender relations and gender roles in a given society (Walby, 2004), but also to the institutionalisation

[1] The 'Gendered Globalization of the Legal Professions' project was carried out between 2015 and 2020, and aimed to study how globalisation affects women's legal careers in France and Switzerland, attempting to determine whether gender inequalities in the legal profession of these two countries are being eroded by the increasing share of women lawyers. It was based on a mixed-methods approach combining a large-scale survey and face-to-face interviews.

of gender inequalities in organisational settings (Acker, 2009; Boni-Le Goff et al., 2019).

Under the Swiss 'neo-maternalistic' gender regime (Giraud & Lucas, 2009) women, particularly mothers, are expected to have a reduced participation in the labour force and to downgrade their professional aspirations. Childcare solutions are limited and expensive, and school hours are also relatively short, in line with a general absence of public support for working mothers (Levy, 2018). The family economy traditionally revolves around a modified male breadwinner model, with women working at most part-time, which also leads to an unequal division of domestic labour (Valarino & Gauthier, 2016). Women therefore have limited access to managerial and professional jobs, and most of them have discontinuous, part-time employment histories.

In France, women are better able to maintain a strong commitment to the labour market throughout their life courses, thanks to high levels of subsidised childcare solutions and parental leave options. Highly qualified women benefit from the existence of a hybrid gender regime (Lépinard, 2018) that simultaneously promotes women's primary roles as mothers and their access to the labour market. In fact, pronatalist family policies have been combined with measures that facilitate women's participation in the labour force, thus facilitating their widespread access to qualified jobs, including those in the legal profession (Le Feuvre & Lemarchant, 2007; Boni-Le Goff et al., 2019). High levels of subsidised childcare solutions and parental leave options enable women—especially those in highly-qualified occupations—to have continuous, full-time labour force participation patterns throughout their lives.

However, in both countries, women struggle to achieve full integration into the legal profession. This suggests that it is not only important to consider the different societal-level gender regimes in question, but also the specific gendered occupational career structures that can be found with respect to the legal profession in the two countries, as well as the interaction between these levels of reality (Boni-Le Goff et al., 2019). Both in France and Switzerland, the Bar—the national association of lawyers, for which membership is compulsory in order to practice law—is deeply segmented by gender, with women over-represented in less prestigious chambers and legal specialisms. Female lawyers nevertheless appear to navigate the legal labour market hierarchy through alternative career paths. In France, despite the relatively favourable societal gender regime, women seem to turn to solo practice in order to maintain a continuous career trajectory and avoid the obstacles to obtaining recognition and full integration into the profession (Le Feuvre & Walters, 1993). In Switzerland, where the gender regime is less favourable to the construction of a professional career, women benefit from the more permeable boundaries between exercising as lawyers and alternative legal jobs in order to stay working in the sector despite their more discontinuous career paths.

Against this background, it is interesting to compare how, in the context of dissimilar gender regimes and occupational career structures, the persistence and perception of gender inequalities relate to the construction of potentially alternative models of professionalism during the early stages of a legal career.

3.2 Data

The online survey was administered in 2016 in collaboration with the French National Bar Council (*Conseil National des Barreaux*) and the Paris Bar (*Ordre des Avocats de Paris*) in France, and with the Bar organisations in Geneva (*Ordre des Avocats de Genève*) and in Lausanne (*Ordre des Avocats Vaudois*), both in the French-speaking part of Switzerland. Alongside the socio-demographic profile of lawyers, the questionnaire asked each respondent about their educational and professional history, current position and job content, career aspirations and projection, discrimination issues encountered and work-family arrangements. After cleaning up the data, the final sample used for our analysis was made up of 982 respondents (319 men, 663 women) from the Paris Bar for France, and 366 respondents (154 men, 212 women) from the Bars in Geneva and Lausanne for Switzerland.

For our analyses, we first selected a list of variables regarding different aspects that contribute to professionalism, drawing on three groups of variables relating to: forms of legal practice, career patterns and types of professional understandings. Taken together, these variables enable us to identify the potential variety that can be reflected by professionalism, understood as the diversity of visions of what constitutes appropriate behaviour for a lawyer and the realities of exercising as one (Wallace & Kay, 2008). In order to distinguish different forms of legal practice, we used the following variables: working hours, type of employment structure (solo practice, small-medium law firm, large corporation), legal domain (administrative, trade, family, work, banking and business, etc.), legal activity (advising and/or litigation), size of portfolio (number of clients), type of clientele (small/medium size firms; large firms/corporations; governmental institutions; associations and no-profits), internationalisation of clientele (national and/or international clients) and supervisory duties. To differentiate between career patterns, we based our analyses on the following variables: professional project after graduation (solo practice; small-medium size law firm; large firm/corporate; bifurcation into another profession/uncertain), number of professional positions held to date, years of professional experience and partnership status. Finally, we addressed the types of professional aspirations through the following variables: current professional projection (planning a change of status within the same profession), career goals (high earnings, career advancement, improving society, achieving work-life balance, life-long learning, etc.), career needs (increasing income, improving work-life balance, having more free time; staying up to date with technological change, etc.), forms of professional engagement (participation in professional associations, such as the Bar, lobbying activities, etc.).

When it came to measuring perceived discrimination, lawyers were asked whether they had personally experienced or witnessed discriminatory practices in their workplaces over the previous five years. They were then asked to state the basis of the discrimination they had experienced or witnessed. Types of discrimination based on sex and pregnancy were those most frequently mentioned by our female respondents: together they represented over 50% of the cases of discrimination reported by these women. Given that in the case of women these two types of discrimination may frequently overlap, we grouped them under one category that we subsequently labelled 'gender discrimination'. Hence, this is the type of discrimination we refer to here. Studies show that, as a result of either one's own personal experiences or the experiences of others with whom one identifies, relatively speaking, people perceive more discrimination against people of their own sex (Gutek et al., 1996). Moreover, objective experiences of mistreatment may differ from perceptions of mistreatment (McCord et al., 2018). Given the different exposure to gender discrimination suffered by men and women in the professional domain, in the case of men, we only retained discrimination that had been witnessed, while for women, we retained cases of both witnessed and experienced discrimination. Thus, our study does not aim to provide a comprehensive measure of discriminatory practices, nor to constitute any kind of basis for formal legal claims, but rather to provide an indication of the subjective awareness of differential treatment received by male and female Swiss and French lawyers in the early stages of their careers. As stressed by Nelson et al. (2019), lawyers' perceptions of discrimination are significant in themselves because they are an indicator of gender inequalities within the legal profession.

3.3 Methods

The aim of this chapter is to provide an explorative study of gendered models of professionalism in the legal profession and establish their relationships to perceptions of gender discrimination. In order to do this, we employed descriptive statistics and cluster analysis.

We first used measures of association (t-tests and chi-square tests) to check which of our selected variables were significantly associated with the sex of the respondent, in order to identify the aspects likely to contribute to the definition of gendered models of professionalism.

Then, we performed separate hierarchical cluster analyses for men and women, using Wald linkage and Gower distance, which is a metric used to measure the dissimilarity of two items (i.e. the lesser the distance, the more similar the items), on the variables that were significantly associated with sex. Cluster analysis is a technique that allows individuals to be classified into groups of related variables. Hence, it is useful for identifying the characteristics that jointly describe models of professionalism for each sex and how individuals are distributed among them. It is important to underline that with this type of technique, the disentanglement of the different groups is subject to the assessment of the researcher, whose choices are both methodologically and theoretically driven. Hence, the number of groups (i.e. distinct models of professionalism) that we identify and present in the following section represents the number that we consider to be analytically relevant with respect to the objectives of our study. That is also why we summarise the main characterising variables of each model, that is, the variables that were closer to each other within the group (those that displayed the lower values for the estimated Gower distance) and that in our view contributed to analytical coherence.

Finally, we used measures of associations to test the relationship between these models and perceived gender discrimination, to assess if alternative models of professionalism were more strongly related to perceptions of gender discrimination, and if so, which ones.

4 Results

4.1 Are Alternative Models of Professionalism Gendered?

Table 4.1 presents the list of variables for which we found statistically significant differences between men and women and their distribution in the two countries under study.[2] The majority of the variables we tested turned out to be significantly associated with sex in both countries, although with some differences between France and Switzerland. This is a first indication of the potential gender differences regarding professionalism in both countries.

This is confirmed by results from cluster analyses, based on the aforementioned list of significant variables, which showed that, despite some similarities, men and women relate differently to the different facets of professionalism represented by each of the selected variables. This confirms the existence of alternative and competing gendered models of

[2] To save space, we have decided not to report the descriptive statistics for all the variables we tested. Likewise, for each country, we only report the distribution of variables for which we found statistically significant differences between men and women (when no values are reported, this means that the variable was found not to be significantly associated with sex in that country).

Table 4.1 Descriptive statistics for the variables significantly associated with sex[a]

		France		Switzerland	
		Men	Women	Men	Women
Forms of legal practice					
Working hours (mean)		51.86	48.73	48.44	45.16
Structure type (%)	Solo practice	20.69	23.32	18.42	9.27
	Small/medium	55.80	56.40	65.79	80.00
	Large/corporate	23.51	20.27	15.79	10.73
Legal domain (%)[b]	Finance and business	10.34	5.28		
	Work	20.38	26.55		
	Family	6.90	19.00	48.70	61.32
	Administrative	15.36	9.65	46.75	29.72
	Trade			61.04	41.98
Client type (%)[b]	Small/medium firms	72.10	65.16	75.52	56.04
	Large/corporate	55.17	44.49	40.56	37.91
	Associations & non-Profit	20.06	13.88	33.57	23.63
	Governmental	17.24	8.90		
Supervisory duties (%)	Yes	41.38	35.14	54.55	42.18
Phases of legal career					
Professional projects after graduation (%)	Solo/small-medium firm	30.90	38.94		
	Large/corporate	34.55	26.01		
	Bifurcation/uncertain	34.55	35.05		
Years of professional experience (%)	Up to 5 years			26.62	40.09
	6–10 years			36.36	33.49
	10+ years			37.01	26.42
Seniority (%)	Partnership status	37.54	31.11	46.19	25.95
Understandings					
Current professional projects (%)	Change of status within the profession	56.64	64.30		
Career goals (%)[b]	Improving society	66.77	74.51		
	Life-long learning	98.12	99.70		
	Career advancement	89.03	94.12		
	High earnings			93.51	85.38
	Work-life balance			96.75	99.53
Career needs (%)[b]	Increasing income			27.97	38.59
	Technologically updated	24.45	17.14	28.67	17.39
	More free time	15.15	23.83		
	Work-life balance	44.51	51.58		
Professional engagement (%)	Participation in professional associations			54.79	65.53
	N	319	663	154	212

[a]Statistically significant differences between men and women at $p < 0.05$

[b]These are groups of variables: percentage values correspond to the share of individuals that indicated 'yes' for each of the variables in the group

professionalism, which differ somewhat between the countries under study. We identify four main models. Their share among men and women in each country, along with their main characterising variables, are summarised in Table 4.2.[3]

As shown in Table 4.2, the first model corresponds to the 'organisational male-centred' model of professionalism, which is found among men and women in both countries. The most salient variables that characterise it are long working hours, career goals centred on career advancement (in France) and high earnings (in Switzerland), and activity in large/corporate firms. These aspects typically represent the professional standards endorsed by the male-based, organisation-driven process of professional identity formation and regulation (Macerollo, 2008; Faulconbridge & Muzio, 2008; Sommerlad, 2016). The fact that this model is found for both sexes in both countries is a further confirmation of its influence over lawyers in the early stages of their careers (Sommerlad, 2016; Santos, 2018). This is also supported by its distribution in the two national samples: over 40% of men and women in France and over one-third of men and women in Switzerland adhere to this model. It is interesting to note that in Switzerland, work-life balance as a career goal is another variable that characterises this model, for men and women alike. This is indicative of the anticipations of early-career lawyers in the context of the Swiss gender regime, where childcare facilities are limited, but where family life is nevertheless considered important.

We labelled the second model 'specialised female-settled'. This model could be identified among both French and Swiss women lawyers, and is characterised by achievement of partnership status through specialisation in terms of mode of practice (solo practice) and of expertise (i.e. legal domain, such as family law in France). For women in France, aspirations for solo practice immediately after graduation are also associated with this model. This indicates that, for women, the achievement of partnership status—still the most important distinction in law practice, and the sign of achieving full integration into the legal profession—is related to the pursuit of a restricted type of law practice with unique organisational

[3] In order to facilitate reading and understanding our results, we have chosen not to include dendrograms here.

Table 4.2 Models of professionalism: share (%) and characterisation by sex and country, and association with perceived gender discrimination[a]

Model of professionalism	Sex and country	Main characterising variables
1. ***Organisational male-centred***	Men, France (44.22%) and Switzerland (33.33%) Women, France (43.41%)[a] and Switzerland (39.61%)	Working hours, work in large/corporate firms, career advancement (France) and high earnings (Switzerland) as career goals In Switzerland, work-life balance is also a career goal for both men and women
2. ***Specialised female-settled***	Women, France (13.19%)[a] and Switzerland (12.64%)[a]	Partnership status, specialisation in terms of activity (solo practice) In France, also specialisation in terms of expertise (family law) and professional project after graduation (solo practice)
3. ***Differentiated male-settled***	Men, France (55.78%) and Switzerland (66.67%)	Partnership status, differentiation in terms of activity (type of structures) and expertise (legal domains, type of clients) In Switzerland, also differentiation in terms of work experience
4. ***Early-stage female-unsettled***	Women, France (43.40%) and Switzerland (47.75%)[a]	In France, professional project after graduation was bifurcation/uncertain, change of status within the profession as current professional project, work-life balance as a career need In Switzerland, limited work experience, differentiation in terms of expertise (legal domains) and participation in professional organisations

[a]Statistically significant association at $p < 0.05$

characteristics, opposed to the one prescribed by the male-centred organisational model of professionalism (i.e. solo vs. corporate practice). This model is represented by a small although not negligible proportion of female lawyers: 12.19% in France and 13.64% in Switzerland.

The third model, which we defined as the 'differentiated male-settled' model, was observed among both French and Swiss men. It is marked by achievement of partnership status through a diversity of modes of practice (structure types) and fields of expertise (legal domains and types of clients). In the case of Swiss men, on top of diverse organisational settings and legal domains, this differentiation extends to different career phases in terms of work experience (medium-term to long-term). This model is in line with the dominant script of highly assertive male lawyers being perfectly suited to the job (Nelson et al., 2019), and is well-represented among men in both countries, accounting for 55.78% of male lawyers in France and 66.67% in Switzerland.

It is interesting to note that, in order to secure their full integration into the profession, men seem to develop quite diverse professional profiles, while women have to work in specific organisational settings (e.g. solo practice) and practice areas (e.g. family law). It is likely that this pattern further prevents female lawyers from accessing the core of legal knowledge and power, as it is conducive to a rhetoric whereby women lawyers cultivate an alternative, 'more caring' approach to the profession (Pierce, 1995; Nelson et al., 2019). This suggests that, beyond national differences in the way the legal profession is structured in France and Switzerland (Boni-Le Goff et al., 2019), professional career paths are linked to gendered models of professionalism in both countries.

The fourth model, which we named the 'early-stage female-unsettled', could be found among both French and Swiss women, although with a different slant in each country. In France, this model is characterised by aspirations for a change of status within the profession and an emphasis on work-life balance as a career aspiration, and it is thus indicative of a struggle to find a place within the profession. This contrasts somewhat with the characteristic of the French gender regime to favour the work-life balance of working women, especially highly qualified professionals. However, this model is also associated with unspecified professional projects after graduation, and with aspirations for professional mobility (either outside law, or to another branch within the legal profession). About 43% of female lawyers in our French sample fall under this model. For Swiss women, this model is marked by limited work experience in a variety of areas of practice (legal domains), suggesting that it is typical of female lawyers in the early phases of exploring their career options. Participation in professional associations is another characteristic of this model, which confirms the blurred boundaries that characterise the occupational structure of the profession in this country. As noted earlier, these are used as resources by women to build an alternative pathway into the profession (Boni-Le Goff et al., 2019). An aspiration for a good work-life balance is not associated with this model in Switzerland, whereas it is in France. This may be related to the fact that female Swiss lawyers in the early stages of their careers are more likely to temporarily leave the labour market when they have children as compared to their French counterparts (Boni-Le Goff et al., 2019). Almost 48% of women lawyers in our Swiss sample fell under this model.

4.2 Gendered Models of Professionalism and Perceptions of Gender Discrimination

Table 4.2 shows that in both countries, perceived gender discrimination was significantly associated with models of professionalism, but only in the case of women.

The first model that is significantly associated with perceptions of differential treatment is the 'organisational male-centred' for women in France. This suggests that female French lawyers in the early stages of their careers know that they are still perceived as deviating from the image of the paradigmatic lawyer even when they comply with the ethos of being fully committed to career success and to the corporate work-organisation paradigm that characterises this model. Stereotypes about women being less competent and committed than men may lead some women, including those who have invested heavily in their careers, to perceive discrimination. Precisely because of normative cultural expectations regarding traditional female roles, employers may still expect women to occupy lower status jobs and second-tier positions, regardless of their human capital and the value they generate for the firm (Benard & Correll, 2010).

The 'specialised female-settled' model is also significantly associated with perceptions of gender discrimination in both France and Switzerland. This is indicative of women's awareness of the different career opportunities that are offered to female lawyers compared to their male counterparts: they are left either to mimic the male-centred professional script or to build themselves an alternative model, restricted to selected areas of activity and expertise (Pierce, 1995; Nelson et al., 2019). Previous qualitative results from our study confirm that solo practice in France represents a functional alternative for women to gain partnership status, whereas the Swiss legal profession has a less competitive occupational structure, with higher availability of partner positions for female lawyers in small-to-medium size firms (Boni-Le Goff et al., 2019). The fact that we found this alternative model to be associated with perceived gender discrimination in both countries confirms the normative power of the male-centred model of professionalism, and the fact that this alternative ultimately limits women's access to the most prestigious positions in the French and Swiss legal occupational hierarchies.

The 'early-stage female-unsettled' model is significantly associated with perceptions of gender discrimination, but only in Switzerland. This suggests that transformations in professional law practices and standards have created categories in the profession that are increasingly exposed to processes of social exclusion and reproduction of gender inequalities (Faulconbridge & Muzio, 2008; Ashley & Empson, 2017; Santos, 2018). Likewise, it reveals the understanding that female Swiss lawyers in the early stages of their careers have what are considered appropriate behavioural norms, values and approaches to professional practice. If read together with the participation in professional associations that are typical of this model, women's awareness of gender inequalities denotes a reluctance to face these normative aspects of professionalism, and suggests that women's temporary shift to alternative types of employment (e.g. as court clerks) could provide an alternative path into a legal career (Boni-Le Goff et al., 2019).

5 Conclusion

The legal profession has traditionally been characterised by strong homogeneity in terms of composition and practices. The feminisation process of recent decades has brought increased diversity to the profile of aspiring lawyers, but it has not eroded the male-oriented model of professionalism. On the contrary, this model has been reinforced by the transformations triggered by globalisation and restructuring and through the implementation of organisational principles and practices that assume the paradigmatic professional to be male and totally committed to his career. Our analysis of gendered models of professionalism in the legal profession in France and Switzerland and their relation to perceived gender discrimination confirms a shift away from this professional norm on the part of women, although this shift is not necessarily associated with new forms of power and sources of legitimacy within legal work (Ashley & Empson, 2017).

Alongside the 'organisational male-centred' model that provides the baseline of professionalism, we found competing models that either offered women alternative, but restricted, ways of building a career path (i.e. 'specialised female-settled'), or mirrored their struggles to find an alternative form of professionalism (i.e. 'early-stage female-unsettled'). These models are indicative of the limited inclusion of women in the legal profession in these two countries and reveal persistent patterns of gendered stratification. Conversely, the 'differentiated male-settled' model testifies to the full integration of male lawyers into the profession and can probably be seen as a pragmatic alternative to the 'organisational male-centred' model. Usually, the paradigmatic male lawyer moves through the normative phases of a legal career (i.e. from law school to a partnership position) without encountering any significant impediments. However, should he be unable to follow this linear progression, deviations from this norm do not prevent him from eventually achieving professional recognition. This confirms the idea that the male-oriented model of professionalism usually retains and reproduces a regulated gendered order within the profession (Evetts, 2003; Macerollo, 2008; Suddaby & Viale, 2011).

These gendered models of professionalism are indicative of the complex tensions structuring professional hierarchies in law practice. In the case of women, we found that all the models were associated with perceptions of gender discrimination. This suggests that women are aware of underlying gender stereotypes and of the ways in which they serve to reinforce masculine standards of professionalism, thus requiring them to negotiate alternative professional identities throughout their careers

(Macerollo, 2008; Sommerlad, 2016). We have identified some female-centred models of professionalism, but have also observed that these tend to reinforce gender segmentation in the legal profession. It is thus unclear whether the increase in the number of women in the profession will serve to modify gender hierarchies within it, notably by challenging the standards and practices on which they are based (Suddaby & Viale, 2011). Women's awareness of gender discrimination and its relation to specific models of professionalism suggest that female lawyers might play a significant part in contesting and challenging the traditionally masculine qualities that are valued within the legal profession. There is some evidence from other countries that women lawyers do indeed elaborate various strategies to cope with their disadvantaged positions and discriminatory professional environments (see Chap. 8 in this volume, for example). The interplay of gender norms, career practices and structural characteristics of national legal labour markets (Boni-Le Goff et al., 2019) will most likely shape the outcomes of these dynamic processes in the future.

Acknowledgement The Swiss National Science Foundation (SNSF) funded the research project on which the chapter is based (project 100017 156390).

References

Acker, J. (2009). From glass ceiling to inequality regimes. *Sociologie du travail, 51*, 199–217.

Ashley, L., & Empson, L. (2017). Understanding social exclusion in elite professional service firms: field level dynamics and the 'professional project.'. *Work, Employment and Society, 31*(2), 211–229.

Benard, S., & Correll, S. J. (2010). Normative discrimination and the motherhood penalty. *Gender & Society, 24*(5), 616–646.

Bolton, S., & Muzio, D. (2008). The paradoxical processes of feminization in the professions: The case of established, aspiring and semi-professions. *Work, Employment and Society, 22*(2), 281–299.

Boni-Le Goff, I., Le Feuvre, N., Mallard, G., Lépinard, E., & Morel, S. (2019). Do gender regimes matter? Converging and diverging career prospects among young French and Swiss lawyers. In M. Choroszewicz & T. Adams (Eds.), *Gender, age and inequality in the professions* (pp. 114–133). Routledge.

Byron, R. A., & Roscigno, V. J. (2014). Relational power, legitimation and pregnancy discrimination. *Gender & Society, 28*(3), 435–462.

Collins, T. A., Dumas, T. L., & Moyer, P. L. (2017). Intersecting disadvantages: Race, gender, and age discrimination among attorneys. *Social Science Quarterly, 98*, 1642–1658.

Evetts, J. (2003). The sociological analysis of professionalism: Occupational change in the modern world. *International Sociology, 18*(2), 395–415.

Evetts, J. (2011). A new professionalism? Challenges and opportunities. *Current Sociology, 59*(4), 406–422.

Faulconbridge, J., & Muzio, D. (2008). Organizational professionalism in globalizing law firms. *Work, Employment and Society, 22*(1), 7–25.

Giraud, O., & Lucas, B. (2009). Le renouveau des régimes de genre en Allemagne et en Suisse: Bonjour 'néomaternalisme'? *Cahiers du genre, 46*, 17–46.

Gutek, B. A., Cohen, A. G., & Tsui, A. (1996). Reactions to perceived sex discrimination. *Human Relations, 49*(6), 791–813.

Kay, F. M., & Gorman, E. G. (2008). Women in the legal profession. *Annual Review of Law and Social Sciences, 4*, 299–332.

Kay, F. M., Alaire, S., & Adjei, J. (2016). Undermining gender equality: Female attrition from private law practice. *Law and Society Review, 50*(3), 766–800.

Le Feuvre, N., & Walters, P. (1993). Égales en droit ? La féminisation des professions juridiques en France et en Grande-Bretagne. *Sociétés contemporaines, 16*, 41–62.

Le Feuvre, N., & Lapeyre, N. (2005). Les 'scripts sexués' de carrière dans les professions juridiques en France. *Work, Knowledge & Society / Travail, Savoirs et Sociétés, 3*, 103–126.

Le Feuvre, N., & Lemarchant, C. (2007). Employment, the family and 'work-life balance' in France. In R. Crompton, S. Lewis, & C. Lyonette (Eds.), *Women, men, work and family in Europe* (pp. 210–229). Palgrave.

Lépinard, E. (2018). The French parity reform. The never-ending quest for a new gender equality principle. In E. Lépinard & M. Rubio-Marin (Eds.), *Transforming gender citizenship. The irresistible rise of gender quotas in Europe* (pp. 62–93). Cambridge University Press.

Levy, R. (2018). Devenir parents ré-active les inégalités de genre : une analyse des parcours de vie des hommes et des femmes en Suisse. *Social Change in Switzerland, N°, 14*.

Macerollo, A. (2008). Power of masculinity in the legal profession: Women lawyers and identity formation. *The Windsor Review of Legal and Social Issues, 25*(1), 121–144.

McCord, M. A., Joseph, D. L., Dhanani, L. Y., & Beus, J. M. (2018). A meta-analysis of sex and race differences in perceived workplace mistreatment. *Journal of Applied Psychology, 103*(2), 137–163.

Muzio, D., & Tomlinson, J. (2012). Editorial: Researching gender, inclusion and diversity in contemporary professions and professional organizations. *Gender, Work and Organization, 19*, 455–466.

Nelson, R. L., Sendroiu, I., Dinovitzer, R., & Dawe, M. (2019). Perceiving discrimination: Race, gender, and sexual orientation in the legal workplace. *Law & Social Inquiry, 44*(4), 1051–1082.

Noordegraaf, M. (2007). From "pure" to "hybrid" professionalism: Present-day professionalism in ambiguous public domains. *Administration & Society, 39*(6), 761–785.

Pierce, J. L. (1995). *Gender trials: Emotional lives in contemporary law firms.* University of California Press.

Reichman, N. J., & Sterling, J. S. (2004). Sticky floors, broken steps, and concrete ceilings in legal careers. *Texas Journal of Women and the Law, 14*(27), 27–76.

Rivera, L. A. (2012). Hiring as cultural matching: The case of elite professional service firms. *American Sociological Review, 77*(6), 999–1022.

Saks, M. (2012). Defining a profession: The role of knowledge and expertise. *Professions & Professionalism, 2*(1), 1–10.

Sandefur, R. (2007). Staying power: The persistence of social inequality in shaping lawyer stratification and lawyers' persistence in the profession. *Southwestern Law Review, 36*(3), 539–556.

Santos, S. (2018). Becoming a lawyer in a large law firm: The idea of the unstoppable worker. *Professions and Professionalism, 8*(3). https://doi.org/10.7577/pp.2285

Sommerlad, H. (2002). Women solicitors in a fractured profession: Intersections of gender and professionalism in England and Wales. *International Journal of the Legal Profession, 9*(3), 213–234.

Sommerlad, H. (2016). "A pit to put women in": Professionalism, work intensification, sexualisation and work–life balance in the legal profession in England and Wales. *International Journal of the Legal Profession, 23*(1), 61–82.

Suddaby, R., & Viale, T. (2011). Professionals and field-level change: Institutional work and the professional project. *Current Sociology, 59*(4), 423–442.

Valarino, I., & Gauthier, J. A. (2016). Paternity leave implementation in Switzerland: A challenge to gendered representations and practices of fatherhood? *Community. Work & Family, 19*(1), 1–20.

Walby, S. (2004). The European Union and gender equality: Emergent variety of gender regimes. *Social Politics, 11*(1), 4–29.
Tomlinson, J., Muzio, D., Sommerlad, H., Webley, L., & Duff, L. (2013). Structure, agency and career strategies of white women and black and minority ethnic individuals in the legal profession. *Human Relations, 66*(2), 245–269.
Wallace, J., & Kay, F. (2008). The professionalism of practising law: A comparison across work contexts. *Journal of Organizational Behavior, 29*, 1021–1047.

5

Are Platforms Changing Professionalism?

Davide Arcidiacono, Ivana Pais, and Giorgio Piccitto

1 Introduction

The main objective of this chapter is to analyse how the digital revolution—as "a general acceleration in the pace of technological change in the economy, driven by a massive expansion of our capacity to store, process and communicate information using electronic devices" (Eurofound, 2018, p. iv)—intertwines with the processes that are transforming professionalism. In particular, we focus on the relationship between professional work and the transition to a new socio-technical system that has been defined as the *platform paradigm* or *platform economy* (MIT, 2018).

D. Arcidiacono (✉)
Department of Political and Social Science, University of Catania,
Catania, Italy
e-mail: dlarcid@unict.it

I. Pais
Department of Sociology, Università Cattolica del Sacro Cuore of Milan,
Milan, Italy
e-mail: ivana.pais@unicatt.it

© The Author(s), under exclusive license to Springer Nature Switzerland AG 2023

L. Maestripieri, A. Bellini (eds.), *Professionalism and Social Change*,
https://doi.org/10.1007/978-3-031-31278-6_5

In doing so, our hypothesis refers to a potential shift from organisational professionalism (Evetts, 2006) to "platform professionalism". Of the three processes of transformation examined in this volume—the post-industrial transition, globalisation, and digitalisation—we focus on the last, with particular attention to the "within" dimension: the role of digital platforms in strengthening the commercialisation of professionalism (Hanlon, 1996, 1998), as well as the related processes of marginalisation of professions (Butler et al., 2012) (see Chap. 1). We ask if the diffusion of technologies is causing fragmentation of labour and loss of professional power, or is instead a mechanism that is reinforcing an already existing trend.

Our research looks at specific segments of the professional labour market: professions whose access is regulated by public regulation and the traditional professionalisation model, based on strong institutions and peer control, and where the interrelation between digitalisation and differentiation of the professional labour market appears most clearly. In particular, we focus on specific professional profiles (architects, lawyers, journalists, and psychologists).

2 From Platform Thinking to (Professional) Platform Work

We live in the era of the *platform economy* (Srnicek, 2017), defined as a digital infrastructure that enables different types of users (clients, suppliers, producers, and professionals) to interact and develop markets together, based on network effect logics (Rietveld & Schilling, 2021) and the algorithmic management (Stark & Pais, 2020) of performances anchored to digital-reputation systems (Origgi & Pais, 2018).

G. Piccitto
Department of Political and Social Science, University of Catania, Catania, Italy

Dipartimento di Scienze Politiche e Sociali, University of Bologna, Bologna, Italy

Platforms act as *multi-sided markets* (Boudreau & Hagiu, 2009; Rochet & Tirole, 2006) that aggregate services and re-intermediate the relationship between supply and demand. As new intermediaries in the labour market, platforms can govern the rules of transactions and directly access the data generated by online interactions. Thanks to this process, they also exercise some form of control over interactions and manage opaque mechanisms to develop trust among users (Gandini et al., 2016).

The growing body of literature in this field focuses on the impact of digital platforms—and, in general, digital technologies—as a disruptive innovation capable of altering the rules in terms of working conditions, career paths, and rewards (Arcidiacono et al., 2021). However, platform companies are developed with a plurality of practices and organisational sub-designs that could generate differentiated sets of opportunities and risks for professionals.

Despite the fact that the tendency to recruit workers via platforms started with less qualified jobs and more repetitive tasks (Lehdonvirta & Ernkvist, 2011), professional jobs (with their flexible contents, implications in terms of autonomy and individualised competition, and need for personal branding) are increasingly in line with the constitutive principles of platforms as intermediation mechanisms, and form a new productive model.

Some scholars have attempted to classify the various forms of platform work. One of the most highly regarded typologies in the literature is provided by De Groen et al. (2016), who distinguish between *online tasks*, based on practices that could be performed exclusively electronically and where the entire working process could be managed entirely online (e.g. Upwork), and *on-location tasks*, which require some physical interaction in an offline space (e.g. Foodora). They also add a further distinction between *low-medium-skill jobs* (e.g. Helpling), which are manual or low-specialised, and *high-skill jobs* (e.g. Zooppa), which require highly specialised skills and certain learning processes obtained through work experience or specific formal credentials. This typology makes it possible to distinguish the heterogeneity of platform work more clearly and to identify the various areas of interest for professional work. However, according to Pesole et al. (2018), in many cases, this classification is insufficient to represent the real heterogeneity of the phenomenon, and they therefore attempt to classify workers based on their status in the labour market, the payment they receive and the number of hours worked, identifying almost 45 combinations of platform work, the majority of which are concentrated in high-skill and highly professionalised sectors.

The research carried out by Wood et al. (2019) on platforms such as Upwork, Fiverr, PeoplePerHour and Freelancer.com. has demonstrated how algorithmic management techniques in platforms tend to offer workers high levels of flexibility, autonomy, as well as varied and complex tasks. But at the same time, these mechanisms result in low pay, social isolation, and self-exploitation. Although it has been widely confirmed that the extrinsic conditions of platform work are often unsatisfactory (e.g. in terms of levels of income or career advancement), professionals and knowledge workers continue to offer their services on platforms, encouraged above all by vocational aspects or by interest in non-material incentives, such as increased visibility and professional reputation (Nemkova et al., 2019).

3 The Transformations of Professionalism in Italy: A "within" Perspective

Starting in the mid-1970s, particularly with Braverman's *Labor and Monopoly Capital* (1988), a major strand of literature advanced the hypothesis of the degradation of work, emphasising deskilling, and task unbundling. In the sociology of professions, this literature has found particularly fertile ground in the debate regarding the end of the "golden age" of professions (Gorman & Sandefur, 2011). Despite this hypothesis of a general decline, professions cannot be conceptualised as equal, homogeneous entities, and are best seen as hierarchically differentiated groups based on varying forms of exclusionary social closure (Saks, 2015). The sociology of professions has highlighted the differentiation within professions in terms of prestige, income, and power (Freidson, 2001), attributed to professional sub-specialities or types of clients (Abel, 1985; Parding et al., 2021).

In more recent years, a new phenomenon has emerged: the outsourcing of professional work. Professionals work outside the boundaries of large organisations while maintaining a de facto dependency on them. This phenomenon is well highlighted, for example, by the case of the *temporary attorney* as a professional with second-class status, performing tasks that are fragmented, deskilled, intensified, and regimented (Brooks, 2011).

In the debate on the decline and differentiation of professional work, the emergence of new technologies and the impact they have on professionalism is not always examined sufficiently. The digitalisation of professional work through platforms represents a discontinuity that requires further interpretative effort. Our aim is try to assess if the diffusion of technologies is causing a new logic of organisation and division of labour, or reinforcing a logic that is already present in the labour market.

The debate over platform work has once again brought to the fore issues that had long been abandoned in the academic literature on the professions, in light of the impact of the digital transition in lowering entry barriers to certain professional fields, allowing even those without formal credentials to opt for jobs and operate in specific qualified segments of the labour market. At the same time, by lowering access barriers and configuring new methods of interaction and matching in professional markets, the platforms act as drivers, changing the characteristics and practices that are necessary to be competitive that are recognised and legitimised in the markets of reference.

According to the existing literature on this issue, the role of digitalisation on professionalism appears ambivalent: some studies minimise the role of the digital world in professional markets, although forms of algorithmic control mean that these professionals working online are granted lower intra-professional status and less professional autonomy. This is due to the low interference in supply and demand between online and offline markets that essentially maintains distinct practices and repertoires of actions, and contains the disruptive effects of digital practices on professional markets (Yao, 2020). Other studies highlight how new technologies have changed the relationship between professionals and clients, modifying attitudes regarding ethical aspects—for example, privacy for doctors (Griebel et al., 2017), or checks on the reliability of information and quality of sources for journalists (Manninen, 2017). Platforms tend to be represented as the ideal "place" for "transitional work" or for multiple job strategies of the *plural careerist* (Caza et al., 2018), in which many workers who already have stable jobs and income streams decide to take on professional digital jobs as "supplemental earners" (Schor, 2020). However, a growing body of research shows that this work appears anything but transitory or residual, but extends over time, making it possible to develop specific professionalisation based on ad hoc repertoires of action and skills (Bosma, 2022; Driel & Dumitrica, 2021). At the same time, the rhetoric of accessory and complementary work does not seem to recognise the growing professionalisation of remote professionals that operate, sometimes exclusively, through platforms (Raval & Pal, 2019).

We hypothesise that the diffusion of platforms that match the supply of professional work to demand for it does not undermine the conditions of professional work. On the contrary, this very transformation of professional work might make the platform model attractive.

Although the platformisation of professional work can be interpreted through all the three analytical dimensions outlined in Chap. 1—within, between, and beyond—the most significant aspect for the discussion of the platformisation of professionalism is "within" (Chap. 1). In particular, we look at the relationship between the diffusion of professional work platforms and inequalities between professionals within the same profession.

The question that guides our analysis is whether platforms can offer new opportunities at the lower levels of the social stratification of the professions, or whether they do the opposite: strengthen the process of the systematic differentiation and decline of professional positions.

Our analysis focuses on the Italian case, where, since the 1990s, the number of professionals has grown quite considerably (Confprofessioni, 2021). Despite this, the effects of digital technology on the professions in Italy have not been sufficiently studied. The academic debate on the effects of platform work on the Italian labour market has focused more on the so-called *riders*, home delivery gig workers, than on highly skilled professionals (Bellini & Lucciarini, 2019).

This chapter attempts to address this gap in the Italian debate by examining a specific segment of regulated professions and the traditional professionalisation model, based on strong institutions and peer control. We selected four regulated professions (architects, lawyers, journalists, and psychologists), both because they present a high level of professionalisation, which allows us to test our hypotheses more clearly, and because of the existing international results that have emerged regarding the digital transformation in the most established professions (Yao, 2020).

4 Research Design and Methods

To analyse the relationship between professionalism and digital platforms, we developed a two-step research design.

The first step was based on the identification of the most important professional work platforms through a general mapping of all work platforms active in Italy, performing Google searches using keywords such as "work online" or "platform work". Having acknowledged the difficulties of accurately quantifying a dynamic and constantly changing phenomenon, from the results that emerged in the first ten pages of results, we selected those that could be defined as work platforms. One hundred and fifty platforms were identified: 46 online/high-skill; 26 online/low-medium-skill; 22 on-location/high-skill; and 62 on-location/low-medium-skill. In the absence of a national or international register of platform companies, this mapping, although it cannot be considered exhaustive in relation to the Italian platform economy, identified the most active platforms (in terms of visibility and number of registered workers) to include in the study.

The second phase was based on 26 semi-structured interviews with four different profiles (platform workers, platform managers, representatives of professional organisations, platform clients of professional services) in the four selected professional markets. We concentrate on the most important platforms in terms of numbers of users and reputation within their professional group of reference (see Table 5.1 for details).

Unlike the research carried out in most of the previous literature, our focus on different platforms and professional groups allowed us to compare internal differences in various regulated/protected professional groups, looking at the relation between professional work and platforms.

Table 5.1 Interviews by gender, role, and platform services

Code	Gender	Role	Services provided
M1	M	Manager, high-skill/On-location platform	Legal
M2	M	Manager, high-skill/On-location platform	Architectural
M3	M	Manager, high-skill/On-location platform	Architectural
M4	F	Manager, low-medium-skill/Online platform	Text Editing
M5	M	Manager, high-skill/Online Platform	Psychology
M6	M	Manager, high-skill/Online and on-location platforms	Architectural
M7	M	Manager, low-medium-skill/Online and on-location platform	Various
M8	F	Manager, high-skill/Online platform	Text Editing
L1	F	Worker, low-medium-skill/Online Platform	Text Editing
L2	M	Worker, high-skill/Online platform	Design
L3	F	Worker, high-skill/Online platform	Architectural
L4	M	Worker, high-skill/On-location platform	Architectural
L5	M	Worker, high-skill/On-location platform	Architectural
L6	M	Worker, low-medium-skill/Online platform	Text Editing
R1	M	Representative of the professional organisation of Milan	Legal
R2	M	Representative of the professional organisation of Tuscany	Journalism
R3	M	Representative of the professional organisation of Piedmont	Psychology
R4	M	Representative of the professional organisation of Liguria	Architectural
C1	M	Platform client – Milan	Architectural
C2	F	Platform client – Aquila	Text Editing
C3	M	Platform client – Lucca	Legal
C4	M	Platform client – Bergamo	Legal
C5	F	Platform client – Bologna	Architectural
C6	F	Platform client – Avellino	Architectural
C7	F	Platform client – Naples	Architectural

We adopted an explorative approach in our research, allowing the interviewees' opinions to emerge with regard to the issue of professional digitalisation (with special concern for the role of digital platforms) and the role of professional organisations and what they achieve. The interviews were carried out remotely, either telephonically or by videoconference. Interviews followed an established protocol, with a common section for all four profiles and a profile-specific section for each one, with targeted questions. The common section puts together the personal profile of each interviewee and their particular positioning with respect to the phenomenon under investigation. The specific section varies with respect to the type of interviewee: the interviews with the managers concentrated on aspects relating to the creation of the platform, such as its design and operating mechanisms, but also reconstructed the motivations of the actors regarding their choice to operate in that specific professional market and the problems they encountered, as well as considering their relationship with professional associations. The interviews with the workers focused on their experience and careers and on the role that the platform played in their professional progression, highlighting advantages and disadvantages. The interviews with professional associations focused on their relationships and positioning with respect to the phenomenon of platforms that brokered professional services in their specific sector. Finally, the client interviews focused more on the perceived advantages and disadvantages of the platform-mediated professional relationship with these professionals. Given the difficulty of exhaustively mapping the field of reference, the preference was to triangulate the mapping activity with a qualitative and interpretative research design.

An in-depth analysis was conducted on the content of the interviews, grouping the answers collected into two fundamental thematic cores: the role of platforms as intermediaries and the peculiarity of the organisational model, in an attempt to outline how these two aspects contributed to transforming and differentiating the working activity of these professional groups with respect to their relationships, both with providers (the platform) and with clients (i.e. the users of digitally mediated services).

The research design and the type of data analysis adopted were seen to be compatible with the exploratory aims of the study, but some problems and issues were highlighted that will require further investigation and the construction of a specific research agenda on these issues.

5 Findings

As mentioned in the previous section, the first step in our research aimed to quantify the digital platforms that were active in Italy in order to have a clearer picture of their features. From our mapping activity, it emerges that there are almost 150 platforms that intermediate labour supply and demand in Italy. 45.3 per cent intermediate high-skill tasks, and 54.7 per cent deal with low-skill activities. Moreover, 53 per cent are based in Italy and 47 per cent are foreign platforms that also operate in Italy. This is made possible by 44 per cent of the mapped platforms intermediating online tasks and not providing on-location services. This provisional data already shows how the public debate on platform work is largely "short-sighted" with respect to the heterogeneity of the phenomenon, focusing above all on on-location and low-skill activities (such as drivers or riders) which, although slightly in the majority, represent only one portion of platform jobs. In fact, if we focus our attention on professional tasks, over half (56.0 per cent) of these platforms intermediate or deal with expert labour, and nearly one out of five (16.7 per cent) manage occupations that are regulated by a professional guild/association. It is also worth noticing that almost two out of three (64.6 per cent) of the platforms involving professional work provide "online" services (entirely or partly).

To understand this evidence more deeply, we interviewed managers, clients, and workers, exploring two different issues: firstly, the platform as a new intermediary for professionals, which, in some way, competes with or complements professional associations; secondly, the platform as a new organisational system with specific characteristics that modify some typical elements of the professionals' status and ways of organising their work.

5.1 The Platform as an Intermediary

Looking at the "within" dimension, our research analyses the regulated labour platforms both as intermediaries for matching demand and supply, and also as a new form of work organisation. From the first perspective, finding professionals—traditionally performed through selection mechanisms such as consulting association registers or the recommendations of trusted people—is now carried out on platforms using assessments made by strangers. In analysing these new forms of matching the supply of professional work with demand, our main question is whether the platform reproduces existing or new criteria.

Some platforms maintain traditional quality signals (such as registers) and use the platform for matching clients only with certified professionals.

> In the last few months, we have started a process of recruiting psychologists. That is, we have launched a call for tender. We have now selected twelve people, who are already qualified psychologists and are about to start a training course. (M5)

The cases in which platforms do not verify the possession of formal credentials, even when these should be required, as in regulated professions, is more problematic and more frequent: this practice questions the principle of the professions' social closure and has been the subject of disputes brought by professional associations.

> Any person who wants to write for us can register on the platform and, in fact, they don't have to be a journalist or a professional editor; the only way we have to classify their competence is through a test. Even when they write "journalist" in their account, it doesn't matter to me. Do you know how many texts I send back to people who are journalists? (M4)

> The register started a big fight with us; they also expelled my partner. They created legal hurdles; this means you have to call a professional from their register, and, in some situations, this artificially distorted the market; so, they viciously attack any company that wants to generate new models. (M2)

Platforms and professional associations differ on the principles they use to assess competence: the former uphold a typical market principle, meritocracy, demonstrated through professional experience and regardless of formal certifications; the latter believe that the customer's choice should be limited to professionals who are pre-selected by peers and should be made exclusively on the basis of the principle of trust.

> You go to an architect because you know them, not because they're the most suitable for you, not because you have seen their work, or because their taste coincides with yours, but because they're your classmate, your sister's ex-boyfriend. In contrast, we have purely meritocratic relations. The

> contest is anonymous: you vote for the best project without knowing who they are, and, later, you find out if they are Italian or Turkish, handsome or ugly, young or old, a woman or a man, and so on. (M2)

> Would you go to a lawyer you can find on the Internet, who nobody knows, someone who maybe offers you a free first consultation? A lawyer is not like a commodity on Amazon where I look at reviews and decide. The right way to find a lawyer is through word of mouth, where a friend tells you about a person you can trust. Reading about someone on the Internet is not enough for me; I prefer recommendations from a friend, a person I trust. (R1)

It is therefore important to analyse the new trust-building mechanisms. This process is related to the shift from credentialism to reputation: it is assumed that, on the platforms, the informal reference system prevails over the expert system and that the regulators allow it. Some authors have noticed that the heterogeneity of clients is the main cause of the internal stratification of the professions, which prevents homogeneous professional communities being formed. If a professional has adopted an expert system of reference, it implies that they feel part of a community (of colleagues), whose rules they will adhere to and whose support they might ask for. On the other hand, if their reference system is an informal one, they will not be that interested in their colleagues' judgment and will be more concerned about what their clients/patients think. They will have completely different opinions on how to define a "good" professional: they need to be pleasant, open, pay close attention to what people say, and be ready to meet their needs. The professionals at the base of the pyramid (or the "trainees" in the stratification theorised by Freidson) will be more inclined to follow an informal reference system (Pais & Palmieri, 2016), and this can further strengthen their presence on digital platforms. Traditional professionalism considers the clients as incompetent, and protects them through social closure mechanisms. The choice to turn to a platform categorises these kinds of clients—in the eyes of a representative of a professional organisation—as a "second-league clientele".

It is not a reliable clientele; I would have some reservations, it means that they are really desperate. (R1)

On the platforms, the opposite is true: the client is considered capable of evaluating the work of the professional, and their evaluation is used as a sign of professionalism for future clients.

Then, of course, you can give a rating, and that becomes the criterion for the algorithm, which geolocates and selects. The algorithm makes its selection based on specialisation, location, and rating. If you have a low rating, you receive fewer requests. (M1)

Customers type in the text they need. Then, they are asked if they have author preferences and to select the type of author they want. So, for example, they can select that they want authors with four stars. Then, they say that, maybe, they want an author who writes about nature because, maybe, the text is about nature. Then they say they only want authors with positive grammar and spelling assessments. And, then, the platform makes a sort of list of all the authors with the required characteristics. Then, from that point onwards, it is the client who chooses one author rather than another, perhaps by going to the profile of each one and reading the evaluations of the texts. (C2)

The trust in a professional generated through reputational mechanisms is combined with trust in the platform. Customers show that they pay attention to signs of reliability.

Some elements such as the VAT number indicated on the website, a series of references that also lead to a registered office... (C3)

It is interesting to highlight how the introduction of artificial intelligence elements (such as chatbots) are perceived by customers as real interactions—probably seen as communicating with a person—and can strengthen trust in the platform.

I was looking on the Internet, and I found this platform [...]. I started to check it out, look, understand... but, it didn't convince me in the sense that

> I didn't trust it, obviously. Then, a girl contacted me… do you know when you go to a website, and you see the chat at the bottom right...? This girl contacted me and said to me: "Hey, what exactly are you looking for? Do you want to try the service?". And I told her a little, but obviously... I was wary. […] Every time I went to the website, the girl contacted me and told me that there had been a lot of positive experiences on the platform. Then, I finally made up my mind […]. I mainly trusted this girl who spoke to me; she inspired me with confidence. (C5)

The spread of platform work is linked to strengthening the market as a dominant regulatory mechanism even in regulated professions. These processes reinforce what Gorman and Sandefur (2011) point to as the emergence of a diversified *professional environment* composed of "commercialized professionalism" (Hanlon, 1996), a "hybrid form of professionalism" (Hodgson et al., 2015).

5.2 The Platform as a New Form of Organising Work

As regards the platform as an organisational model, our research shows that the platforms are based on *taskification*, mainly matching fragments of professional work to workers. This is a process preceded by exceptional practices, such as the case of franchise law firms offering standardised services to a relatively low-income clientele, which have adopted a highly routinised approach to organising work (Van Hoy, 1995).

While platform managers and representatives of professional associations agree with this analysis, they, do, however, attribute different meanings to it: for managers, it opens up new markets at a time when demand is falling; for professional associations, it lowers the quality of professional services.

> If lawyers were easy to reach, we would go to them ten times a month for our daily problems. Those who are against the possibility of promoting themselves are the generations of old lawyers who have a position that they do not want to lose. (M1)

> Would you go to a doctor you found on the Internet? Maybe for your corns but not for something serious. For lawyers, platforms are for minor issues: a road accident, a condominium conflict, small medical responsibilities. (R1)

From a broader perspective, a central question is whether this taskification process is inherent to the platform and, therefore, destined to last, or if ways of recomposing work can also be carried out through the platform. From the interviews carried out, one platform seems to be moving precisely in this direction:

> I would like to guarantee the professionals, above all the young professionals, a solid core of hours that allows them to have a decent income every month, and, therefore, have other experiences because, in any case, this is a big problem in our professional sector. That is, we have average incomes, especially in the early years, which are appallingly low. (M5)

This process is also related to one of the central attributes of professionalism (Gorman & Sandefur, 2011): the importance of the indeterminate nature of expert knowledge. However, the knowledge mediated by platforms needs to be easily codified, and it cannot uphold a profession's legitimacy. This is the paradox of platformisation of professionalism: on the one hand, it offers market opportunities for marginalised professionals; on the other, it highlights the growing polarisation of work conditions within each profession.

6 Conclusions

Our findings confirm the hypothesis that platform work, instead of being the driver of the processes that are transforming professions—in a perspective of technological determinism—is a mechanism that reinforces dynamics that are already in place in the expert labour segment, and leads to the emergence of what may be termed "platform professionalism" as a variant of organisational professionalism (Evetts, 2006).

The spread of professional platform work is not undermining the conditions of professional work. In fact, the transformations of professional work might have made the platform model attractive due to intra-professional competition and the processes of marginalisation (Butler et al., 2012) that are linked to the erosion of prerogatives such as high salaries, high levels of autonomy, job security, and social status. Similar to what happened in the 1960s and 1970s, a post-industrial transition has changed the nature of professional work and has made the interpenetration of organisational logic with professionalism possible. This should not lead to an analysis that is guided by perspectives of social determinism. On the contrary, from the analysis of the interaction between technological and social transformations in professional labour markets, we have observed the emergence of new paradoxes and tensions *within* (but also *between* and *beyond*) professions and their social contexts.

From the data collected, it clearly emerges that the market of professional services represents a significant share of platform work, despite the debate often centring on low-skilled manual workers such as riders or drivers. In particular, the expansion of platforms for professional services mostly concerns all professions that do not benefit from a regulatory and protection system run by a professional association and, therefore, are more exposed to such a "plat-firming" trend. However, even within the more "protected" professions, we can note the importance of platforms in reinforcing internal differentiation.

As new intermediaries, platforms contribute to a shift from credentialism to reputation as a more informal system of evaluating professional skills and capabilities. This process strengthens internal differentiation in professional markets by encouraging a "race to the bottom" by further segmenting customers, and a further division of labour among a given profession's scope of practice. The clientele of platform services is increasingly low value, price-oriented, and gives little recognition to fair and high-quality service.

As new forms of organisation, through the taskification and codification processes typical of algorithmic management, platforms reduce the complexity of the tasks performed by professionals, undermining the legitimacy of professional workers as holders of expert knowledge and exposing them even further to market competition and to impoverished working conditions.

In this scenario, professionals who work mainly online consider the platform as a showcase and self-promotion tool above all. Greater visibility on the platform is perceived as an essential tool to ensure employability over time. On the other hand, qualified professionals who work on on-location platforms are characterised by a greater individualisation of risks because they must balance the need to remain competitive within the platform (where pay tends to be lower) and the image and reputation that they must maintain offline, in order not to devalue acquired competences and professionalism. In fact, platforms tend to attract professionals who are less experienced or marginal in the labour market. These professionals use platforms as a place to "train" and to overcome access barriers in the professional labour market. However, this is not without risks because the platforms often try to limit the usability of the human and social capital acquired outside the platform, diminishing the autonomy of such professionals.

In conclusion, it can be assumed that platforms tend to relate to workers as "users" of these services, similar to the way they see their clients, transforming the nature of work from a right to a service (Arcidiacono et al., 2021). This is an approach that is consistent with further liberalising professional markets and raises the issue of the regulatory dimension of platforms, which take advantage of the legislative vacuum to put themselves forward as "private regulators" (Cutolo et al., 2019), in potential conflict with professional associations. Accordingly, it would be particularly interesting to go more deeply into assessing the regulatory role of professional associations as actors that—so far—have acted conservatively, but are beginning to consider the possibility of becoming, in their turn, the promoters of a new model of digital organisation for professional services.

Acknowledgements Davide Arcidiacono's contribution to the study is part of the Starting Grant project "INNOVIT – DIGITAL INNOVATION BETWEEN REGULATION AND ORGANIZATIONAL RESISTANCE" within the Pia.ce.ri. Research Plan 2020/2022 of the University of Catania. For the interviews with platform clients, we would like to thank the student, Federica Lepore, who supported the research team.

References

Abel, R. L. (1985). Comparative sociology of legal professions: An exploratory essay. *American Bar Foundation Research Journal, 10*(1), 5–79. https://doi.org/10.1111/j.1747-4469.1985.tb00496.x

Arcidiacono, D., Pais, I., & Piccitto, G. (2021). La qualità del lavoro nella platform economy: Da diritto a servizio. *Social Policies, 8*(1), 75–98. https://doi.org/10.7389/100587

Bellini, A., & Lucciarini, S. (2019). Not only riders. The uncertain boundaries of digital creative work as a frontier for emerging actors in interest representation. *PACO –Partecipazione e Conflitto, 12*(3), 845–870.

Boudreau, K., & Hagiu, A. (2009). Platforms rules: Multi-sided platforms as regulators. In A. Gawer (Ed.), *Platforms, markets and innovation* (pp. 163–191). Cheltenham.

Bosma, J. R. (2022). Platformed professionalization: Labor, assets, and earning a livelihood through Airbnb. *EPA: Economy and Space, 54*(4), 595–610. https://doi.org/10.1177/0308518X211063

Brooks, S. L. (2011). Meeting the professional identity challenge in legal education through a relationship-centered experiential curriculum. *University of Baltimore Law Review, 41*(3), 395–440.

Butler, N., Chillas, S., & Muhr, S. L. (2012). Professions at the margins. *Ephemera, 12*(3), 259–272.

Caza, B., Moss, S., & Vough, H. (2018). From synchronizing to harmonizing: The process of authenticating multiple work identities. *Administrative Science Quarterly, 63*(4), 703–745. https://doi.org/10.1177/0001839217733972

Confprofessioni. (2021). Osservatorio delle libere professioni, Rapporto 2021 sulle libere professioni in Italia. Roma: www.confprofessioni.eu.

Cutolo, D., Kenney, M., & Zysman, J. (2019). Platform-dependent entrepreneurs as private regulators in the platform economy. BRIE Working paper.

De Groen W.P., Maselli I., & Fabo, B. (2016). The digital market for local services: A one-night stand for workers? An example from the on-demand economy. CEPS Paper, Centre for European Policy Studies. Retrieved March 25, 2022, from https://www.ceps.eu/ceps-publications/digital-market-local-services-one-night-stand-workers-example-demand-economy/

Eurofound. (2018). Automation, digitalisation and platforms: Implications for work and employment. Publications Office of the European Union. Retrieved March 25, 2022, from https://osha.europa.eu/en/oshnews/automation-digitisation-and-platforms-work-implications-work-and-employment-eurofound

Evetts, J. (2006). The Sociology of Professional Groups: New Directions. *Current Sociology, 54*(1), 133–143.

Freidson, E. (2001). *Professionalism, the third logic: On the practice of knowledge.* University of Chicago Press.

Gandini, A., Pais, I., & Beraldo, D. (2016). Reputation and trust on online labour markets: The reputation economy of Elance. *Work Organisation, Labour & Globalisation, 10*(1), 27–43. https://doi.org/10.13169/workorgalaboglob.10.1.0027

Gorman, E. H., & Sandefur, R. L. (2011). "Golden age," quiescence, and revival: How the sociology of professions became the study of knowledge-based work. *Work and Occupations, 38*(3), 275–302. https://doi.org/10.1177/0730888411417565

Griebel, L., Kolominsky-Rabas, P., Schaller, S., Siudyka, J., Sierpinski, R., Papapavlou, D., Simeonidou, A., Prokosch, H., & Sedlmayr, M. (2017). Acceptance by laypersons and medical professionals of the personalized eHealth platform, eHealthMonitor. *Informatics for Health and Social Care, 42*(3), 232–249. https://doi.org/10.1080/17538157.2016.1237953

Hanlon, G. (1996). "Casino capitalism" and the rise of the "commercialised" service class-an examination of the accountant. *Critical Perspectives on Accounting, 7*(3), 339–363. https://doi.org/10.1006/cpac.1996.0038

Hanlon, G. (1998). Professionalism as enterprise: service calss politics and redefinition of professionalism. *Sociology, 32*(1), 143–163.

Hodgson, D., Paton, S., & Muzio, D. (2015). Something old, something new? Competing logics and the hybrid nature of new corporate professions. *British Journal of Management, 26*(4), 745–759. https://doi.org/10.1111/1467-8551.12105

Lehdonvirta, V., & Ernkvist, M. (2011). Knowledge map of the virtual economy: Converting the virtual economy into development potential. World Bank working series. Retrieved March 25, 2022, from https://openknowledge.worldbank.org/handle/10986/27361

Manninen, V. J. E. (2017). Sourcing practices in online journalism: An ethnographic study of the formation of trust in and the use of journalistic sources. *Journal of Media Practice, 18*(2–3), 212–228. https://doi.org/10.1080/14682753.2017.1375252

MIT. (2018). Platform Strategy Summit-report. Retrieved March 25, 2022 from http://ide.mit.edu/sites/default/files/platform-2018-v05_0.pdf

Nemkova, E., Demirel, P., & Baines, L. (2019). In search of meaningful work on digital freelancing platforms: The case of design professionals. *New*

Technology, Work and Employment, 34(3), 226–243. https://doi.org/10.1111/ntwe.12148

Origgi, G., & Pais, I. (2018). Digital reputation and mutual admiration society. *Studi di Sociologia, 56*(2), 175–194. https://doi.org/10.26350/000309_000035

Pais, I., & Palmieri, A. (2016). Professional communities online: Toward a third reference system? *Journal of Technologies in Knowledge Sharing, 11*(4), 1–11. https://doi.org/10.18848/2381-9235/CGP/v11i04/1-11

Parding, K., McGrath-Champ, S., & Stacey, M. (2021). Governance reform in context: Welfare sector professionals' working and employment conditions. *Current Sociology, 69*(1), 119–139. https://doi.org/10.1177/00113921209098

Pesole, A., Brancati, U., Fernández-Macías, E., Biagi, F., & Gonzalez Vazquez, I. (2018). Platform workers in Europe. Publications Office of the European Union. Retrieved March 25, 2022, from https://publications.jrc.ec.europa.eu/repository/handle/JRC112157

Raval, N., & Pal, J. (2019). Proceedings of the ACM on Human-Computer Interaction 3(CSCW): 1–17.

Rietveld, J., & Schilling, M. (2021). Platform competition: A systematic and interdisciplinary review of the literature. *Journal of Management, 47*(6), 1528–1563. https://doi.org/10.1177/01492063209697

Rochet, J. C., & Tirole, J. (2006). Two-sided markets: A progress report. *RAND Journal of Economics, 37*(3), 645–667. https://doi.org/10.1111/j.1756-2171.2006.tb00036.x

Saks, M. (2015). Inequalities, marginality and the professions. *Current Sociology, 63*(6), 850–868. https://doi.org/10.1177/001139211558

Schor, J. (2020). *After the gig: How the sharing economy got hijacked and how to win it back*. University of California Press. https://doi.org/10.2307/j.ctv125jrwn

Stark, D., & Pais, I. (2020). Algorithmic Management in the PlatformEconomy. *Sociologica, 14*(3), 47–72.

Srnicek, N. (2017). *Platform capitalism*. John Wiley & Sons.

Van Driel, L., & Dumitrica, D. (2021). Selling brands while staying "authentic": The professionalization of Instagram influencers. *Convergence: The International Journal of Research into New Media Technologies, 27*(1), 66–84. https://doi.org/10.1177/1354856520902

Van Hoy, J. (1995). Selling and processing law: Legal work at franchise law firms. *Law and Society Review, 29*, 703–729. https://doi.org/10.2307/3053919

Yao, Y. (2020). Uberizing the legal profession? Lawyer autonomy and status in the digital legal market. *British Journal of Industrial Relations, 58*(3), 483–506. https://doi.org/10.1111/bjir.12485

Wood, A. J., Graham, M., Lehdonvirta, V., & Hjorth, I. (2019). Good gig, bad gig: Autonomy and algorithmic control in the global gig economy. *Work, Employment and Society, 33*(1), 56–75. https://doi.org/10.1177/0950017018785616

6

Learning and Differentiation within Professions—The Cases of Teaching and Nursing

Karolina Parding and Anna Jansson

1 Introduction

This chapter is situated in both the Sociology of Professions and the Workplace Learning fields,[1] and focuses on welfare sector professionals'[2] conditions for learning. It is well established that continuous learning is an essential aspect of the work of members of professions, as a way of continuously developing not only an individual's competences, but also further consolidating the profession itself (Billett et al., 2014). There have

[1] The Sociology of Professions field focuses on professions and professionals, and their conditions for work and employment. The Workplace Learning field focuses on the conditions for learning, in, at, and for work, including formal and informal learning. We use the terms learning and workplace learning interchangeably.

[2] We use the terms welfare sector and welfare sector professionals. By welfare sector, we refer to education and healthcare in particular, but also include social services for instance. By welfare sector professionals, here we refer to professional groups of teachers and nurses that deliver services to citizens.

K. Parding (✉) • A. Jansson
Luleå University of Technology, Luleå, Sweden
e-mail: karolina.parding@ltu.se; anna.jansson@ltu.se

© The Author(s), under exclusive license to Springer Nature Switzerland AG 2023

L. Maestripieri, A. Bellini (eds.), *Professionalism and Social Change*,
https://doi.org/10.1007/978-3-031-31278-6_6

been profound changes over the last decades in the context in which welfare sector professionals are situated—the welfare sector labour market—which is in part due to the influx of the New Public Management (NPM) agenda. As an example, we examine teachers and nurses, as professionals situated in the education and the healthcare sectors. In Sweden, these sectors used to be, and are still to a large extent publicly run: typical for a social democratic system (Esping-Andersen, 1999). In line with ideas of NPM, such as efficiency and effectiveness, reforms have been implemented, involving, for example, private actors entering the arena as "additional" employers of welfare sector professionals. More specifically related to work in the welfare sector are shifts in the provision of welfare services via reforms in terms of devolution, privatisation, marketisation, consumer choice, and competition. This implies more choice for not only users of these services, but also for the professionals working in them. There may be both positive and negative aspects to this situation. For instance, many nurses actually prefer to work for staffing agencies, as their employment and working conditions are seen as more attractive.

There are also contradictory trends in the governance and organisation of professional work, such as standardisation, audits, and accountability, which can be seen as shifts towards centralisation. Alvehus and Andersson (2018) discuss this, saying that there are "seemingly contradictory coexisting features of modern welfare professions" (p. 91), with the education and healthcare sectors being examples. They argue that entangled institutional logics can be identified, with "a paradoxical relationship between centralization and decentralization" (p. 92). Taking this as its starting point, the aim of this chapter is to discuss welfare sector professionals' learning conditions in relation to the current variations in employers, both private and public. The research questions guiding the chapter are: what differentiating aspects of conditions for learning can be identified in professional work in the welfare sector? And how can these be understood?

It is relevant to examine and discuss welfare sector professionals' working conditions in general, in relation to current labour market trends, as they are said to have a crucial role in society (Bourgeault et al., 2009; Kamp, 2016). In fact, these are large occupational groups and they deliver essential services to citizens based on democratic principles, with the mission of providing equal services to everyone. In the context of professional work, discussing specific conditions for learning is crucial as it has been argued that the continuous development of competences is essential, and also that within professions, it is the professionals themselves that lead the profession's consolidation of knowledge (Billett et al., 2014; Freidson, 2001). Moreover, in their seminal work on enabling and constraining factors for a good work environment, Karasek and Theorell (1990) found that good learning conditions can act as a buffer in a strained work situation.

Previous research has tended to focus on single professions, and in fact, for quite some time there have been calls for comparative studies, as well as studies that include several professions (c.f. Adams, 2015; Brante, 2013). This piece is thus a contribution to the shortage of multi-profession approaches in the Sociology of Professions research. This approach identifies both differences and similarities, with the possibility of drawing conclusions that are relevant beyond one single profession, highlighting more general trends regarding conditions for work and learning among welfare sector professionals. Indeed, some theories of comparison suggest that studying cases that have both similarities and differences can be useful in exploring and explaining differences (Burau, 2007).

The chapter is structured as follows: firstly, we describe the key labour market reforms linked to the two cases. Then we illustrate how conditions for learning appear to become differentiated within the two professional groups. Subsequently, we discuss what this means for teachers' and nurses' learning conditions in particular, and welfare sector professionals' working conditions in general. Finally, we suggest practical implications as well as directions for further research.

2 Key Reforms and Their Implications

As the reforms make up the context in which we discuss the professionals' conditions for learning, rather than forming the object of study itself, what we present here is a simplified explanation. Reforms often take place within rather intertwined processes, and clear distinctions may be difficult to make without going into close detail. However, before we go into the two cases, we offer an overarching description of the public sector in Sweden.

Over the last decade, there has been an increase in public sector purchases of services from private actors. For example, the regions'[3] purchases of services from private actors increased from 7.9% to 13% from 2006 to 2020, with the corresponding figures for municipalities being 7.2% to 12.8% (Ekonomifakta, 2021).

The education sector reform affecting teachers is known as the *school choice reform*,[4] and paved the way for further differentiation. This reform was introduced in the early 1990s, and with it, a voucher system was launched: each student was assigned a voucher that was allocated to the school where the student was admitted. With this reform, non-public employer organisations were also introduced. This reflected a significant change, as practically all teachers had previously been employed in the public sector. The number of new privately run schools has risen at a rapid pace, from virtually none prior to the reform being implemented at the beginning of the 1990s, to employing some 25 per cent of the teachers at upper secondary level in 2020–2021 (SNAE, 2021). However, the percentage differs substantially between different municipalities, from zero to approximately 60 per cent. Each employer decides on how to organise training, including organising formal as well as non-formal and informal learning. Similar initiatives focusing on privatisation and choice in education can be found elsewhere to, for instance in Australia, the US, and Chile (e.g. see Ladd & Fiske, 2019).

Within the nursing profession on the other hand, private hiring of personnel for profit has been permitted in Sweden since 1993. This meant that the number of private employers increased within the Swedish

[3] In Sweden, a significant proportion of all public services are provided by municipalities and regions that finance themselves mainly by taxes and which, compared with other EU member states, have wide-ranging responsibilities. Municipalities and regions may procure services from private companies and thus, private providers are also financed by tax revenues. For example, regarding healthcare, the 290 municipalities are responsible for elderly care, home care, and social care, while the 21 regions are responsible for all individual health services (primary, psychiatric, and specialist healthcare). While many primary care (municipal level) providers are private, most Swedish hospitals (regional level) are publicly owned (with both publicly and privately owned healthcare facilities being publicly funded).

[4] It should be noted that the education sector also has been subject to a devolutionary reform, from being state governed, to being devolved to the approximately 290 different municipalities.

healthcare system. In contrast to the education sector reforms discussed above, this mirrors a reform that affects the entire labour market, and thereby different occupational groups, that is, not only nurses. However, since nurses in Sweden have traditionally been employed primarily by public employers (municipalities and regions), this reflects an interesting change in their sector. In fact, over the 2011–2018 period, the hiring of temporary agency staff (mainly doctors and nurses) increased quite dramatically within Swedish healthcare regions. During this period, the total costs for hiring of temporary staff rose from approximately 2.5 billion to 5.4 billion krona (SALAR, 2019). Recent figures also show how the total costs for temporary agency nurses increased by 24 per cent over 2021 (the corresponding figure for doctors is 8.4 per cent) (SALAR, 2022). Although these latest figures are affected by the COVID-19 pandemic, they still illustrate how the hiring of nurses is still on the rise. Similar trends have been noted elsewhere, for example, in the UK and Australia. Agency nurses are employed by temporary work agencies. However, they carry out their work at a client organisation, which purchases their labour from the temporary work agency for a fixed, limited time. The management relationship with these nurses lies with the client organisation, where issues regarding daily work and working conditions are handled. This implies that the responsibility for formal learning activities, such as courses, can be assumed to be handled by the employer (i.e. the temporary work agency), whereas informal learning activities, since they are connected to daily work and working conditions, can be assumed to be more connected to the client organisation. However, in practice, each temporary work agency (employer) *and* each client organisation decides on how to organise an employee's work, including organising formal as well as non-formal and informal learning.

To sum up, we have described how reforms affecting education and healthcare affect employment arrangements, as professionals can now work for more and different employers. In the case of the education sector, teachers now work for either private or public sector education providers. In the case of the healthcare sector, temporary agency staffing has been introduced for nurses, giving them the opportunity to work for a temporary work agency (a private employer) performing daily work in a client organisation (most often public) that is responsible for their daily management, as well as for "traditional" public employers. Thus, the very same workplace can be manned by staff employed directly by the client organisation and temporary agency staff concurrently. This in turn, seems to have implications for learning conditions in the two cases, which we will now elaborate.

3 Teachers' and Nurses' Learning Conditions Amid the Key Reforms

Based on our previous empirical research, we see indications that welfare sector professionals' conditions for learning have changed. It seems the reforms described above can be interpreted as initiatives that accentuate a differentiation between professionals within the very same professions. Below we discuss our findings in terms of differentiated conditions for learning.

3.1 Conditions for Learning in the Teaching Context

In our own previous research over the last decade, we have identified indications of increasingly differentiated conditions for teachers' work, not least in terms of conditions for learning. Overall, and across the board, and not only in our own previous research, it has been argued that one major implication of the Swedish education system reforms, which are partly based on privatisation, but also partly on devolution, lies in that the teaching profession's possibilities of influencing conditions for learning (on a collective level) have been diminished; this is related to the shift in responsibility from the national state level to local municipalities around the country (SOU, 2014, p. 5). To further complicate the situation, the responsibility lies not only with each of the 290 municipalities, but with the many private employers of teachers that have been established as a result of the school choice reform. Each employer thus decides on what formal and informal learning is provided.

In a recent study, based on qualitative interviews with upper secondary teachers in one geographical region in Sweden, in eight different schools, public and non-public—situated in three different market types,[5] we found that the geographical location and budgetary situation of workplaces, along with their size and age, were linked to how teachers experienced their working conditions, including learning conditions (Parding et al., 2017, 2021). The differences could not be explained simply through the lens of public and non-public employers. Rather, regional and local characteristics seemed to be of primary importance. For example, geographical differences exist throughout the country in terms of urbanisation levels, including population density and proximity to larger towns or cities. These circumstances seem to affect possibilities to partake in formal learning activities, as courses are usually given in bigger towns or cities, thus tending to exclude teachers in geographically distant and economically challenged, often rural, schools. The interviewees' answers could be linked to their school's geographic location and related budgetary conditions, but also their workplace size and age. The workplace's geographic location, together with its budgetary conditions, seemed to be more strongly related to formal learning, while the workplace's size and age appeared to be more closely related to informal learning. A key finding was that the conditions for learning, in the context of the school choice reform, can be described as differentiated. This means that the local and regional circumstances of a workplace must be considered when examining the conditions for learning among welfare sector professionals—reforms appear to have complex consequences on various levels. Moreover, it seems that local circumstances (geographical, social, economic, etc.) affect the schools and teachers' conditions for work and learning, but also that the educational circumstances may affect the local community more generally.

In a related paper (Parding & Berg-Jansson, 2018), based on the very same empirical data, we show how the teachers interviewed identified their subjects as the most important to learn more about. Moreover, we

[5] The Swedish National Agency for Education (SNAE) (2012) identified six *types* of school markets: large city areas (34), larger regional centres (27), smaller regional centres (87), larger local centres (56), smaller local centres (70), and municipal centres (16). We have chosen the three most common market types; one example of a smaller regional centre (SRC), one example of a larger local centre (LLC) and one example of a smaller local centre (SLC). These market types are based on the local school market's size in terms of number of students and other regional characteristics (SNAE, 2012).

found spatial and temporal aspects of the local organisation of work to be important, including practical issues such as positioning of work stations and schedules, which seemed to influence the conditions for subject learning. The current organisation of work seems to contrast with how the interviewees would have preferred the work to be organised, as to provide better conditions for informal learning. These findings are supported by, for instance, Hoekstra et al. (2009), who claimed time and proximity to teacher colleagues as being central in order to encourage informal learning to take place. Other scholars have identified similar results. Lohman (2006) has argued that lack of time, lack of proximity to colleagues' work areas, and insufficient funds are organisational factors that constrain teachers' informal learning. This line of argument mirrors our own previous research (Parding & Abrahamsson, 2010), regarding the importance of subject focus and organisation of work, and also signals that the priority of the interpretation lies within the organisation rather than the profession. Lastly, and of specific relevance here, our findings also illustrate conditions for learning being experienced differently both between and even within workplaces in different subjects. This can certainly be seen as differentiation within the teaching profession, which we link to a differentiated education sector, where local workplace characteristics nowadays appear to shape learning and development conditions.

Finally, we also carried out a large-scale survey, including 58 questions that focussed on upper secondary teachers' working conditions, including a section on conditions for learning (Parding et al., 2018). By and large, the respondents seemed dissatisfied with the conditions for learning, in particular teachers working in the public sector. These results mirror results from "The Teaching and Learning Survey" (TALIS), where it has been found that teachers in Sweden partake in fewer learning activities on average than their colleagues in the other 44 participating countries (SNAE, 2014). We found, for instance, that when asked whether the professional development provided by the employer covered a teacher's needs, only 26 per cent of the publicly employed teachers agreed, compared to 40 per cent of the privately employed teachers. This points to problematic numbers of teachers being dissatisfied, but also to a difference between sectors. Moreover, asked whether their daily work is organised in a way for teachers to learn from each other, 35 per cent of the publicly employed teachers agreed that it was, compared to 46 per cent of the privately employed teachers.

To sum up, based on our own literature overviews and empirical studies, which use both qualitative and quantitative methods, as well as other existing research and data, the conditions for teachers' learning seem unsatisfactory, and—something that is relevant here—they seem to be rather different depending on where one works, which we here link to two main reforms. There is a clear difference between publicly and non-publicly employed teachers in terms of conditions for professional development. Moreover, where the specific workplace is situated—mainly its economic and geographical circumstances—also seems to impact on conditions for learning.

3.2 Conditions for Learning in the Nursing Context

As described above, since 1993, when the private hiring of personnel for profit was permitted in Sweden, nurses could now choose to work as agency nurses. In this way, the number of temporary work agencies, that is, private employers, has also grown. Our research focused on working and learning conditions for both nurses with public employers and agency nurses with private employers, and showed some differences between these different categories of nurses (Berg Jansson & Engström, 2017, 2022; Berg Jansson et al., 2020). Indeed, these are differences which we interpret as illustrations of how temporary agency staffing leads to differentiated learning conditions between these different categories of nurses.

Our own previous research indicates that agency nurses judge their working conditions as better when agency employed, than when employed directly by a public employer (Berg Jansson & Engström, 2017). This can be explained by the fact that nurses, due to their high employability, can be assumed to make an active and voluntary choice to work as agency nurses. Indeed, deRuyter et al. (2008) discuss higher financial rewards and improved flexibility as strong pull-factors into agency nursing. Secondly, today occupational groups that "...require complex skills and retraining" (Augustsson, 2016, p. 522) are part of the temporary workforce, exemplified here by agency nurses. To sum up, this is relevant since conditions for learning for temporary agency workers have been found difficult to organise, and have oftentimes been considered insufficient (see, e.g. Håkanson & Isidorsson, 2015; Garsten, 1999).

In a study focusing on nurses' experiences of working with or as agency nurses, interesting results linked to conditions for learning emerged (Berg Jansson & Engström, 2017). The analysis showed similarities and differences regarding daily work and working conditions among nurses employed directly by the client organisation and agency nurses; how agency nurses were not always familiar with specific routines, local service organisation, and so on, and therefore described their work as more limited than nurses employed directly by the client organisation. Interestingly, the agency nurses express this as positive as this allowed for more patient-related work. Indeed, although nurses employed directly by the client organisations described agency nurses as competent, ambitious, and generous, they also mentioned how they themselves took overall responsibility for documentation, planning, and development work. This is supported by the findings of Cicellin et al. (2015) who discuss how more long-term tasks such as developing procedures are assigned only to staff employed directly by the client organisation, while more urgent tasks and routine tasks are assigned to both nurses employed directly by the client organisation and agency nurses (see also Augustsson, 2016). Furthermore, agency nurses described how they were not part of a "group" or local organisation, and how they therefore worked even more independently as temporary staff. This resembles Allvin et al.'s (2003) description of the work of nurses employed directly by the client organisation as more "boundless" than the work of agency nurses, since working for the organisation directly implies more administration and planning, for instance.

In a related paper, we discuss conditions for learning in relation to temporary agency staffing, with a focus on agency nurses' and nurses employed directly by the client organisation's experiences of social relations (Berg Jansson et al., 2020). Regarding individual agency nurses, conditions for more long-term and work-related feedback, emphasised as decisive for informal learning (Ellström, 2011), and formal learning (such as courses), are less clear-cut for agency nurses than for nurses employed directly by the client organisation. However, this must be put into perspective, since nurses employed directly by the client organisation express that they are not always either fully satisfied with the conditions for feedback and learning, but they also ask for more of this in their work. Despite this, that is, although they say that they would like more learning, the learning experiences of nurses employed directly by the client organisation appeared to be *more* organised and structured by their employers, and implied opportunities to participate in training work and some formal learning activities. At the same time, work as an agency nurse is described as providing good opportunities for informal learning through variation of tasks and opportunities to work in different workplaces. Hence, the analysis signals partly differentiated learning conditions between nurses employed directly by the client organisation and agency nurses in terms of fewer opportunities for agency nurses to receive long-term and work-related feedback and participation in formal learning (Berg Jansson et al., 2020). Indeed, as stressed by Håkansson and Isidorsson (2016), temporary work agencies and client organisations (in general) follow different logics, each one clearly affecting conditions for learning. "The logic in the employment relationship is to contract temporary agency workers out to client organisations, thus there is no time for formal training. The logic in the management relationship lies in making temporary agency workers profitable as soon as possible, encouraging shortcuts in training and instruction; thus, temporary agency workers risk being left with a lack of clarity regarding what to do and how to do it" (Håkansson & Isidorsson, 2016, p. 340).

The results of a recent study (Berg Jansson & Engström, 2022) focusing on agency nurses' conditions for learning is in line with the results of the above-mentioned studies. That is, they show unclear conditions for formal learning and difficulties for agency nurses to receive work-related and long-term feedback and participate in organisational processes at client organisations/in their daily work. This is also in line with Augustsson's (2016) discussion of how client organisations do not use the full potential of the knowledge of highly skilled temporary staff (such as nurses). On the other hand, the analysis indicated relatively satisfactorily conditions for informal learning. Furthermore, the results show how the conditions for learning among the agency nurses to a large extent depends on the specific temporary work agencies and client organisations in question; we see great variation between them. Neither of them offers any clearly set out opportunities for learning. We interpret this as indications of individualisation of the responsibility for learning among agency nurses (Berg Jansson & Engström, 2022), as well as a sign of differentiation..

To sum up, we have shown how reforms in the education and health-care sectors particularly, and on the labour market generally, impact on the professionals; exemplified by changed conditions for learning among teachers and nurses. New employment arrangements, as an implication of the reforms, brings differentiation in learning conditions. This line of argument will be further developed in the discussion section below.

4 Discussion

The line of argument in this chapter—that current reforms bring differentiating processes in relation to the conditions for professional work, more specifically in terms of teachers' and nurses' conditions for learning—certainly corroborates with the thesis on differentiation process in professional work (Chap. 1). It should be noted that while the two examples used in this chapter illustrate new, private employers being added as employers; although this has happened in different ways for the two professions, they have many similarities. The case of teachers illustrates professionals being employed by different employers, and thus different workplaces, in different sectors; public and non-public, where both the specific employer, and the local and regional surrounding context seems to amplify differentiation in conditions for learning. The case of nurses on the other hand illustrates professionals being employed by different employers, but working side by side in the very same workplace. Our research also shows differences in learning conditions for agency nurses and nurses employed directly by the client organisation, and also differentiation *among* agency nurses.

Of course, there have always been different conditions for work, depending on specific employers and workplaces, for instance. Just as

Adams (2020, p. 102) argues, "internal divisions within professions" are not new. However, changed circumstances for professions bring "new challenges with implications for professional collegiality, identity, and unification". Thus, we argue, via our two cases, that privatisation labour market reforms seems to accentuate differentiation among professionals. Starting from the two cases described in this chapter, we raise more general questions regarding what the amplified differentiation in conditions for learning in particular, and working conditions in general, can come to mean for professionals, groups of professionals, and professions altogether. With a greater variety of types of employers, and types of employment, as well as a greater diversity in terms of conditions for both employment and working conditions, not least conditions for learning, it could be argued that different groups of professionals will have very different experiences and varying needs and agendas. This can possibly make the collective voice of professions weaker, as has also been discussed in Parding et al. (2021) and Adams (2020) who, based on an empirical analysis of engineers, argues that there are signs of "stratification, division, and even, at times, hostility, between professionals in managerial roles and employee roles" (p. 102). Adams argues that this can potentially lead to intra-professional division and conflict. More research is needed to follow the current processes within professions as they relate to differentiation. This is relevant first and foremost to monitor ways in which professionalism is developing.

5 Concluding Remarks

The current situation has been discussed in terms of possible concerns. However, the picture is complex. Both drawbacks and potentials can be identified, both on the level of individual professionals as well as professions as collectives. Indeed, professions today are faced with—and surrounded by—changed conditions, mirroring developments in society in general, and the labour market in particular. On an individual level, working as a temporary agency worker may bring ample opportunities for individuals in terms of learning, as moving between different workplaces gives insights into different routines and ways of working (Berg Jansson & Engström 2017, 2022; Berg Jansson et al., 2020). At the same time, with the complex triadic relationship for temporary agency workers, formal learning opportunities seem to fall between stools (cf. Håkansson & Isidorsson, 2016). Being a regular employee, on the other hand, may mean better opportunities for structured formal learning. Also with bearing for the individual level, when it comes to the current choice and competition circumstances in the education sector, learning possibilities can become hampered; the incentives for sharing knowledge with colleagues can be reduced if colleagues are seen as competitors (Parding & Berg Jansson, 2016; Silins et al., 2002). In future research, the implications of differentiating processes and their results need to also be examined on an organisational level as well as a collective level (that of professions).

To conclude, it is essential that further studies of professions and professionals, as they relate to conditions for work in general, and conditions for learning in particular, apply a geographically informed frame of reference, in order to decipher if and how processes of differentiation develop in different contexts and relate to the central concept of professionalism. This direction corroborates previous research on the conditions for professional work, where it has been claimed that the specific workplace context has often been left out of the analytical process, as if conditions were always homogenous. Indeed, calls for more contextualised studies have been made (cf. Svensson, 2008; Muzio et al., 2013; Adams, 2015).

Despite the differences between the two cases and the respective reforms, they seem to share similarities regarding differentiated learning conditions. This in turn emphasises the thesis on differentiation in professional work. Thus, with this chapter, we have contributed an illustration of how welfare sector professional work is seemingly becoming increasingly differentiated. While having particular relevance and importance in the Swedish context, we argue that the line of argument put forward in this chapter highlights a more general change in conditions for professional work, across professions and across national borders.

References

Adams, T. L. (2015). Sociology of professions: International divergences and research directions. *Work, Employment and Society, 29*(1), 154–165.

Adams, T. L. (2020). Professional employees and professional managers: Conflicting logics, hybridity and restratification. *Journal of Professions and Organizations., 7*(1), 101–115.

Allvin, M., Jacobsson, A., & Isaksson, K. (2003). *Att avgränsa det gränslösa sjuksköterskearbetet: en intervjustudie om sjuksköterskors villkor och valmöjligheter i bemanningsbranschen [To delimit boundless nursing work: an interview study of nurses' conditions and options in the staffing industry]*. Arbetslivsinstitutet.

Alvehus, J., & Andersson, T. (2018). A new professional landscape: Entangled institutional logics in two Swedish welfare professions. *Nordic Journal of Working Life Studies, 8*(3). https://doi.org/10.18291/njwls.v8i3.109542

Augustsson, G. (2016). The client company marginally utilizes the knowledge of highly-skilled temporary staff. *Journal of Education and Work, 29*(5), 519–539.

Berg Jansson, A., & Engström, Å. (2017). Working together: Critical care nurses experiences of temporary agency staffing within Swedish health care. A qualitative study. *Intensive Critical Care Nursing, 41*, 3–10.

Berg Jansson, A., & Engström, Å. (2022). Conditions for workplace learning among professional 'temps': A qualitative study of temporary Agency nurses in Sweden. *Vocations and Learning, 15*(1), 155–176. https://doi.org/10.1007/s12186-022-09283-x

Berg Jansson, A., Parding, K., & Engström, Å. (2020). What about learning? A study of temporary agency staffing and learning conditions in Swedish healthcare. *Journal of Workplace Learning, 32*(1), 63–75.

Billett, S., Harteis, C., & Gruber, H. (2014). Introduction. In S. Billett, C. Harteis, & H. Gruber (Eds.), *International handbook in professional and practice-based learning* (pp. xvii–xxi). springer.

Bourgeault, I., Benoit, C., & Hirschkorn, K. (2009). Introduction: Comparative perspectives on professional groups. Current issues and critical debates. *Current Sociology, 57*(4), 475–485.

Brante, T. (2013). The professional landscape: The historical development of professions in Sweden. *Professions and professionalism, 3*(2).

Burau, V. (2007). *Comparative health research*. In M. Saks & J. Allsop (Eds.), *Researching health: Qualitative, quantitative and mixed methods* (pp. 368–383). Sage Publishing.

Cicellin, M., Pezzillo Iacono, M., Berni, A., & Esposito, V. (2015). Dealing with resistance in temporary agency nurses: The role of fear in identity building processes. *Journal of Health Organization and Management, 29*(3), 298–316.

deRuyter, A., Kirkpatrick, I., Hoque, K., Lonsdale, C., & Malan, J. (2008). Agency working and the degradation of public service employment: The case of nurses and social workers. *The International Journal of Human Resource Management, 19*(3), 432–445.

Ekonomifakta. (2021). Offentlig sektor i privat regi. https://www.ekonomifakta.se/Fakta/Valfarden-i-privat-regi/Privata-aktorer-i-offentlig-sektor/ (Retrieved April 24, 2022).

Ellström, P.-E. (2011). Informal learning at work: Conditions, processes and logics. In M. Malloch, L. Cairns, K. Evans, & B. N. O'Connor (Eds.), *The SAGE handbook of workplace learning*. Sage.

Esping-Andersen, G. (1999). *The three worlds of welfare capitalism*. Polity Press.

Freidson, E. (2001). *Professionalism: The third logic*. Policy Press.

Garsten, C. (1999). Betwixt and between: Temporary employees as liminal subjects in flexible organizations. *Organization Studies, 20*(4), 601–617.

Håkansson, K., & Isidorsson, T. (2015). Temporary agency workers—precarious workers? Perceived job security and employability for temporary agency workers and client organization employees at a Swedish manufacturing plant. *Nordic Journal of Working Life Studies, 5*(4), 3–22. https://doi.org/10.19154/njwls.v5i4.4841

Håkansson, K., & Isidorsson, T. (2016). Between two stools: Occupational injuries and risk factors for temporary agency workers. *International Journal of Workplace Health Management, 9*(3), 340–359.

Hoekstra, A., Korthagen, F., Brekelmans, M., Beijaard, D., & Imants, J. (2009). Experienced teachers' informal workplace learning and perceptions of workplace conditions. *Journal of Workplace Learning, 21*(4), 276–298.

Kamp, A. (2016). Welfare professions in transition. *Nordic Journal of Working Life Studies, 6*(S1), 1–6. https://doi.org/10.19154/njwls.v6i1.4882

Karasek, R., & Theorell, T. (1990). *Healthy work: Stress, productivity, and the reconstruction of working life*. Basic Books.

Ladd, H. F., & Fiske, E. B. (2019). International perspectives on school choice. In M. Berends, A. Primus, & M. Springer (Eds.), *Handbook of research on school choice* (pp. 87–100).

Lohman, M. C. (2006). Factors influencing teachers' engagement in informal learning activities. *Journal of Workplace Learning, 18*(3), 141–156.

Muzio, D., Brock, D. M., & Suddaby, R. (2013). Professions and institutional change: Towards an institutionalist sociology of the professions. *Journal of Management Studies, 50*(5), 699–721.

Parding, K., & Abrahamsson, L. (2010). Learning gaps in a learning organization—Professionals' values versus management values. *Journal of Workplace Learning, 22*(5), 292–305. https://doi.org/10.1108/13665621011053208

Parding, K., & Berg-Jansson, A. (2016). Teachers' working conditions amid Swedish school choice reform: Avenues for further research. *Professions & professionalism, 6*(1), 1–16.

Parding, K., & Berg-Jansson, A. (2018). Conditions for workplace learning in professional work: Discrepancies between occupational and organisational values. *Journal of Workplace Learning, 30*(2), 108–120. https://doi.org/10.1108/JWL-03-2017-0023

Parding, K., McGrath-Champ, S., & Stacey, M. (2017). Teachers, school choice and competition: Lock-in effects within and between sectors. *Policy Futures in Education, 15*(1), 113–128. https://doi.org/10.1177/1478210316688355

Parding, K., Sehlstedt, T., Johansson, A., Berg-Jansson, A., & Jakobsson, M. (2018). Lärares arbetsvillkor i kontexten av marknadisering, privatisering, val och konkurrens – beskrivande data. Report. Luleå: Universitetstryckeriet. ISBN: 978-91-7790-024-5 http://urn.kb.se/resolve?urn=urn:nbn:se:ltu:diva-67117

Parding, K., McGrath-Champ, S., & Stacey, M. (2021). Governance reform in context: Welfare sector professionals' working and employment conditions. *Current Sociology, 69*(1), 119–139. https://doi.org/10.1177/0011392120909859

SALAR. (2019). Projekt - oberoende av inhyrd personal. Rapport från det nätverksgemensamma projektet 2016–2018. https://skr.se/download/18.544e1c0b1784a90739252ad/1616401747464/Rapport%20Oberoende%20av%20inhyrd%20personal.pdf (retrieved April 24, 2022).

SALAR. (2022) Kostnader för inhyrd personal i hälso- och sjukvården 2021. Jämförelser av helåret 2021 samt halvår 2/2021. Fördjupad analys. https://skr.se/download/18.eb74a4a17f44902bce40129/1646720568525/Kostnader-for-inhyrd-personal-i-halso-och-sjukvarden_2021.pdf (retrieved April 22, 2022).

Silins, H., Zarins, S., & Mulford, B. (2002). What characteristics and processes define a school as a learning organisation? Is this a useful concept to apply to schools? *International Education Journal, 3*(1), 24–32.

SNAE (Swedish National Agency for Education). (2012). *Mapping the school market: Synthesis of the Swedish National Agency for Education's school market projects*. Swedish National Agency for Education.

SNAE (Swedish National Agency for Education). (2014). *TALIS 2013: En studie av undervisnings- och lärmiljöer i årskurs 7–9, rapport 408* [A study of teaching and learning environments in years 7–9, report 408]. Swedish National Agency for Education.

SNAE (Swedish National Agency for Education). (2021). Gymnasieskolan – personalstatistik. https://siris.skolverket.se/reports/rwservlet?cmdkey=common & geo=1 & report=gy_personal & p_sub=1 & p_flik=G & p_ar=2020 & p_lankod= & p_kommunkod= & p_skolkod= & p_hmantyp= & p_hmankod=.

SOU (Swedish government's recent official report/Statens offentliga utredningar). (2014:5). *Staten får inte abdikera—om kommunaliseringen* [The State must not abdicate—About municipalisation]. Stockholm: Ministry of Education and Research.

Svensson, L. G. (2008). Profesjon og organisasjon [Profession and organization]. In A. Molander & L.-I. Terum (Eds.), *Profesjonsstudier [Studies on the professions]* (pp. 130–143). Universitetsförlaget.

Part II

Between

7

Changing Professional Status in Evolving Professional Systems: Towards Using a Descriptive Lens to Analyse Multi-layered Transformation Processes

Jean-Luc Bédard, Marta Massana Macià, and Christophe Groulx

7.1 Introduction

In a context of changes in professional mobility at the international level, professional regulatory jurisdictions and systems need to review frameworks for professional practice, and their standards and practices concerning the admission and entry into practice of foreign-trained professionals (FTPs). Access to regulated professions for FTPs is an issue that mobilises the efforts of several actors in the public, para-public, and private sectors, both internationally and locally. In a given jurisdiction,

J.-L. Bédard (✉) • C. Groulx
Department of Education, TÉLUQ University, Montreal, QC, Canada
e-mail: jean-luc.bedard@teluq.ca

M. Massana Macià
Groupe d'expertise pour le développement des cités interculturelles au Québec (GEDCIQ), Montreal, QC, Canada

© The Author(s), under exclusive license to Springer Nature Switzerland AG 2023

L. Maestripieri, A. Bellini (eds.), *Professionalism and Social Change*,
https://doi.org/10.1007/978-3-031-31278-6_7

with its own legal particularities, while certain issues regarding admission to the profession and entry into practice are common to all FTPs, significant differences appear depending on the nature of the profession. In our examination of the situations of FTPs, we focus on admission to the profession and entry into practice as two related but distinct processes, the first being a necessary first step and the latter being the final objective in the immigration process, from a professional point of view. This article examines variations in trajectories depending on the characteristics of the labour market, according to whether the market in question is public or private. These differences create specific tensions that contribute to a series of problems for FTPs both in being admitted into the profession and in them entering into practice. How do these public and private markets structure FTPs' experiences of admission and entry into professional practice? To answer this research question, this chapter presents two cases of regulated professions (doctors and engineers) that both benefit from mutual recognition arrangements (MRAs) between France and Quebec. Since 2011, these regulation devices have aimed to facilitate mobility between both jurisdictions for some 26 self-regulated professions. Our analysis looks at how the implementation of these arrangements differ, however, according to whether the profession is practiced in public organisations (doctors) or in private ones (engineers), and also depend on the varying nature of the actors engaged in overseeing this practice. In addition to these differences, we will also focus on common issues regarding FTPs' admission and entry into practice in the case of these regulated professions in Quebec. We will also document and analyse how the notion of protecting the public is invoked by the various actors, at different levels, to justify measures for controlling professional admission and entry into practice.

7.2 Theoretical Context of the Research

Various research studies on the sociology of professions provide insight regarding the workings of the regulated professions and their relationships with other social institutions. This study is anchored in Abbott's (1988) theory of jurisdiction, as well as Freidson's (2001) perspective on professionalism as knowledge-centred logics that influence the relationships between professions, the State, and the market. We also rely on Douglas' (1986) view on institutions as forms of cognitive apparatus, and use it to ground our analysis of the various institutional actors' positions and justifications in managing mobility and its related risks while they validate the protection of the public through specific measures.

Abbott (1988) underscored the importance of the processes of engaging in turf battles and establishing boundaries and jurisdictions regarding expertise within a profession (specialisations) and between neighbouring professions, such as nurses and doctors, or architects and engineers. At the same time, each profession asserts the scope of its work and justifies its processes for opening or closing up, for example, towards FTPs.

As for Freidson (2001), he emphasises each profession's relationships with the State and the market, and the consequences of these relationships for negotiating changes in standards for protecting the public. In North America, professional self-regulation processes are again being called into question (Adams, 2016). Neoliberal-inspired critics contend that, as closed markets, self-regulating professions curtail competition and are incapable of effectively regulating transnational work and, consequently, professional malpractice can occur more easily. The many research studies in the literature that call self-regulating professions into question can be grouped under three themes: (1) neoliberal and pro-globalisation ideologies, (2) oversight and professional malpractice, and (3) changes in the orientation of public policies.

Neoliberal ideologies celebrate the role of the market, and promote eliminating barriers in order to improve competition, flexibility, and efficiency (Merino et al., 2010; Nancarrow, 2015). Permits to practice and professional regulation are considered as restrictions to commerce: barriers that increase prices while reducing the supply of practitioners (Kleiner, 2006) and limiting organisational flexibility (Nancarrow, 2015). Self-regulating professions are criticised for having created "unnecessary obstacles" for businesses, having hindered competition and restricted consumer choice (Kleiner, 2006; Paton, 2008).

Furthermore, as Freidson (2001) points out, the relationships the professions maintain with the State affect their behaviour. The case of professional malpractice illustrates this well: with the soaring cost of malpractice litigation, professional autonomy in exchange for low-cost self-regulation is becoming less attractive to the State. It is evident that cost management is emerging as a major concern for State actors, particularly when public health systems are involved, as is the case in Canada and the United Kingdom. Public healthcare costs are skyrocketing, and these actors are seeking to curb rising costs by exercising more oversight over health professionals and the organisation of their work.

Finally, changes in approach and to public policies have a significant effect on the position occupied by regulated professions. The onerous costs of legal proceedings and, more generally, of the administration of justice, have led to changes in the regulation of professions. State actors can break up professional monopolies and amend regulatory powers for the purpose of controlling government expenditure. While self-regulating professions were once regarded as contributing to governance, closely following a Foucauldian approach, since the 1990s, they have increasingly been viewed as placing an inefficient burden on government finances, and as threatening to challenge the government's plans rather than supporting them (Saks & Adams, 2018). However, some authors emphasise the importance of regulations, this time in the sense of re-regulation (see Burau & Vrangbaek, 2008, p. 29; Bellini & Maestripieri, 2018).

We turn to Douglas' (1986) perspective for a relevant frame to analyse these institutional actors' positions. Drawing on the work of Durkheim (1984), her approach insists on the justifications given by institutions: "rooted in nature, the sacred emerges at key points, in order to defend any classifications and theories that maintain institutions". Following Durkheim, the "sacred" becomes a "social artefact", a collective representation that defines the division of work, and in the case that interests us here, that identifies the professionals who are said to be capable of protecting the public, and those who should be disallowed. This helps us better grasp "how professional orders think". How do they understand and legitimise the notion that is the foundation of their practices, that is, the notion of protecting the public? How does this vary between professional regulators of doctors and engineers? Furthermore, Durkheim identifies three characteristics of sacredness in any institution:

1. its dangerous nature; if the sacred is made profane, serious consequences will ensue, and the offender will be punished accordingly. In fact, in the notion of protecting the public, in addition to the aspect of danger, there also appear to be impassioned defensive responses and opportunities for explicit demonstrations of its tangible properties (evidence).
2. any attack on the sacred provokes impassioned defensive responses, here founded in scientific terms and seen through the lens of rational public policy. The notion of the protection of the public is regularly invoked to justify the status quo, whereas an objective analysis might show that a proposed change is actually well founded.
3. the sacred is the subject of explicit invocations that make it tangible, in this case through regulations that limit access to the order and allow entry into practice only if time is spent in lengthy and costly training and internships.

As described by Kuhlmann et al. (2016), each profession can be characterised, at least in part, by a path dependency that reflects its specific institutional, political, and social settings. These perspectives are especially useful when analysing the admission processes of FTPs into the local, self-regulated workforce. Therefore, our analysis fits into the broader perspective of the current diversity of professionals who negotiate their positions with other professionals, as well as with their changing work and management environments, as Dent et al. mention in their "General introduction" (Dent et al., 2016, pp. 2–6). Our data and analysis do not directly concern the managerial inflexion of professionalism, but we do consider governance pressures that question how regulation operates, especially in admitting FTPs and allowing them to enter professional, self-regulated practice.

We will see how these factors take shape in the cases of doctors and engineers, with various institutional actors intervening in these processes of entry into practice, stemming mainly from the predominance of public or private actors.

7.3 Ethnographic Context of the Research

7.3.1 On the International Level

Globalisation and the international movement of professionals, promoted by neoliberal policies, raise challenges for self-regulating professions. In the United Kingdom, these professions operate nationally, whereas in Canada and the United States, their regulatory bodies operate regionally (at the provincial or state level). These bodies were created to govern local practices, but face the challenges of regulating professionals working within transnational corporations, as well as the entry of FTPs into local markets (Suddaby et al., 2007; Flood, 2011; Gorman, 2014). FTPs find themselves in a complex regulatory environment and are potentially subject to an array of national and international regulations (Quack & Schußler, 2015). This presents problems for professionals seeking to enter practice, but also for the capacity of companies and businesses to meet the needs of their clientele. For this reason, FTPs try to find ways to navigate—and even circumvent—these regulations (Flood, 2011; Gorman, 2014). They explicitly adopt strategies "to avoid local regulatory problems" (Flood, 2011, p. 513); one example of this is how large commercial law firms have succeeded in bringing about change in professional regulation in the United Kingdom with a view to maximising their autonomy. While the various problems that arise for FTPs and the solutions proposed primarily concern regulated professions mainly operating in the private sector, the barriers for FTPs entering into practice can also be obstacles to the practice of professions regulated by the public sector. Such is the case for doctors in Quebec where, in spite of the historical shortage of doctors and difficulties in accessing a family doctor, the regulation of this profession itself contributes to the situation of scarcity.

7.3.2 On the Local Level

Many factors can limit the access of immigrants to professional practice (Blain et al., 2018): gender, age, national origin, immigration status, membership of a visible minority, language, period of immigration or, for that matter, “the very fact of seeking to practice a regulated profession, and the costs associated with the professional recognition process, as well as professional non-recognition” (Blain et al., 2018) [our translation].

Barriers to accessing employment can be attributed to a combination of intersecting and accumulating factors (Chicha, 2009, 2012). Reducing the remaining obstacles can be achieved by mobilising the different actors involved (employers, the government, training institutions, local organisations, etc.). This is even more important when it comes to recognition of prior learning and skills, as well as access to professional orders. In comparison with the other Canadian provinces, the match rate in Quebec for immigrants who would like to practice a regulated profession appears to be the lowest in Canada. Although significant progress has been made since the 2000s, a gap persists between Quebec and the other provinces (CIQ, 2019; Homsy & Scarfone, 2016).

7.4 Presentation of Results

7.4.1 The Publicly Funded Health System and Practice of the Medical Profession in Quebec

There has been a persistent problem of accessing doctors in Quebec, at least since the 1990s, resulting in long waiting lists. In this context of an insufficient number of doctors, it seems crucial to understand the regulatory conditions for access to the profession, and the limitations placed on the issue of permits to practice.

The following diagram provides an overview of the structure of the professional system that governs access to the medical profession in Quebec for FTPs (Diagram 7.1):

Quebec’s publicly funded health system determines the position of actors in the professional system, as well as that of the doctors themselves. Doctors are hired by the MSSS [Quebec’s Ministry of Health and Social Services], which controls funding for the province’s workforce: currently 21,000 doctors. The number of positions is not determined by the professional order nor by the medical unions, but by the MSSS. Most of

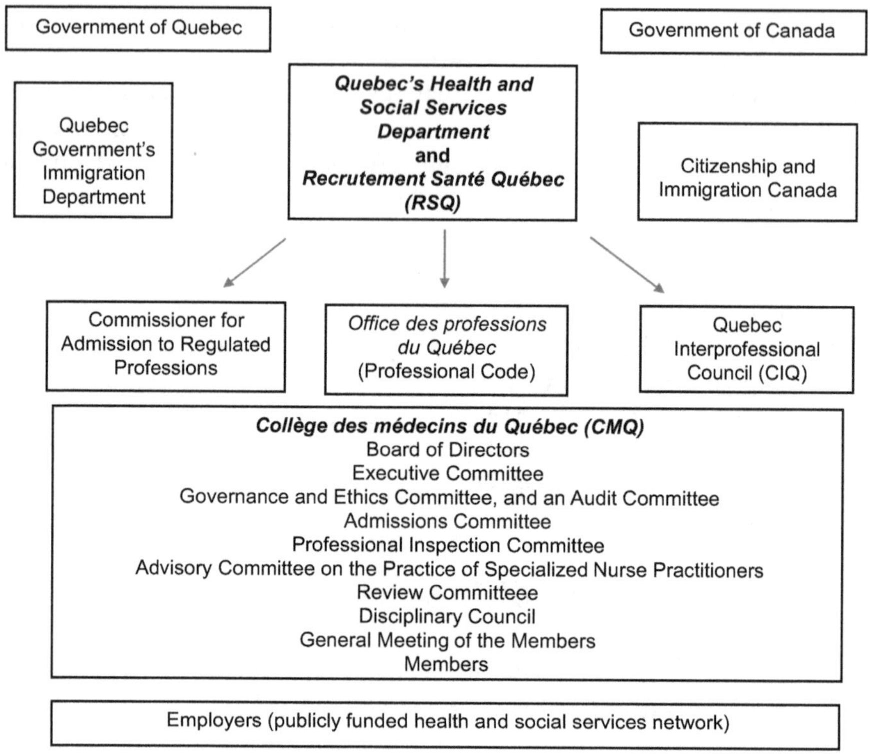

Diagram 7.1 Structure of regulation governing access to the medical profession for FTPs

these doctors are employed by the public system, with a negligible proportion (2–3 per cent) working in the private sector.

Furthermore, ministerial and departmental managers contend with significant budgetary constraints, a phenomenon that has been exacerbated by the increases in earnings granted to Quebec doctors over the last decade. As a result, in 2016, 7.1 per cent of the Government of Quebec's budget was taken up by the fees paid to some 20,000 doctors (Hébert et al., 2017); these accounted for 0.4 per cent of the labour force in 2019 (ISQ, 2019). Increasing the number of new positions for doctors therefore became more difficult considering the budgetary constraints arising from these agreements negotiated with medical associations. It should be noted that, unlike professional orders such as the *Collège des Médecins du Québec*, medical associations work explicitly in the interests of doctors.[1]

7.4.2 The Role of the Private Market in the Engineering Sector in Quebec

The situation is entirely different with respect to engineers and the general perception regarding the self-regulation of their practice. Of Quebec's 56 regulated professions, the *Ordre des ingénieurs du Québec* (OIQ) is the second largest professional order in terms of number of members (62,000). For the most part, its members practice in the private sector. Throughout the decade of the 2000s, a series of scandals tarnished the reputation of engineering firms, with some of them convicted under laws regarding the funding of political parties and the awarding of government contracts. The work of a public inquiry (the Charbonneau Commission, 2011–2015) shed light on what had happened. In this context, a series of measures were undertaken under the imposition of a trusteeship on the OIQ; this restructured the order and its practices and regulations, including its practices relating to inspection, investigation, and continuing education.

Trusteeship was imposed by the Government of Quebec from July 2016 to February 2019, following an analysis of the OIQ's situation by the *Office des professions du Québec* [Quebec Professions Board or OPQ]. This decision stemmed from the public inquiry, which revealed unlawful strategies enabling some firms to receive government contracts in return for contributing funds to political parties, through schemes to circumvent the laws on funding political parties and awarding government contracts. Even if these scandals only involved a few businesses, public trust in the profession and in its mechanisms for self-regulation were shaken. At the end of the trusteeship in 2019, as the OIQ states on its website, its

[1] A proportion of the doctors represented by these associations have expressed their disagreement with the pay rises, considering the shortfall of doctors and the rising costs leading to the inability of the government to fund an increase in the number of positions to bridge it. These doctors express their views primarily through the *Association des médecins pour un régime public* [Association of doctors for a public system].

processes had been reviewed, the inspection rate of members had increased dramatically, and a narrower range of activities was accepted under the terms of mandatory continuing education. The annual membership fees increased by 50 dollars, mainly to allow for the funding of increased professional inspection activities.

The reason that led to us choosing these two orders (doctors and engineers) for our analysis was the fact that the dynamics between the profession, the State and the market operate quite differently for each of them. As the CIQ pointed out:

> [...] Each order encompasses a distinct professional world in itself that must take into account a specific dynamic that includes its own requirements [...] a dichotomy can be seen between the public and private sectors [...] the professions that are most connected to the private sector following the changes in supply and demand, [...] whereas the orders associated with the public sector are necessarily dependent on government reforms and administrative decisions in the public sector. (CIQ, 2019:18)

On the one hand, 97 per cent of doctors work in the public system, in which the State decides the number of positions, their locations, and allocations by specialties. Above all, it assigns budgetary allocations that enable the health network to function; in particular, it allows some internships to be supervised in practice settings.

> The number of people chosen to enter into practice in medicine is based on the positions for doctors that the government decides to open up as part of its own plan. Therefore [the Ministry] does not need foreigners to fill these positions, since in the decree it has already decided beforehand how many students will be accepted in each of the specialties based on its plan. (Female, 57, representative of the Collège des Médecins du Québec) [our translation]

As for engineers, most are employed in the private sector. Engineering graduates must pass an exam to be admitted to the OIQ. Next, private organisations employ these new engineers, in coordination with the professional order.

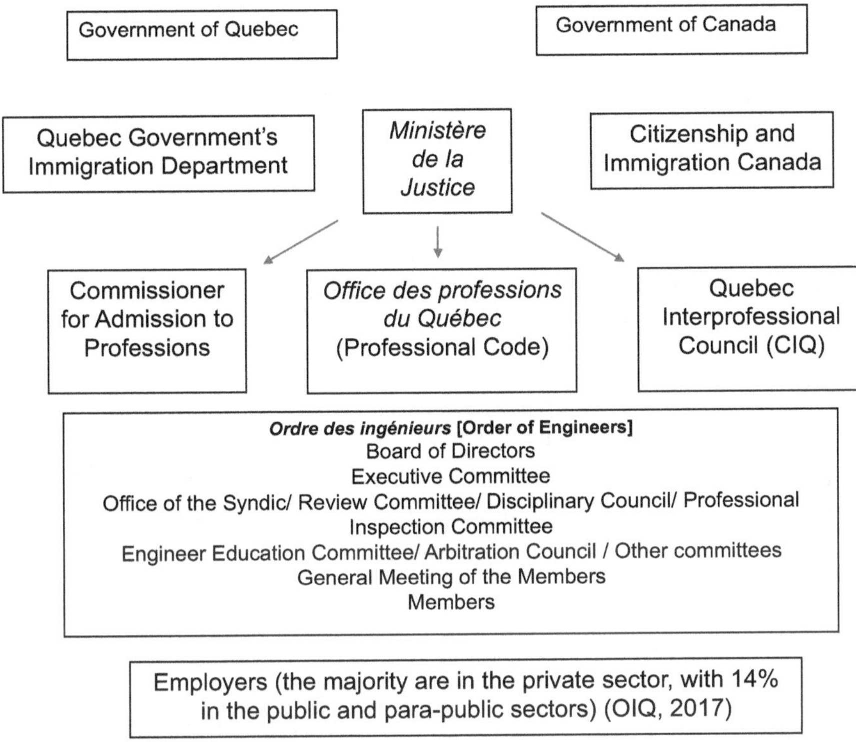

Diagram 7.2 Structure of regulation governing access to the engineering profession for FTPs

The following diagram illustrates the main actors involved in FTPs' paths to recognition and admission into the engineering profession in Quebec (Diagram 7.2):

Despite the manifest differences between these two professions and the ways in which they are regulated, in both cases, it is possible to observe (1) barriers to enter professional practice,[2] and (2) the pervasiveness of the notion of protection of the public as a principle that forms the basis

[2] Since the 2010–2011 fiscal year, of all foreign-trained candidates applying for admission to the OIQ (excluding those resulting from a Mutual Recognition Arrangement (MRA) in accordance with the Agreement between France and Quebec), an average of 34 per cent of candidates have given up during the application process.

of the professional orders' existence. This notion of protection of the public is at the heart of the raison d'être of professional orders, in the context of self-regulating professions under State supervision. The *Office des professions du Québec* confirms this in its revised notion of protection of the public (OPQ, 2012), and this is a position that is again taken up by the orders in their objectives and as the foundation of their actions.

7.4.3 Desacralising the Notion of Protection of the Public

Our analysis addresses obstacles to entry into professional practice that could be abolished or modified without calling into question the notion of protecting the public. This is inspired by recommended coordination strategies, measures, and practices between the various actors and institutions involved, as we will see later. These coordination measures and practices correspond to several of the recommendations set out by the OECD,[3] regarding the recognition of qualifications and skills.

In terms of waiting periods for the training or internship being offered, a recent survey conducted by the CIQ with the ten professional orders that receive the highest number of applications for recognising qualifications from abroad found that "the waiting period for retraining varies between 3 and 18 months (the average was 7 months)" (CIQ, 2019, p. 15). The orders surveyed considered that "among the principal obstacles to obtaining a permit to practice (…), access to retraining and internships are the most important factors" (CIQ, 2019, p. 16).

Regarding internships, those performed by engineers and doctors are both paid. In the case of engineers, the internship takes place in a private setting, and in the case of doctors, in a public setting. The Access to Training Coordination Hub (2019) has observed that there is a significant shortage of doctors' internships, that is more or less acute depending on the specialty.

[3] This document puts forward ten recommendations for the recognition of qualifications and skills based on innovative practices in various countries of Europe, Australia, Canada, the United States, and elsewhere (OECD, 2017).

In view of the shortage of doctors that has existed in Quebec for several decades, it may seem inconsistent, in terms of protecting the public, not to make enough internships available for the doctors who are eligible to undertake them, thus contributing to prolonging the shortfall in the provision of medical services in the public health system. Of course, these internships require supervision and therefore have costs attached, including the costs of material and human resources. Medical resources therefore need to be shifted to cover these training needs. However, supervising foreign-trained interns makes it possible to obtain doctors who are recognised as competent to practice locally much faster than applicants who are undergoing complete medical training. Moreover, these foreign-trained doctors have experience in contexts that could prove to be useful in the Quebec context, depending on the particular circumstances of his/her practice.

In addition to the issues concerning access and supply, there are other issues emerging from failures in coordination between actors responsible for setting requirement criteria in terms of knowledge and experience, and for setting compensation.

> As matters stand, the French hold a number of things against us: first, that we do not recognize their recommendations regarding qualification boards; second, our insisting on a three-month adaptation internship. (…) Our registration complaints commissioner conducted an investigation which found that there were indeed substantial differences and that we should keep it. Except that his recommendation was that 'you should adjust the duration of your internships depending on specialities, individuals, and this and that.' That means a slide rule and that you allow just about anything. (Male, 55, representative of the Collège des médecins du Québec)

In the case of doctors, a proposal has been made to introduce a supervised internship instead, which would allow for a longer assessment of the actual work of the candidate, while at the same time allowing him/her to experience practice settings in Quebec. Nevertheless, the 13-week internship that is currently under way has revealed, among other things, inevitable occasions when the subjectivity of the internship supervisor comes into play, particularly where assessment is concerned. Thus, targeted training based on actual needs would make it possible to assess candidates on the relevant subjects.

Thus far, our analysis has helped to illustrate how the behaviour of the actors who have a role in the entry into practice of FTPs varies significantly according to whether the job market for these professionals is based in the public or the private sector. This is particularly the case in the steps leading to the recognition of skills, including the discourse of the actors when they justify their practices, with the results varying based on this public or private anchoring.

7.4.4 A Need for Sustained Coordination Between the Actors and Institutions Involved

We have highlighted two major findings: (1) the recognition and entry into practice of FTPs is not the responsibility of one single actor or institution, but of a chain of actors and institutions of varying natures (political, administrative, private, etc.) acting on different levels (international, national, and local); (2) in the case of regulated professions, improvements are needed in the governance of issues concerning the recognition and entry into practice of FTPs. This governance requires an intersectoral, multilevel approach that allows all stakeholders to intervene and participate in dialogue (the government, training institutions, professional orders, employers, etc.). This converges with the conclusions of the Commissioner for Admission to Professions (CPMRCP, 2015, 2016), made after analysing the connection between the professional orders' requirements for the training of FTPs on the one hand, and college or university training institutions' offer, on the other. Intersectoral, multilevel governance and investment in the necessary resources (human and financial) would also lead to coherent professional retraining suited to the demand for training and to the needs of the market.

In addition, our data also shows the need for quality information and dissemination, mostly for private employers. Many of these were not aware of the MRAs for engineers, even a few years after their implementation, despite the initiatives led by professional regulators to make these known. Some employers have therefore asked FTPs to work as apprentices, not recognising the validity of the internships they had carried out under the supervision of the engineers' regulating body, the OIQ.

7.4.5 Centralising Information

In this regard, our data shows: (1) the scarcity of resources made available to FTPs concerning the procedures for obtaining recognition and entry into practice; (2) the broad range of information, sometimes contradictory, available in the various communication channels; (3) a lack of transparency in the information transmitted to FTPs, particularly abroad. This leads to situations of *imperfect* or *incomplete information* (Krafft, 1999) that limit the ability of FTPs to make informed decisions and take appropriate actions.

Offering centralised information in a "one-stop service" is crucial for countering the negative effects of the lack of clear instructions and to provide easily identifiable resources for finding expert information.

7.4.6 Towards a Benevolent Use of the Notion of Protecting the Public

Protecting the public is the fundamental justification of the system of regulated professions and its structures to which the State delegates its powers of surveillance. The way the professional orders refer to this principle bestows on it an almost sacred status, to use the words of Durkheim (1984). As Olson argues in his *Logic of Collective Action* (1965), the notion of protecting the public was conceived of as a "public good". This hybrid concept legitimises action taken in the public interest, on the pretext of acting for the common good—something which no one can oppose. The sacred dimension lends the concept a symbolic, yet empirical force.

However, our research shows that by claiming the protection of the public as a justification, certain requirements and procedures set out by professional orders limit or restrict the entry of foreign-trained professionals into practice, with no evidence of any threat to the public's protection. Rather, the procedures and requirements put in place are the result of practical accommodations that meet institutional and organisation constraints. In other words, in seeking to facilitate the entry into practice of FTPs, the modifications introduced attempt to please all sides: they deal with organisational difficulties that have little to do with protection of the public. They propose solutions that avoid short-term investments but that, in the medium and long term, prove to be costly and not very effective for facilitating the entry into practice of FTPs. Instead, in effect, they tend to advocate the adoption of a "plan B", whereby the initial plan of practicing one's initial profession is abandoned and instead, one takes up more technical trades, or even precarious but readily accessible work.

Therefore, our analysis leads us to discard argumentation that can be associated with forms of sacredness through the notion of protection of the public. The promotion and operationalisation of this notion in a more flexible and decentralised context would allow for a clearer discussion on what is suitable for protecting the public, beyond the usual and convenient practices for institutional actors. Moreover, history has shown that the sacred principle of protection of the public has not prevented instances of corruption in some regulated professions, instances that have required State intervention. In other instances, the evaluation of candidate's profiles has led to automatic requirement for uniform additional training, ignoring variations between different candidates' profiles. In other words, the structures overseeing the delegation of State powers, similarly to the system of self-regulating professions, are not immune to straying into territory that runs counter to the protection of the public, and instead serves organisational or even corporate interests.

We also suggest a review of the procedures and processes used by professional orders with respect to FTPs in order to ensure that they are not discriminatory, and that these orders have the necessary tools to act in an increasingly diversified context. This was in fact an observation made by the Commissioner for Admission (2017):

> It appears essential to us for the staff responsible for admission to orders who provide reception services, information, assessment and orientation for immigrants in the context of the steps of their application to the order,

> to have skills in the area of intercultural relations. Indeed, a lack of awareness of cultural codes may result in misunderstandings and a failure to understand that could be detrimental to the processing of the files of immigrants (p. 21 – item 2.4).

In this regard, the reform of the Professional Code (C-26) (2019) made it possible to include new obligations for professional orders, including the obligation to offer training to their members on ethnocultural diversity management (Section 62.0.1, paragraphs 4 and 5). It remains to be seen whether such regulatory changes will bring effective results.

7.4.7 Assessment: Review of Practices and Reduced Waiting Times

It has been shown that the structure of the admissions committees entrusted with evaluating the files of candidates for admission to certain professional orders could raise some questions (Commissioner for Admission (2017, January: 13):

> (…) a single committee member was tasked with evaluating files and making a decision. This means that the decision rests on the judgment of a single person. How can we be sure that this person proceeded rigorously, or that the evaluation was fair and impartial? In the philosophy of regulation, setting up a committee is designed to ensure that files are studied, and conclusions shared with a degree of collegiality, precisely to prevent a decision on a file being based on the conclusions of a single individual.

Finally, regarding the timelines for processing applications, our data reveal that these need to be reviewed or offset by measures allowing applicants to meet their daily needs and those of their families during this period. In this respect, the OIQ's 2019 survey found that the average processing time for an application for the permit required by FTPs was between six months and two years. This average does not consider candidates who dropped out when faced with the prospect of these long waiting periods.

7.5 Conclusions

Our analysis brings to the fore specific factors associated with entry into practice in the private sector (engineers) and the public sector (doctors). These actors need to have frameworks adapted, in turn, to the reality of their sectors of practice.

Similarly, the use of the notion of protecting the public takes different forms depending on the sector. These issues remain to be examined; we were able to address the tension between private interests and the protection of the public. A more in-depth analysis of how engineers negotiate professionalism and increased productivity would show how institutional and professional mechanisms do or do not allow for reconciling their interests with the interests of protecting the public, as suggested by Adams (2020).

The path followed by FTPs who want to practice medicine in Quebec also presents a combination of challenges. Internship placements, the availability of supervisions and, ultimately, the public health system's levels of funding are central issues. These FTPs face the institutional obstacles mentioned above, in that they cannot bypass public structures when they wish to gain access to professional practice. These structures have very little intrinsic autonomy, and hence their ability to be innovative and flexible is limited. In the case of engineers, specific structures and actors are also found to exist, but given the relative independence of the areas of practice, there is some degree of fragmentation of these structures, despite their being regulated by the professional system.

Finally, we saw that the latest regulatory reforms of the professional system have led the orders and some of their structures (disciplinary and inspection committees, etc.) to modernise their practices to include cultural diversity training. This reflects the evolution of professional systems locally and globally, in professions practising in both the public and private sectors.

References

Abbott, A. (1988). *The system of professions. An essay on the division of expert labour*. Chicago University Press.

Adams, T. (2020). Professional employees and professional managers: conflicting logics, hybridity, and restratification. *Journal of Professions and Organization, 7*(1), 101–115. https://doi.org/10.1093/jpo/joaa005

Adams, T. (2016). Professional self-regulation and the public interest in Canada. *Professions & Professionalism, 6*(3), 1–15. https://doi.org/10.7577/pp.1587

Bellini, A., & Maestripieri, L. (2018). Professions within, between and beyond. Varieties of professionalism in a globalising world. *Cambio, 8*(16), 5–14. https://doi.org/10.13128/cambio-24947

Blain, MJ. et al. (2018) Synthèse du rapport de recherche: Portrait de l'intégration professionnelle des personnes immigrantes au Québec: expériences et points de vue croisés sur les obstacles systémiques, les éléments facilitants et les ressources.

Burau, V., & Vrangbaek, K. (2008). Global markets and national pathways of medical re-regulation. In E. Kuhlmann & M. Saks (Eds.), *Rethinking professional governance: International directions in healthcare* (pp. 29–43). Policy Press.

Chicha, M.-T. (2012). Discrimination systémique et intersectionnalité: la déqualification des immigrantes à Montréal. *Canadian Journal of Women and the Law, 24*(1), 82–113. https://doi.org/10.3138/cjwl.24.1.082

Chicha, M.-T. (2009). *Le mirage de l'égalité: les immigrées hautement qualifiées à Montréal.* Fondation canadienne des relations raciales.

CIQ (Conseil interprofessionnel du Québec). (2019). *Enjeux et solutions. L'intégration professionnelle des personnes immigrantes. Sondage des dix ordres recevant le plus de demandes de reconnaissance d'équivalence sur les enjeux reliés à l'intégration professionnelle des immigrants.* Conseil interprofessionnel du Québec.

Professional Code. (2019). RLRQ c C-26, http://canlii.ca/t/6cb8p. Retrieved on 2020-05-08.

Commissaire à l'admission aux professions. (2017). *Portrait des mécanismes de reconnaissance des compétences professionnelles.* Office des Professions du Québec.

CPMRCP (Commissaire aux plaintes en matière de reconnaissance des compétences professionnelles). (2016). *L'organisation et le financement de la formation d'appoint à l'université en réponse à la prescription d'un ordre professionnel.* Office des professions du Québec.

CPMRCP. (2015). *L'organisation et le financement de la formation d'appoint à l'université en réponse à la prescription d'un ordre professionnel.* Office des professions du Québec.

Dent, M., Bourgeault, I. L., Denis, J.-L., & Kuhlmann, E. (2016). General introduction. In M. Dent, I. L. Bourgeault, J.-L. Denis, & E. Kuhlmann (Eds.), *The Routledge companion to the professions and professionalism* (pp. 1–10). Routledge.

Douglas, M. (1986). *How institutions think.* SUNY Press.

Durkheim, É. (1984). *The division of labour in society* (WD Halls, Trans.). Macmillan. (Original work published 1893).

Flood, J. (2011). The re-landscaping of the legal profession: Large law firms and professional re-regulation. *Current Sociology, 59*(4), 507–529. https://doi.org/10.1177/0011392111402725

Freidson, E. (2001). *Professionalism, the third logic: On the practice of knowledge.* University of Chicago Press.

Gorman, E. H. (2014). Professional self-regulation in North America: the cases of law and accounting. *Sociology Compass, 8*(5), 491–508. https://doi.org/10.1111/soc4.12152

Hébert, G., Sully, J.-L., & Nguyen, M. (2017). *L'allocation des ressources pour la santé et les services sociaux au Québec: état de la situation et propositions alternatives.* Institut de recherche et d'informations socioéconomiques.

Homsy, M., & Scarfone, S. (2016). *Plus diplômés que nous, mais sans emploi. Comparer Montréal: le paradoxe de l'immigration montréalaise.* Institut du Québec.

Institut de la statistique du Québec. (2019). *Québec Handy Numbers* (2019th ed.). Institut de la statistique du Québec.

Kleiner, M. (2006). *Licensing occupations: Ensuring quality or restricting competition?* W.E. Upjohn Institute for Employment Research.

Krafft, J. (1999). « Information imparfaite », p. 485-488, in R. Le Duff, Encyclopédie de Gestion. Paris: Dalloz.

Kuhlmann, E., Agartan, T., & von Knorring, M. (2016). Governance and professions. In M. Dent, I. L. Bourgeault, J.-L. Denis, & E. Kuhlmann (Eds.), *The Routledge companion to the professions and professionalism* (pp. 31–44). Routledge.

Merino, B. D., Mayper, A. G., & Tolleson, T. D. (2010). Neoliberalism, deregulation and Sarbanes-Oxley: The legitimation of a failed corporate governance model. *Accounting, Auditing & Accountability Journal, 23*(6), 774–792. https://doi.org/10.1108/09513571011065871

Nancarrow, S. A. (2015). Six principles to enhance health workforce flexibility. *Human Resources for Health, 13*(9), 1–12. https://doi.org/10.1186/1478-4491-13-9

OECD. (2017). *Making integration work: Assessment and recognition of foreign qualifications, making integration work*. OECD.

Office des professions du Québec (OPQ). (2012). *Le rôle de surveillance de l'Office des professions: un tournant guidé par l'actualisation de la notion de protection du public*. Office des professions du Québec.

Olson, M. (1965). *Logic of collective action*. Harvard University Press.

Paton, P. (2008). Between a rock and a hard place: The future of self-regulation - Canada between the United States and the English/Australian experience. *Journal of the Professional Lawyer, Symp. Issues*, 87–120.

Quack, S., & Schußler, E. (2015). Dynamics of regulation of professional service firms: National and Transnational Developments in Law and Accounting. In L. Empson, D. Muzio, J. P. Broschak, & B. Hinings (Eds.), *The Oxford handbook of professional service firms* (pp. 48–70). Oxford University Press. https://doi.org/10.1093/oxfordhb/9780199682393.013.3

Saks, M., & Adams, T. (2018). Neo-Weberianism, professional formation and the state: Inside the black box. *Professions & Professionalism, 9*(2), 1–14. https://doi.org/10.7577/pp.3190

Suddaby, R., Cooper, D. J., & Greenwood, R. (2007). Transnational regulation of professional services: Governance dynamics of field level organizational change. *Accounting, Organizations and Society, 32*(4–5), 333–362. https://doi.org/10.1016/j.aos.2006.08.002

8

Professionalism in Everyday Work: Women Lawyers' Strategies to Exercise Control over Their Work in Finland, French Canada, and Poland

Marta Choroszewicz

1 Introduction

The disadvantaged position of women lawyers in the legal profession is an ongoing topic of research. This study approaches the phenomenon through the lens of professionalism and, specifically, its touchstone: professional autonomy. Autonomy has been regarded as central to the interlinked concepts of professions and masculinity—that is, professions have been considered masculine projects rooted in qualities and values culturally assigned to men (Davies, 1996; Hearn et al., 2016). Autonomy permits professionals to control the future of their own professions and to conduct their work in line with professional values and interests (Freidson, 1986, 2001). In contrast to their male colleagues, women in male-dominated professions have faced numerous challenges in exercising their professional autonomy (Davies, 1996; Hearn et al., 2016; Choroszewicz & Adams, 2019).

M. Choroszewicz (✉)
University of Eastern Finland, Joensuu, Finland
e-mail: marta.choroszewicz@uef.fi

© The Author(s), under exclusive license to Springer Nature Switzerland AG 2023

L. Maestripieri, A. Bellini (eds.), *Professionalism and Social Change*,
https://doi.org/10.1007/978-3-031-31278-6_8

Because of the historical disadvantage women lawyers have experienced in pursuing their careers, the legal profession offers an important case study to examine women's strategies to attain and maintain their professional autonomy. While globally, the feminisation of legal professions has significantly improved over the past 30 years (Michelson, 2013), it has not yet led to full gender equality (Kay, 2019; Choroszewicz & Kay, 2022). The culture and structures of the legal profession continue to undermine women lawyers' integration into the profession and their recognition as professionals. For instance, women lawyers are more likely than their male colleagues to work in the public sector than in the private sector and in lower-status legal specialties and positions, some of them precarious (Sommerlad, 2016; Kay, 2019). They are also more likely to leave the profession (Kay et al., 2013, 2016). Their unequal treatment and limited career opportunities in legal professions have relegated them to work that reflects gender-specific expectations in which they experience more control over their work (Bolton & Muzio, 2007; Choroszewicz, 2014, 2018). The ongoing commercialism in the legal profession has further challenged lawyers' autonomy to control their work. Today, lawyers must accommodate the commercial pressures of being business-like and entrepreneurial while remaining loyal to professional values and interests (Wallace & Kay, 2008; Dinovitzer et al., 2014; Collier, 2015). Lawyers are increasingly employed—and thus controlled—by organisations, and they therefore enjoy less professional autonomy and authority than they had in the past (Flood, 2011; Muzio & Faulconbridge, 2013).

This chapter contributes to the **"between"** dimension of professionalism (Bellini & Maestripieri, 2018; Chap. 1) by examining the ways in which women lawyers from three civil law systems circumvent the obstacles and barriers to their professional autonomy and strive to control their work within the highly competitive professional market. In Canada, professional regulations vary across provinces (see Chap. 11). French Canada covers the province of Quebec and has a civil law system, in contrast to the rest of Canada that belongs to the common law tradition. In French Canada, Finland, and Poland, the growth in the number of women lawyers has coincided with increased competition due to the high number of qualified lawyers and the expanding supply of legal services (Dinovitzer & Dawe, 2020; Gadowska, 2020). The proportion of women lawyers is higher in civil law countries—for example, in Quebec and Poland, women make up 50 per cent of lawyers (Redzik, 2018; Choroszewicz & Kay, 2022). Traditionally, in civil law countries, the state has provided legitimacy and leeway for professionals to exercise market control (Abel, 2020). However, due to concerns about equal opportunities for disadvantaged social groups in accessing legal professions, in the last three decades or so, civil law countries have expanded public education and increasingly recognised private universities (Abel, 2020). While Poland, Finland, and French Canada all have civil law systems, there are important differences in their professional structures and cultures. For instance, in Canada, women leave private practice in larger numbers and earlier in their careers than men, and small firms are even less successful in retaining women lawyers (Dinovitzer & Dawe, 2020). Also in Canada, women lawyers are also more likely than their male counterparts to report actively seeking new employment outside of law practices (Dinovitzer & Dawe, 2020). When they practice in law firms, Canadian and Polish women must fit into existing working norms (Dinovitzer & Dawe, 2020; Gadowska, 2020). In Finland, women lawyers experience less pressure to conform to masculine ideals of an uninterrupted career, face time at the office and long working hours (Choroszewicz, 2014). Flexible working arrangements are also less popular in Canada and Poland compared to Finland (Kay et al., 2013; Choroszewicz, 2014, 2016, 2018).

2 Women and Changing Professionalism in the Legal Profession

Scholars have pointed out the masculine character of professional projects (Davies, 1996), including the legal profession (Leiper, 2006; Bolton & Muzio, 2007). Even though the work of lawyers is performed under different national regulations and cultures, women uniformly share a disadvantaged position due to the gendering processes on which the masculine character of legal professionalism is built.

The two ideas of professionalism—specifically its "third logic" (Freidson, 2001) and "organisational" professionalism (Evetts, 2006,

2011)—discussed in this chapter can also be considered as rooted in the cultural ideas of masculinity, specifically with regard to authority over professionals' own work, clients, and other occupations. Yet, the marketisation of professional work and professions has prompted changes to the authority of professionals. Sociologist Eliot Freidson (2001) defined occupational professionalism as the "third logic"—a method of organising work based on the key notion that professionals organise and control their work by drawing on their social recognition. Freidson perceived professions as occupations capable of creating exclusive shelters for practitioners through the monopolisation of educational training and credentials, which guarantees professionals privileged access to the market. These institutional mechanisms enable professions and their members to maintain control over their own tasks and behaviours as well as the production and management of professional bodies of knowledge (Freidson, 1986, 2001).

In the case of lawyers, their power and autonomy historically originated from the high social status of the legal profession, the monopolisation of educational training and credentials, a commitment to public service, and privileged access to the legal market. The core of their knowledge is proficiency in legal regulations and the capacity to convert them into reasoned argumentation in both speech and writing (Leiper, 2006, p. 31). Yet, this form of "third logic" professionalism has been contested in the legal profession in the face of ongoing commercialism and deregulation, making lawyers more susceptible to the influence of their clients and their workplaces, lessening concerns about their professional conduct and career advancement (Heinz et al., 2005; Faulconbridge & Muzio, 2008; Muzio & Faulconbridge, 2013). Evetts (2006, 2011) coined the idea of "organisational" professionalism to account for changes in occupational control related to hierarchy, bureaucracy, output, performance measures, and the standardisation of work practices. These changes have been well documented by scholars of the legal profession, who have noted that commercial pressures are especially strong in private law practice, where law firms and professional service firms operate as the primary locus for professional socialisation and development (Faulconbridge & Muzio, 2008; Flood, 2011). The emergence of professional service firms and global law firms has also intensified competition in the market for legal services, increasingly subordinating lawyers to the values of efficiency and entrepreneurialism, and employing the language of the market in assessing lawyers' performance and commitment to their careers (Wallace & Kay, 2008; Sterling & Reichman, 2016). "Organisational" professionalism has exposed lawyers to market forces and rendered them less capable of resisting the pressure to be available for work 24/7 in the interest of maximising their firms' profits. Lawyers, especially those in private practices, have become increasingly subject to the economic power of clients (Heinz et al., 2005). Professional autonomy has thereby become subject to social forces within professional workplaces, including relations with clients, law firm partners, and other lawyers (Dinovitzer et al., 2014).

These changes in the legal profession have further hindered the integration of minority members, increasingly subjecting them to treatment as a "disposable resource" (Sommerlad, 2016). Women and ethnic and sexual minorities continue to face barriers to their career choices and career progress (Choroszewicz & Kay, 2022). Behavioural scripts, values and attributes, as well as work and career patterns, have been re-capitalised in the promotion of male lawyers' legal careers (Choroszewicz, 2020a). Organisational practices that determine compensation and promotion continue to hinder the advancement of women, who also suffer from a lack of transparency about key performance metrics and reward structures (Sterling & Reichman, 2016; Choroszewicz & Kay, 2022). Women are specifically discriminated against when they are unable to conform to male working patterns and career models (Boni-Le Goff et al., 2019; Plickert, 2019; Chap. 4). Thus, women who stay in the profession develop alternative ways of working or create enclaves in which their work and expertise can be better recognised (Biese & Choroszewicz, 2018; Kay, 2019).

In the face of the ongoing transformation of the legal profession, it is important to comprehend how historically disadvantaged members of the profession—specifically women lawyers—navigate different forms of professionalism in their everyday work to circumvent obstacles and barriers to their professional autonomy. I have therefore examined the strategies through which women lawyers mobilise particular resources that relate to "third logic" professionalism and "organisational" professionalism to exercise control over their work and the professional market.

3 Data and Methods

Women lawyers from private law practices in Finland, French Canada, and Poland provide an interesting case study for investigating the ways in which contemporary lawyers attempt to attain and maintain control over their work. The data sets used for the analysis originated from two separate projects on lawyers. The first project was conducted in 2009–2014 and focused on the careers of female lawyers in Finland and Poland. The second project was conducted in 2016–2018 and focused on how lawyers reconciled their legal careers and family life in Finland and French Canada. In total, 76 semi-structured interviews were conducted with 34 male and 42 female lawyers from the largest cities in Finland, Poland, and French Canada (Helsinki, Warsaw, and Montreal).

All women interviewees were middle-class, highly-educated professionals between the ages of 30–81. The majority of interviewees (65 per cent) were either married or cohabiting. At the time of the interviews, 16 interviewees worked in solo practices, 10 in small law firms, and 14 in medium-sized or large law firms, while two interviewees had left private law practice to work as legal academics.

The scope of thematic data analysis for this chapter is based on the interviews with the women lawyers, since they are more likely to face barriers in pursuing their legal careers (for more, see e.g. Kay et al., 2013, 2016; Sommerlad, 2016; Choroszewicz & Kay, 2022). The focus of thematic data analysis was on the micro-dynamics of women lawyers' work practices and strategies as recounted by interviewees, using an inductive approach. The data analysis proceeded in three stages and was guided by the following research question: how do women lawyers across three civil law countries cope with the constraints regarding their control over the organisation of their work and the professional market? The first analytical stage identified interview passages relevant to the research question. The second stage involved reading and organising these passages into different strategies related to the interviewees' decisions concerning their work organisation, workplace, and encounters with clients. In the third stage, the empirical material was reread in light of "third logic" and "organisational" professionalism and the masculine character of professional projects. During this stage, five strategies were identified and examined for differences and similarities related to professional systems, structures, and cultures.

4 Results: Women Lawyers' Strategies

The results yielded insights into five strategies through which women lawyers exercise control over their everyday work practices and the professional market: (1) highlighting the status of the profession, their additional educational qualifications, and the title of law firm partner, (2) highlighting altruistic aspects of legal work, (3) the "typing" of clients and cases, (4) personalising relationships with clients, and (5) establishing joint law offices with friends and sharing office space. Each of these strategies is discussed below.

4.1 Highlighting the Status of the Profession, Additional Educational Qualifications, and the Title of Law Firm Partner

Women lawyers in all three countries appeared to specifically mobilise different aspects central to the "third logic" of professionalism (Freidson, 1986, 2001), including high social status, legal knowledge, educational credentials, and job titles, in order to acquire more credibility and authority as lawyers in encounters with powerful clients. This pattern was characteristic of those interviewees who worked in originally male-dominated legal specialties, such as criminal and corporate law.

For example, Finnish and Polish interviewees referred to the internal hierarchy within legal professions, in which obtaining the title of attorney-at-law is considered a status symbol in itself because it involves additional credentials and bar membership.

> *I have always perceived the profession of attorney as more prestigious (...) although I also knew that it is difficult to obtain admission to an attorney apprenticeship.* [Polish, 40, partner in a large law firm].

But I think it is a great profession, it is an old profession, and to me the title 'attorney' means a lot and I am proud that I am not just a lawyer but an attorney because that brings some history and a kind of professional pride in what you do and it kind of also gives you expectations that you have to follow certain rules of behaviour that society expects of you. [Finnish, 34, senior associate in a medium-sized law firm].

In addition, Polish solo practitioners argued that additional educational qualifications, such as doctoral degrees, can be a powerful resource, especially for women lawyers who work as solo practitioners:

Undoubtedly for a woman attorney, this title of Doctor of Law will help me to gain people's trust, especially in my legal specialisation, as I exclusively work with criminal law. So it will mean I do not need to spend two hours convincing my clients that I know something, but they will see that I have this title of Doctor of Law, so it will speak for itself, I think. [Polish, 34, solo practitioner]

In Canada, it was argued that the title of "partner" in a law firm improved women's career opportunities by giving them more credibility in the eyes of clients even though they acted as non-equity partners:

It gives you… more status in front of clients. From the outside, they assume that if this big firm is willing to make you a partner, I am in good hands. (…) That helps you in terms of credibility to be able to develop business as well. (…) that when you are working at a big firm, being a partner, it gives you a stamp of approval from a client's perspective. [Canadian, 53, partner in a large law firm]

4.2 Highlighting Altruistic Aspects of Legal Work

A commitment to public service is an important feature of professional work (Freidson, 1986). Lawyers fulfil this commitment by providing legal services to poor and/or disadvantaged members of society or to non-profit organisations. This commitment can be undertaken through state-sponsored legal aid and pro bono—that is, free of charge—work (see, e.g. Choroszewicz, 2020b). Pro bono legal services can be provided by lawyers individually or through their law firms. This form of public service is also increasingly endorsed and remunerated by law firms (Kay & Granfield, 2022).

For women lawyers, pro bono work emerged as a source of control over their decisions about what types of legal cases to accept, and generated a feeling that they were doing meaningful work. Specifically, women lawyers from larger law firms across the three countries argued that pro bono work provided them with a sense of doing socially valuable work, which they did not necessarily feel when serving corporate clients.

> *Actually, I started to do a little of it [pro bono] because I think now, at this point, I can even afford to do it (...) It makes you feel good, it gives you a good conscience in a different way than just finalising a new transaction.* [Finnish, 42, associate in a large law firm]

Furthermore, Polish solo practitioners admitted that pro bono work provided them with new career prospects and strengthened their reputations, especially when they handled publicly important cases. This is particularly salient in Poland, where attorneys are not allowed to promote their legal services by distributing business cards or taking out advertisements. Some of the Polish interviewees stated that they had already begun to give free legal counselling when they were at law school with the expectation of acquiring practical legal skills and accessing networks of potential clients. For instance, one interviewee argued:

> *But once, at my department, I learned that an association needed volunteers to help accident victims. I got there like that (...) I worked there as a volunteer and, at some point, we established a civil-law partnership outside that association. (...) I can't deny that I counted on the fact that some of the people I would meet there would later come back to me as my clients in this office.* [Polish, 35, solo practitioner]

While state funding in all three countries gives support to their legal aid systems, Finnish and French Canadian lawyers have no obligation to work on legal aid cases (Choroszewicz, 2020b; Dinovitzer & Dawe, 2020). Thus, the Polish interviewees appeared to be more critical of pro bono work because mandatory legal aid cases are imposed on attorneys in

Poland. Furthermore, legal aid cases are more financially rewarding in Finland and French Canada, and thus appeared to be favoured by those Finnish and French Canadian interviewees who worked as solo practitioners, for whom legal aid cases guaranteed a stable income. However, more professionally established women lawyers in all three countries tended to avoid these cases, instead opting for pro bono work remunerated by their law firms.

4.3 The "Typing" of Clients and Cases

Commercial pressures and the need to resolve them while remaining loyal to professional values were mentioned by interviewees from all three countries. These pressures were specifically related to clients' wishes or demands for more customised, personalised, and tailored legal services, which appeared to challenge the lawyers' autonomy in fulfilling their professional roles (Faulconbridge & Muzio, 2008; Wallace & Kay, 2008; Dinovitzer et al., 2014). This issue appeared to be particularly important in legal specialties and law firms that dealt with wealthy and prestigious clients, with whom it was also important to retain long-lasting lawyer-client relationships (Heinz et al., 2005).

Some of the women interviewed appeared to cope with commercial pressures through the so-called "typing" of clients and cases. This strategy encompassed the lawyers' autonomy to use their market power to select their clients. This strategy appeared to be more popular with well-established solo practitioners and lawyers working in small law firms in all three countries than with lawyers in larger law firms. The women lawyers who chose this strategy argued that in the course of their careers they have learned to recognise and avoid clients and cases that might generate more problems than benefits. These interviewees tended to have more authority in their lawyer-client relationships, as they dealt with fewer powerful and predominantly individual clients. For instance, one interviewee recommended avoiding nervous and anxious clients, walks-ins, and self-represented clients:

> *Most walks-ins are not great cases. They don't really have a legal problem or they've waited too long to do anything about it (...) at the beginning I needed to take all cases. I could not say to a client that 'No, I don't want your case, I don't like you, I don't like your personality'. Now I don't mind saying that. Now when I talk to them and I don't get the feeling that I can trust them, I don't take the case and I refer them to someone else. I just kind of flush out everybody that I don't like.* [Canadian, 34, solo practitioner]

> *We don't need to take all the cases, so I have the courage to refuse a case when I see there might be some problems [...] I try to avoid difficulties with clients beforehand.* [Finnish, 46, small law office]

Another tactic that fell under the typing of clients and cases were price variations. Specifically, the Polish and French Canadian interviewees argued for the use of price variations to target their services to a certain type of client. This, however, was possible only for women lawyers who were already professionally well-established and so had the luxury of carefully selecting the recipients of their legal services. For example, some of them established extremely high fees for their services in order to exclude groups of clients they wanted to avoid and who would be unable to afford them. As one interviewee admitted:

> *One of the reasons I started to increase my hourly rate is because I do not want to work so hard anymore. So I figured if I increase my rate, I will have less people and maybe avoid the problematic clients.* [Canadian, 62, owner of a small law office]

4.4 Personalising Relationships with Clients

Commercial pressures have made it necessary for lawyers to engage in boundary work between rainmaking, client services, quality assurance, managing teams of lawyers, and complying with the expectation of 24/7 availability (Dinovitzer et al., 2014; Sterling & Reichman, 2016). The latest technological advances have contributed to an emphasis on good-quality client services, such as promptly responding to clients' emails and calls as well as making oneself almost constantly available to answer clients' inquiries (Choroszewicz & Kay, 2020). Furthermore, as lawyers' professional roles are no longer predominantly only to respond to clients' needs but now also include the creation of the need for legal services, lawyers are expected to be increasingly flexible and fluent in so-called soft skills (Choroszewicz, 2020a).

Some of the women interviewed coped with the commercial pressures caused by increasingly demanding lawyer-client relationships by establishing meaningful and trusted connections with their clients, which provided them with more control to decide on the frequency and conditions for communicating with them. They argued that good personal relationships with clients helped to make clients more understanding concerning the commercial expectation of 24/7 availability. This was especially possible for women lawyers from solo practices and small law firms in French Canada and Poland who had more leeway not to give their private phone numbers to clients, but instead instructed them to contact them via email. Others argued that it was sometimes enough to provide some of their clients with opportunities to contact them whenever they wanted so that they felt important. For example, one interviewee argued:

> *All clients would want that [to be able to reach their attorneys in the evenings] and you need to let some do that [...] Some [clients] like, for some reason, to contact us in the evenings, so as I said, you need to let some of them do that and you should not let others do it.* [Polish, 34, owner of a small law office]

By contrast, in larger law firms, the commercial pressure to be constantly available appeared to be stronger, and thus the interviewees from all three countries argued that they felt obliged to communicate with clients even on weekends and during their holidays. Yet, maintaining good relationships with clients allowed them to better evaluate whether or not they needed to react immediately to clients' requests:

> *My clients know that I am available for real emergencies. Normally, I can easily recognise if it is a real or fake emergency. If it is real, I get it done even if it is the weekend. Otherwise I just try to tell them that I will send them a reply that 'Okay, I will look over your file by Wednesday morning or something like that'. Usually this works.* [Canadian, 42, senior associate in a medium-sized law firm]

4.5 Establishing Joint Law Offices with Friends and Sharing Office Space

Women lawyers have been put at a great disadvantage by the male networking and socialising patterns prevalent in law firms (Leiper, 2006; Kay & Gorman, 2008). Thus, in countries like Poland and Canada, women lawyers are more likely to work in small law firms or as solo practitioners. This is in contrast to Finnish women lawyers, most of whom, in this study, were employed in larger law firms (Choroszewicz, 2014; Dinovitzer & Dawe, 2020).

The results indicated that the Finnish, Polish and French Canadian women solo practitioners, aiming for a more pleasant and collaborative working environment and lower expenses for their solo practices, established joint law offices or shared office space with trusted female friends or colleagues. They also often shared secretarial staff. These interviewees also established their own forms of collaboration and work organisation. In this way, they remained independent practitioners but, if they needed to consult others on particular legal cases, they had trusted female colleagues nearby whose advice they could seek.

> *Here, we work together in a co-working space, but each of us has our own solo practice. At the moment, we are three women here (…) We are a really well-matched team. We often meet just to have a chat. We also have common projects. Recently, as a co-working space, we issued a legal guidebook together (…) We have many meetings just like that in order to be together and invite other people, to keep in contact with other people, judges and prosecutors in order to keep these relations friendly, because these are often also people from university. It kind of helps [to keep in contact with them].* [Polish, 35, solo practitioner]

The women lawyers argued that these shared office spaces or joint law practices afforded them more opportunities for assistance in case they fell ill or when trials were re-scheduled at short notice and they needed help with trial preparation or substitution. Furthermore, sharing office space or running a joint law practice appeared to also help expand their pool of clients and grow professionally, since these women lawyers learned from one other and referred clients to each other when their cases did not match their own legal expertise or there was some kind of conflict of interest.

> *I find sharing an office very useful for planning together, bouncing some ideas off each other, and then doing it and debriefing after. I have noticed that I have improved as a lawyer so much faster because of sharing an office.* [Canadian, 37, solo practitioner]

5 Discussion and Conclusion

This study identifies five strategies through which Finnish, French Canadian, and Polish women lawyers strove to act as resourceful agents to exercise professional autonomy by mobilising different logics of professionalism over their everyday work practices and the professional market. Their strategies are as follows: (1) highlighting the status of the profession, additional educational qualifications, and the title of law firm partner, (2) highlighting altruistic aspects of legal work, (3) the typing of clients and cases, (4) personalising relationships with clients, and (5) establishing joint law offices and sharing office space with other women lawyers. These results contribute to the **"between"** dimension of professionalism (Bellini & Maestripieri, 2018; Chap. 1), by advancing our understanding of how women lawyers' strategies are embedded not only in the increasingly business-like and hyper-competitive market of legal services but also in the differential professional systems, structures, and cultures of the legal profession across these three civil law systems.

The first two strategies draw on the mobilisation of core elements of "third logic" professionalism (Freidson, 1986, 2001), which include legal knowledge and educational qualifications, the high social status of the legal profession, the title of law firm partner and the lawyers' commitment to public service. Educational qualifications and titles appear to be particularly effective for solo practitioners and lawyers of small law firms (see also, e.g. Schultz, 2003, p. xliv). In larger law firms, lawyers' control over their work and careers is related more to job titles and being business-like (see, e.g. Collier, 2015; Sterling & Reichman, 2016). Regarding the strategy of highlighting altruistic aspects of legal work, Finnish and French Canadian women lawyers are more positive about the altruistic character of legal work because, in contrast to Poland, legal aid cases in these two countries are taken up by lawyers voluntarily. Furthermore, for some interviewees in all three countries, pro bono work serves as a strategy to accrue professionally critical resources at the early stages of their careers (see also Dinovitzer & Garth, 2009). For experienced interviewees from larger law firms, pro bono work serves as a way to reconcile the traditional principle of public service with the commercial pressure of generating profits for their firms (see also Wallace & Kay, 2008).

The third strategy (picking and choosing clients) is related to the commercial pressures of "organisational" professionalism (Evetts, 2006, 2011), and is intended to help women lawyers cope with their clients' influence over their ability to act as autonomous professionals and fulfil their professional roles. Through this strategy, women lawyers seek to gain more authority in their encounters with clients and over the legal cases on which they chose to work. The results show that the experienced solo practitioners and lawyers from small law firms in all three countries appear to have more autonomy in choosing clients and cases compared to the lawyers from larger law firms. This capability is especially important in French Canada and Poland, where clients can represent themselves in simpler civil cases and are therefore not accustomed to consulting lawyers unless they are obliged to do so (Dinovitzer & Dawe, 2020; Gadowska, 2020). Self-representation and lack of being accustomed to consult lawyers appear to be particularly problematic for the French Canadian and Polish interviewees who, due to discriminatory professional structures and cultures, choose to work in small law offices and in solo practices more often than their Finnish colleagues.

The strategy of personalising relationships with clients appears to also be beneficial for women lawyers in larger law firms, especially in Poland and Canada, with regard to gaining more understanding concerning clients' expectations of round-the-clock availability. In Finland, these expectations appear to be lower due to, among other factors, the popularity of flexible work arrangements and less pressure regarding face time at the office.

The joint law office and shared space strategy in particular points to women lawyers establishing their own patterns of networking and socialising, which can help them overcome the professional disadvantage of a masculine professional culture and structure. Networking and socialising are popular especially among women lawyers in Canada and Poland, where the professional landscape of the legal profession is dominated by small law offices and solo practices. Thus, in these countries, women lawyers create gender enclaves, such as small all-women law offices specialising in family law, to gain greater control over their working conditions.

The last two strategies also relate to valuing connectedness—an attribute that has been culturally associated with femininity in contrast to authority, which is regarded as a culturally masculine attribute (Davies, 1996). These strategies highlight mutual support and collaboration among women as central to the successful performance of legal work and as an alternative to male networking and socialising patterns.

This study demonstrates that even though Finnish, French Canadian, and Polish women lawyers operate in the global economy, which exposes them to market-oriented competition over client services and business development, differences in professional systems, structures and cultures impact their strategies for circumventing barriers and obstacles to their professional autonomy. Future research should examine the strategies male lawyers use to defend their professional autonomy and, more specifically, whether the strategies identified in the present study are also relevant for them. Finally, further studies could compare professionals' strategies across a number of professions and their impact on the professionals' collective claims to professional autonomy.

References

Abel, R. L. (2020). Comparative sociology of lawyers, 1988—2018: The professional project. In R. L. Abel, O. Hammerslev, H. Sommerlad, & U. Schultz (Eds.), *Lawyers in 21st-century societies. Vol. 1: National reports* (pp. 879–897). Hart Publishing.

Bellini, A., & Maestripieri, L. (2018). Varieties of professionalism in a globalising world: New theoretical perspectives and analytical approaches. *Cambio, 8*(16), 5–14.

Biese, I., & Choroszewicz, M. (2018). Creating alternative solutions for work: Experiences of women managers and lawyers in Poland and the USA. In S. Taylor & S. Luckman (Eds.), *The 'new normal' of working lives: Critical studies in contemporary work and employment* (pp. 309–325). Palgrave Macmillan.

Bolton, S., & Muzio, D. (2007). Can't live with'em. *Can't live without'em: Gendered segmentation in the legal profession' Sociology, 41*(1), 47–61.

Boni-Le Goff, I., Le Feuvre, N., Mallard, G., Lépinard, E., & Morel, S. (2019). Do gender regimes matter? Converging and diverging career prospects among young French and Swiss lawyers. In M. Choroszewicz & T. L. Adams (Eds.), *Gender, age and inequality in the professions* (pp. 114–133). Routledge.

Choroszewicz, M. (2014). *Managing competitiveness in pursuit of a legal career. Women attorneys in Finland and Poland* (Dissertations in social sciences and business studies 74). Publications of the University of Eastern Finland.

Choroszewicz, M. (2016). Women and gendered processes in law firms in Helsinki. *Sosiologia, 53*(2), 122–137.

Choroszewicz, M. (2018). Gendering processes and women's sensemaking of opportunity structure in the legal profession in Poland. *Kultura i Spoleczenstwo, 62*(4), 113–153.

Choroszewicz, M. (2020a). The centrality of soft skills in sustaining masculine ideals in lawyers' career progression in Finland and Quebec. In K. Aavik, C. Bland, J. Hoegaerts, & J. Salminen (Eds.), *Men, masculinities and the modern career* (pp. 89–108). De Gruyter.

Choroszewicz, M. (2020b). It is also about helping people'. Women attorneys' commitment to public service and incentives for pro bono work in Finland and Poland. In N. Foulkes Savinetti & A.-J. Riekhoff (Eds.), *Shaping and re-shaping the boundaries of working life* (pp. 111–122). Tampere University Press.

Choroszewicz, M., & Adams, T. L. (2019). *Gender, age and inequality in the professions*. Routledge.

Choroszewicz, M., & Kay, F. M. (2020). The use of mobile technologies for work-to-family boundary permeability: The case of Finnish and Canadian male lawyers. *Human Relations, 73*(10), 1388–1414.

Choroszewicz, M., & Kay, F. M. (2022). Understanding gender inequality in the legal profession. In R. L. Abel, H. Sommerlad, O. Hammerslev, & U. Schultz (Eds.), *Lawyers in 21st century societies. Vol. 2: Comparisons and theories* (pp. 127–150). Hart Publishing.

Collier, R. (2015). Naming men as men in corporate legal practice: Gender and the idea of 'virtually 24/7 commitment' in law. *Fordham Law Review, 83*(5), 2387–2406.

Davies, C. (1996). The sociology of the professions and the profession of gender. *Sociology, 30*(4), 661–678.

Dinovitzer, R., & Dawe, M. (2020). Canada: Continuity and change in a modern legal profession. In R. L. Abel, O. Hammerslev, H. Sommerlad, &

U. Schultz (Eds.), *Lawyers in 21st-century societies. Vol. 1: National reports* (pp. 65–88). Hart Publishing.

Dinovitzer, R., & Garth, B. G. (2009). Pro bono as an elite strategy in early lawyers careers. In R. Granfield & L. Mather (Eds.), *Private lawyers and the public interest: The evolving role of pro bono in the legal profession* (pp. 115–134). Oxford University Press.

Dinovitzer, R., Gunz, H., & Gunz, S. (2014). Corporate lawyers and their clients: Walking the line between law and business. *International Journal of the Legal Profession, 21*(1), 3–21.

Evetts, J. (2006). Short note: The sociology of professional groups: New directions. *Current Sociology, 54*(1), 133–143.

Evetts, J. (2011). A new professionalism? Challenges and opportunities. *Current Sociology, 59*(4), 406–422.

Faulconbridge, J. R., & Muzio, D. (2008). Organisational professionalism in globalizing law firms. *Work, Employment & Society, 22*(1), 7–25.

Flood, J. (2011). The re-landscaping of the legal profession: Large law firms and professional re-regulation. *Current Sociology, 59*(4), 507–529.

Freidson, E. (1986). *Professional powers: A study of the institutionalization of formal knowledge*. University of Chicago Press.

Freidson, E. (2001). *Professionalism: The third logic*. University of Chicago Press.

Gadowska, K. (2020). Poland: Opening the legal professions. In R. L. Abel, O. Hammerslev, H. Sommerlad, & U. Schultz (Eds.), *Lawyers in 21st-century societies. Vol. 1: National reports* (pp. 309–330). Hart Publishing.

Hearn, J., Biese-Stjernberg, I., Choroszewicz, M., & Husu, L. (2016) Gender, diversity and intersectionality in professions and potential professions: Analytical, historical and contemporary perspectives. In M. Dent, J-L. Denis, & E. Kuhlmann (Eds.), *The Routledge companion to the professions and professionalism* (pp. 57–70). Routledge.

Heinz, J. P., Nelson, R. L., Sandefur, R. L., & Laumann, E. O. (2005). *Urban lawyers: The new social structure of the bar*. The University of Chicago Press.

Kay, F. M. (2019). Launching careers in law: Entry to first jobs after law school. In M. Choroszewicz & T. L. Adams (Eds.), *Gender, age and inequality in the professions* (pp. 95–113). Routledge.

Kay, F. M., & Gorman, E. H. (2008). Women in the legal profession. *Annual Review of Law and Social Science, 4*, 299–332.

Kay, F. M., & Granfield, R. (2022). When altruism is remunerated: Understanding the bases ofvoluntary public service among lawyers. *Law and Society Review, 56*, 1–23. https://doi.org/10.1111/lasr.12586

Kay, F. M., Alarie, S., & Adjei, J. (2013). Leaving private practice: How organisational context, time pressures, and structural inflexibilities shape departures from private law practice. *Indiana Journal of Global Legal Studies, 1*, 223–1260.

Kay, F. M., Alarie, S., & Adjei, J. (2016). Undermining gender equality: Female attrition from private law practice. *Law & Society Review, 50*, 766–801.

Leiper, J. M. (2006). *Bar codes: Women in the legal profession*. UBC Press.

Michelson, E. (2013). Women in the legal profession, 1970-2010: A study of the global supply of lawyers. *Indiana Journal of Global Legal Studies, 20*, 1071–1137.

Muzio, D., & Faulconbridge, J. (2013). The global professional service firm: "One firm" models versus (Italian) distant institutionalized practices. *Organization Studies, 34*(7), 897–925.

Plickert, G. (2019). A life course approach to workplace discrimination and employment: Evidence from a US national sample of women and men lawyers. In M. Choroszewicz & T. L. Adams (Eds.), *Gender, age and inequality in the professions* (pp. 134–154). Routledge.

Redzik, A. (2018). Droga kobiet do zawodu adwokata. *Allerhand Law Review, 1*(1–2), 163–171.

Schultz, U. (2003). Introduction: Women in the world's legal professions: Overview and synthesis. In U. Schultz & G. Shaw (Eds.), *Women in the world's legal professions* (pp. xxv–lxii). Hart Publishing.

Sommerlad, H. (2016). 'A pit to put women in': Professionalism, work intensification, sexualisation and work–life balance in the legal profession in England and Wales. *International Journal of the Legal Profession, 23*(1), 61–82.

Sterling, J. S., & Reichman, N. (2016). Overlooked and undervalued: Women in private law practice. *Annual Review of Law and Social Science, 12*, 373–393.

Wallace, J. E., & Kay, F. M. (2008). The professionalism of practising law: A comparison across work contexts. *Journal of Organisational Behavior, 29*(8), 1021–1047.

9

The Professionalism, Accountability, and Work of Teachers in Different Regulatory Regimes

Lluís Parcerisa, Antoni Verger, Marcel Pagès, and Natalie Browes

1 Introduction

In recent decades, much has been written about how New Public Management (NPM) reforms have transformed welfare sector professions, and in particular, the teaching profession (Parding et al., 2012). NPM reforms in the public sector have transformed the roles, practices and identities of teachers, and have generated a new understanding about what it means to be a teacher (Apple, 2001). This includes substantial organisational and managerial changes being made to teachers' work, but also the transformation of societal expectations, norms, and professional

L. Parcerisa (✉)
Department of Teaching and Learning and Educational Organization, Universitat de Barcelona, Barcelona, Spain
e-mail: lluisparcerisa@ub.edu

A. Verger • N. Browes
Department of Sociology, Universitat Autònoma de Barcelona, Bellaterra, Spain
e-mail: antoni.verger@uab.cat

© The Author(s), under exclusive license to Springer Nature Switzerland AG 2023

L. Maestripieri, A. Bellini (eds.), *Professionalism and Social Change*,
https://doi.org/10.1007/978-3-031-31278-6_9

values associated with the teaching profession (Ball, 2016). Thus, NPM reforms are shaping the teaching profession from the inside as well as from the outside (Evetts, 2009).

Shaping the teaching profession from the outside implies the use of specific policy instruments, such as the devolution of responsibilities to schools, the definition of core learning standards, outcomes-based management, and new forms of accountability, usually linked to students' performance in national large-scale assessments (NLSAs). NLSAs have become a pivotal data-intensive policy tool that enables multiple and complementary education policies to be articulated. Namely, the definition of learning standards, the articulation of school autonomy, and the activation of accountability mechanisms (Verger et al., 2019b). Together, these policies crystallise in performance-based accountability (PBA) systems that alter fundamental aspects of the teaching profession and teachers' work all around the world.

PBA tends to focus on core learning areas (such as numeracy and literacy), implementing a standardisation that enables schools and teachers to be directly compared and monitored, and thus becoming a tool for external control and regulation. Despite PBA instruments having been adopted in most educational systems, this does not mean that they have been used in the same way everywhere. On the contrary, the intensity of the accountability (high stakes or low stakes), the direction of the accountability relationship (vertical or horizontal), and the nature of the consequences (e.g. reputational or material incentives and sanctions) attached to test results vary between countries (Verger & Parcerisa, 2017; Högberg & Lindgren, 2021). These different policy options can strongly condition the enactment and effects of PBA policies on teachers' work.

The education literature usually distinguishes between high-stakes and low-stakes accountability systems (see Hamilton et al., 2002). In

M. Pagès
Department of Sociology, Universitat Autònoma de Barcelona, Bellaterra, Spain

Department of Pedagogy, Universitat de Girona, Girona, Spain
e-mail: marcel.pages@uab.cat

high-stakes systems, students' test results are often tied to rewards and sanctions for the school, but also for individual teachers (e.g. teacher promotion or performance-based pay) (Verger et al., 2019b), whereas in low-stakes systems, there are no official or formal administrative consequences; instead, evaluation results merely offer descriptive information (Thiel et al., 2017). Nonetheless, low-stakes accountability may still result in significant reputational impacts for both schools and teachers (Bunar & Ambrose, 2016).

PBA instruments are being adopted in countries that regulate the teaching profession in different ways, and that have accountability arrangements in place of different natures (bureaucratic, market, professional, and so on). Previous accountability arrangements do not always fit well with the emerging PBA approach, and they sometimes interact with PBA in ways that generate new forms of hybrid accountabilities with unexpected outcomes for the teaching profession. With this in mind, the chapter is guided by the following questions: how do different regulatory models for the teaching profession mediate the enactment of PBA policies? And how do these regulatory models generate, exacerbate, or constrain inequalities and differences between professionals (teachers) in different settings?

Methodologically, the research is based on a systematic literature review (Petticrew & Roberts, 2006) that focuses on recent literature (2017–2020) about PBA and teacher professionalism. To carry out this review, we used two scientific databases: SCOPUS and the Web of Science (WoS). The search strategy followed an iterative process that helped develop the search syntax. In total, 566 articles were obtained. After reading the title and the abstract of each article, we selected papers according to their thematic fit with the objectives of the research. After applying the first screening, 197 articles were selected. In a second stage, two researchers reviewed the articles separately and identified those that had empirical evidence about the subject studied. A total of 101 pieces that focussed on PBA and teacher professionalism were included in the final sample. Data were collected using a review form for each of the papers that included the following main sections: theoretical framework, methods, main characteristics of the policy, and findings (mediating factors and effects on teachers' identities, work, and professionalism).

Subsequently, we organised and analysed the findings of the papers based on how the countries fit into different regulatory models for teachers.

2 Teacher Professionalism: Trends and Regulatory Regimes

2.1 Managerial Reforms and New Forms of Teacher Professionalism

The concept of teachers' professionalism should be understood not as something static or universal, but as an ideological construct that can be adapted according to particular interests (see Ozga & Lawn, 1981). The "classical" discourse of professionalism emphasises the attributes and components of specific occupations which share a specialised knowledge base, strong service ethics, and altruistic orientations, as well as a strong collegial control of professional work (Goodson & Hargreaves, 1996).

However, external performance pressures that have come with NPM reforms have reshaped what it means to be a teaching professional, and have contributed to the emergence of new forms of "managerial professionalism". According to Evetts (2009), NPM reforms have promoted a shift from occupational towards organisational professionalism. While occupational professionalism is based on collegial authority and professional autonomy, organisational professionalism emphasises managerial control, external regulation of work, accountability, standardisation, and rational-legal forms of authority (Evetts, 2009). This emergent professionalism is shaped by agendas of efficiency, accountability, performativity, and competition. To strive in this environment, teachers are increasingly required to become more like "technicians" than autonomous "professionals", which is an occurrence that challenges their professional identities (Day, 2002).

While these general analyses provide a useful way of understanding the broad changes that are taking place within the teaching profession, we do not assume that these transformations have the same weight everywhere. We are interested in better understanding what teachers in different policy contexts do, and how they feel about their work in an era in which PBA has become ever more central in the governance of educational systems. That is, we aim to analyse the "differentiation between" professionals who belong to the same professional group but to different professional systems (Bellini & Maestripieri, 2018, p. 8).

According to Evans (2008), professionalism and teacher professionalism could be operationalised according to three distinct dimensions. Namely: a behavioural component, which relates to "what professionals do in their working lives", an attitudinal dimension which refers to "how and why they do it", and the cognitive or intellectual sphere, involving everything concerning "what they know and understand" about their professional practice (Evans, 2008, p. 855). Beyond these separate analytical dimensions, we should also consider divergent expressions of teachers' professionalism, distinguishing between the professionalism required of them that is born of particular reform agendas, prescribed professionalism related to normative assumptions, and enacted professionalism that is based on actual teaching practices (Evans, 2008). In this chapter, we adapt Evans' operationalisation and use enactment theory (Ball et al., 2011) to understand how teachers' professionalism crystallises into different administrative traditions and professional regulatory systems. Combining Evans' dimensions and the enactment approach, we define teachers' professionalism as the interpretation of the prescriptions concerning what a teacher should know, be, and do, and how this all translates into their actual professional practices.

2.2 Regulatory Models of the Teaching Profession

This chapter is based on the premise that the design, calibration, and enactment of accountability instruments, as well as the effects of these instruments on teachers' professionalism, are contingent to the regulatory regimes for teachers that prevail in each context. Based on Voisin and Dumay's (2020) work, we distinguish between models based on the market (1), training (2), rules (3), and professional skills (4).

1. To a significant extent, the PBA approach fits quite clearly within a *market regulatory model*, where performance-oriented forms of accountability emerged in the 1980s to favour school competition and school choice. The market model includes early-adopter countries of NPM (such as the United Kingdom, Chile, and the US) that conceive high-stakes accountability as a means of promoting competition and pressure to perform among schools. The market model is oriented by the principles of labour flexibility and mobility. This model favours different pathways for entering the profession, but also contemplates differences in salaries and workloads according to productivity and other criteria (Voisin & Dumay, 2020). The regulation of teachers' work and its quality relies on centrally defined standards, and individual teachers' autonomy tends to be much more restricted than in other regulatory contexts.
2. Beyond the market model, PBA instruments were subsequently taken up in other countries, generally following a quality assurance rationale where other regulatory models predominate, such as the so-called *training model*. According to Voisin and Dumay (2020), the training model, "puts occupational control, expertise, and professional autonomy at its center" (p. 2). This model predominates in the Nordic countries in Europe and is characterised by having a very demanding and selective training system that provides future professionals with the necessary skills to perform complex tasks that require the exercise of discretion. In these contexts, teachers have a high level of professional autonomy, and educational authorities and users tend to trust their professional expertise. This high level of autonomy and professional space is rooted in a long-standing governance tradition and has been intentionally favoured by public authorities. PBA policies would apparently contradict this emphasis on professional autonomy and the long-established policy of professional accountability.
3. The *rules model* includes countries that have a bureaucratic tradition of teachers' governance and softer and input-oriented forms of accountability. The rules model is predominant in southern European countries, including Portugal, Spain, France, and Italy, where the implementation of accountability policy instruments in the education sector has often been framed under the rhetoric of quality assurance

and modernisation. However, its implementation has been uneven, has often been resisted by school actors and teachers' unions, and has experienced administrative and political obstacles (Verger et al., 2019a). Indeed, the PBA approach clashes with the bureaucratic accountability tradition, where there is more focus on compliance with rules than on assessing performance outcomes.

4. Finally, the *professional skills model* is a regulative approach to the teaching profession, and is typical in East Asia, including countries such as South Korea, Hong Kong, and Singapore. According to Voisin and Dumay (2020), this model is formally characterised by a combination of bureaucratic rules, professional standards, and practical expertise. Under this model, various forms of accountability are combined, including managerial, hierarchical, and professional accountability. The professional skills model may appear quite similar to the training model, although some important particularities need to be highlighted, for instance "its emphasis on practical knowledge and on-the-job training" (p. 8). Moreover, while the training model is characterised by a "low regulation of the [teaching] labour market", aligned with a tradition of professional autonomy and trust, the professional skills model implies "both a strong bureaucratic regulation of the teaching workforce and professional (accountability and careers) schemes emphasising continuous development linked to career ladders" (p. 9). In the next section, we organise the findings of the chapter following the four regulatory models mentioned.

3 Findings: PBA in Different Professional Contexts

3.1 Market Model: Constrained Professional Autonomy and Tensions in Contexts of Accountability Pressures

Within the market model, PBA policies have acquired an incremental dynamic. The uses and consequences of the policies have expanded over time, as well as the metrics and school grades directly impacted by accountability. In many of the countries that are part of the market regulatory model (e.g. England, USA, Australia, and Chile), PBA instruments are increasingly used to evaluate and assess teachers' work and to decide on whether they are promoted.

In the context of the market-based regulatory model, accountability pressures have strongly shaped instructional practices and curricular decisions (Avalos et al., 2020), and are seen as undermining both teachers' creativity (Appel, 2020) and their agency in educational planning (Farvis & Hay, 2020). Ingersoll and Collins (2017), using data from the Programme for International Student Assessment (PISA) established by the Organization for Economic Co-operation and Development (OECD), show that teachers in the US have less influence over key decisions than the OECD average. Other studies indicate a deterioration of this situation over time. Berkovich (2019) conducted a longitudinal study with PISA data, concluding that, over the years, teachers are experiencing less control over the content of curricula. A recent study conducted in the US Midwest confirms these trends, finding that PBA instruments decreased teachers' professional satisfaction and diminished their sense of control over classroom activities (Kaynak, 2020).

Performance pressures also impact the attention that teachers give to specific groups of students. Diagnostic practices are widely reported in high-stakes accountability systems. Teachers use test data to identify students that underperform, and provide them with additional assistance in an effort to boost their performance (Hardy, 2019; Hardy et al., 2019). Testing thus becomes a core instrument to categorise students and develop ability-grouping practices.

Nonetheless, teachers tend to be aware of the tensions that PBA generates in their everyday work and approach to teaching. Numerous studies report that teachers feel that the way in which the curriculum is covered for the purpose of test preparation conflicts with deep learning and richer ways of working with the subject matter (Thompson & Cook, 2017; Bradford & Braaten, 2018; Simpson, 2017). Not surprisingly, different forms of resistance to PBA are frequently documented. Warren and Ward (2021) see teachers' activism as an act of re-professionalisation and an attempt to open the possibility of balancing teacher autonomy with external demands made by the accountability system (Ben-Peretz, 2012;

cited in Warren & Ward, 2021, p. 12). Falabella (2020), in the Chilean context, identifies a group of teachers "who refuse to be assessed depending on their students' results in trial tests" (p. 16).

However, PBA has also generated logics of consent. Decades of datafication and accountability in education have favoured the emergence of new "teacher subjectivities thoroughly responsive and reactive to data" (Lewis & Hardy, 2017, p. 231). Similarly, Holloway (2019) points out that, over time, there is less space for dissension due to "the increasing alignment between teacher training, evaluation, professional development, and discipline" (p. 1986). In this sense, Paufler et al. (2020) observe that a majority of the teachers they approached reported that standardised testing had a positive impact on their practices, and that it encouraged them to be more reflective and innovative. Holloway (2019) considers that, over time, the possibility of resistance to PBA is diminishing.

The effects of PBA described are especially well documented in relation to socially disadvantaged school settings. Teachers in schools with privileged student populations do not need to adapt their educational and organisational practices to PBA demands so strictly (Fujishiro et al,. 2017). Wronowski (2020) shows that teachers in urban public schools in the US with higher percentages of disadvantaged students "are more likely to perceive a sense of de-professionalization and demoralization", which is something he attributes to the "increased accountability pressure" these schools experience (p. 20; see also Keddie, 2018).

3.2 Training Model: Enacting Agentic Professional Autonomy and Accommodating PBA Demands

The training model is dominant in most Nordic European countries; here, standardised testing has been adopted in recent years for quality assurance and teacher-training purposes and to facilitate data use among schools and teachers (Kelly et al., 2018). In the Nordic countries, PBA is characterised as having soft consequences for both teachers and schools, and it usually adopts a quality assurance logic (Verger et al., 2019a). In these countries, both public authorities and society put considerable trust in teachers, who generally enjoy higher levels of collective and individual professional autonomy, and experience fewer constraints in their professional practice (Voisin & Dumay, 2020).

However, despite the initial predominance of soft accountability designs in these countries, in recent years, the reputational stakes associated with PBA have been raised due to the adoption of new policy tools, such as the publication of performance results and league tables. An emerging body of literature has analysed the effects of PBA on teachers' sense of professionalism, as well as on their professional practice. In contrast to the market model, teachers who work in Nordic countries seem to have higher levels of professional autonomy to accommodate external demands from the PBA system within their own ethical and pedagogical beliefs, both at the individual and collegial levels. The literature reviewed finds a predominance of mixed perceptions about PBA and performance metrics in these countries. Recent investigations show that teachers tend to experience higher levels of professional autonomy in such contexts, which allow them to appropriate and re-contextualise external metrics in meaningful ways, using them to serve their students' interests (Camphuijsen, 2021; Da Silva & Mølstad, 2020; Gunnulfsen & Roe, 2018; Kelly et al., 2018; Mausethagen et al., 2020; Werler & Færevaag, 2017).

Existing research in Nordic countries shows that teachers can adopt various responses to cope with external controls and performance pressures derived from PBA (Gunnulfsen & Roe, 2018; Kelly et al., 2018). It is in Norway that PBA reforms have perhaps generated the most controversy and tension. Norwegian teachers tend to show mixed feelings and perceptions about their professional autonomy: they perceive high levels of decision-making power regarding "their classroom practices", but at the same time, they experience constraints in their pedagogical autonomy (Da Silva & Mølstad, p. 125). Another study finds that teachers perceive PBA instruments as constraining their professional autonomy, forcing them to spend time on test preparation activities and reducing the time they have available to support vulnerable students (Werler & Færevaag, 2017). Sometimes, teachers perceive the use of external data to orient teachers' practices as de-professionalising. In this sense, Da Silva and Mølstad (2020) note that to overcome these external constraints, Norwegian teachers deploy covert forms of resistance towards external metrics, continuing to rely on their own professional judgment to plan their teaching activities.

The strong welfare state tradition is one of the keys to understanding the re-contextualisation of PBA policies in Nordic countries. This tradition predisposes governments to put more emphasis on equity than on market competition and, crucially, attenuates the social and professional side-effects of PBA. In this regard, Kelly et al. (2018) find that in Nordic countries such as Denmark, the publication of results obtained by schools has a less severe pedagogical and curricular effect than in England. Nevertheless, this same research also identified that PBA increased reputational pressure among Danish school principals and triggered effects that governed teachers' work.

3.3 Rules Model: Erratic Policy Trajectory, Uneven Professional Impacts

In southern European countries, where the rules model predominates, the transformation of teacher professionalism through new metrics of performance and accountability appears to be contentious. Some studies found that in these contexts, the accountability system is more contested and hence has a weaker capacity for changing the nature of the teaching profession. Other researchers highlight how, despite significant obstacles, PBA is already part of the policy discourse and practices in the education sector, and therefore the teaching profession is experimenting with other regulatory models.

In France, the literature suggests that accountability policy instruments have had only a modest impact on the teaching profession due to the weak legitimacy of the performance-based accountability approach (Maroy et al., 2021). In fact, some researchers suggest that changes in accountability have only been implemented rhetorically, with most teachers resisting the use of external accountability tools in their daily professional practice (Maroy & Pons, 2019). The impact of accountability policies in France appears to be mediated by local and contextual factors and to have limited effects on teachers' everyday lives, although they seem more salient for principals and school leaders (Buisson-Fenet & Pons, 2019; Maroy et al., 2021).

Following a similar dynamic, the so-called "Good School" reform in Italy introduced new accountability policy instruments and a more managerial logic into the education system (Capano & Terenzi, 2019). This new education evaluation agency and its assessment tools encountered strong opposition and resistance from teachers and their unions (Mincu, 2018). Beyond the reactions of open rejection and political contestation, schools and teachers adhered to the new accountability system unevenly and with diverging responses, according to different "professional cultures" (Landri, 2021). Other authors highlight the key role of principals and school leaders in limiting the potential bureaucracy associated with accountability systems, instead providing the opportunity for "enhancing the school organisation as a professional learning community" (Paletta, 2019, p. 392) as well as promoting "meaningful change in professional practices and teaching in schools" (Paletta et al., 2020, p. 157). In addition, Bronzini and Spina (2018) notes that in the Italian case, "neither of the proposed models of professionalism seems dominant and the current phase appears to be blurred" (p. 96).

In Portugal, a new teacher evaluation model was implemented in 2008, following important public controversies and policy changes. According to Flores (2018), the model that was generated increased bureaucracy and workloads, and the principals interpreted that this system generated "increased individualism amongst teachers, decrease in teacher motivation, and the deterioration of the school climate and of professional relationships in general" (Flores, 2018, p. 240). With similar results, Flores and Ferreira (2019) outline that, as a result of these reforms, "principals and teachers deal simultaneously with bureaucratic intensification and control of their work and increasing demands of accountability and performativity" (p. 146).

In Spain, new accountability mechanisms that could potentially affect the regulation of the teaching profession have been adopted in different regions. In Catalonia, "teaching has been slightly but continuously changing in the last decade in the context of educational reforms focusing on accountability and school autonomy measures", shifting teachers' professionalism from an occupational to an organisational model, at least at the regulatory level (Verger & Pagès, 2018, p. 132). In Andalusia, some researchers suggest that recent endo-privatisation reforms, including external accountability mechanisms, are generating an emerging "performative experience based on quantification, classification and datafication", (Molina-Pérez & Lunego, 2020, p. 66). Accordingly, these policy changes are transforming teaching work into an increasingly technical profession, generating "discomfort and weariness" among teachers (p. 71). In a survey conducted in different Spanish regions, 78 per cent of teachers in the Madrid area suggested that external tests have some negative effects for teachers, students or the school in general. However, their direct impact on teaching work appears to be more modest. Madrid is the region that has suffered the greatest impact in this regard, with 22 per cent of the respondents there stating that the external tests altered their teaching work, and 19 per cent stating that the tests affect the classroom environment (Monarca & Fernández-Agüero, 2018, pp. 262–263).

Overall, the impacts of PBA in the teaching profession within the bureaucratic model appear to be uneven. Similar impacts to other models are reported in some research, while other studies suggest that the administrative bureaucratic legacy strongly mediates and mitigates the impact of PBA on the teaching profession.

3.4 Professional Skills Model: Enhancing Performance Through a Culture of Testing?

Over the last decades, accountability mechanisms have gained importance in the professional skills model. This has implied an increasing use of standardised and external tests to make teaching professionals more accountable to various actors. However, the use of metrics and other data-driven devices to regulate the teaching profession is not—solely—the result of the neoliberal reform approach. Instead, it should be understood as a particular configuration of a global education policy that is re-contextualised within a Confucian culture. Tan (2018) has labelled this particular policy translation as the "East Asian Educational Model (EAEM), […] grounded in and governed by Confucian habitus, and [relying] on educational harmonisation to achieve high performance" (Tan, 2018, n.p.).

Performance-based policy instruments have generated notable impacts on the teaching profession in this context, eroding teachers' autonomy and control over their work, and promoting instructional practices driven by testing cultures based on datafication and performance. In Hong Kong, for instance, accountability pressures have resulted in a transformation of teaching tasks and priorities, giving more importance to administrative-oriented objectives, generating lack of control for teachers over their work, increasing workloads, and limiting instructional time (Tsang & Kwong, 2017, p. 851). Similar impacts are reported by other authors in the same context, suggesting that the accountability regime has resulted in increased workloads and stress, but also in the reconfiguration of the teaching profession, as accountability policy instruments tend to "define and redefine the ways teachers define themselves and what they expect about their own and others' work" (Lee et al., 2020, p. 646). In Singapore, Ro (2020) has analysed the policy discourse of teacher professionalism, characterised by a combination of managerial and professional approaches that neglect a transformative view of teacher professionalism. This form of policy discourse limits the work of teachers to merely implementing a prescribed curriculum. Similar results are found in South Korea, where in a policy context of high-stakes testing and test-based accountability, a model of managerial professionalism has been consolidated, "emphasizing bureaucratic control over teachers' work to maximise their efficiency and performance" by means of focusing on teaching to the test and other instructional activities that do not require "in-depth knowledge or creative teaching strategies" (Ro, 2019, p. 144).

4 Conclusions

Our investigation shows that the effects of PBA on teachers' professionalism and teaching practices are not linear, but are contingent on teachers' regulatory regimes. Administrative traditions associated with specific models of regulating the teaching profession strategically mediate the re-contextualisation and formulation of PBA policy, and facilitate the emergence of differentiation processes between different professional systems. More specifically, the chapter notes the key role of the regulatory models that teachers work under in order to understand PBA effects on the teaching profession and its reconfiguration. The analytic lens of teachers' regulatory regimes allows us to gain a better understanding of the changes experienced by teachers and the teaching profession in different settings. The very nature of teachers' work is being challenged by new modes of "organisational professionalism", which enhance external forms of work control through standardisation and accountability mechanisms. However, teachers' regulatory contexts modulate the depth, trajectory, and impact of these transformations. In countries where the market model is prevalent, the professionalism of teachers is experiencing a more drastic shift towards organisational professional models. Meanwhile, the training model that predominates in Nordic countries seems to mitigate such transformations—thus preserving important professional space and institutional autonomy for teachers. For their part, countries where teachers' professionalism is configured under the rules model report uneven impacts, given the erratic policy trajectory of accountability reforms in these countries. And lastly, countries that follow the professional skills model appear to be experiencing important changes for teachers' professionalism due to a combination of accountability policy models and cultural educational values that place great importance on academic excellence and performance in exams.

The effects of PBA on teachers' professionalism can be identified at different levels: the knowledge base of teachers' work (e.g. the definition of the curriculum, learning standards, and evaluation), professional commitment (beliefs and practices regarding how students' needs should be addressed), autonomy (effects on the power of decision-making and discretion), and individual and collective identities. The effects on each of these dimensions are frequently reported in the context of the high-stakes accountability systems that prevail within the market model. An abundant educational literature published in countries such as Chile, the US, England, and Australia reports that PBA has effects on teachers' practices, such as teaching to the test, narrowing the curriculum and grouping by ability. Nonetheless, this literature does not always make explicit the connection between the effects of accountability and changes in the teaching profession. Interestingly, our review shows that undesired effects and pressures on teachers' work similar to those reported within the market model are increasingly being identified in countries with soft and low-stakes accountability policies.

Finally, we consider it important to underline the limitations of this study and suggest some further lines of research to address them. First, due to an explosion in the publication of academic literature on this topic in recent years, we were forced to limit the temporal scope of the systematic literature review. Unfortunately, this has meant that we had to exclude relevant pieces of research published earlier. Second, despite the numerous advantages of this methodological approach, it tends to reproduce the over-representation of some countries (mainly English-speaking countries) in the academic literature, to the detriment of literature focusing on countries in the Global South. Despite these limitations, the chapter also opens up new avenues of research on the relationship between teachers' professionalism and educational reform, and encourages the production of literature in under-researched contexts.

Acknowledgements This work was supported by the European Research Council under Grant 680172; FJC2020-045847-I/MCIN/AEI/10.13039/501100011033/"NextGenerationEU"/PRTR

References

Appel, M. (2020). Performativity and the demise of the teaching profession: The need for rebalancing in Australia. *Asia-Pacific Journal of Teacher Education, 48*(3), 301–315. https://doi.org/10.1080/1359866x.2019.1644611

Apple, M. W. (2001). Markets, standards, teaching, and teacher education. *Journal of Teacher Education, 52*(3), 182–196. https://doi.org/10.1177/0022487101052003002

Avalos, M. A., Perez, X., & Thorrington, V. (2020). Comparing secondary English teachers' ideal and actual writing practices for diverse learners: Constrained professionalism in figured worlds of high-stakes testing. *Reading & Writing Quarterly, 36*(3), 225–242. https://doi.org/10.1080/10573569.2019.1635056

Ball, S. J. (2016). Neoliberal education? Confronting the slouching beast. *Policy Futures in Education, 14*(8), 1046–1059. https://doi.org/10.1177/1478210316664259

Ball, S. J., Maguire, M., & Braun, A. (2011). *How schools do policy: Policy enactments in secondary schools*. Routledge. https://doi.org/10.4324/9780203153185

Bellini, A., & Maestripieri, L. (2018). Professions within, between and beyond. Varieties of professionalism in a globalising world. *Cambio. Rivista sulle Trasformazioni Sociali, 8*(16), 5–14. https://doi.org/10.13128/cambio-24947

Ben-Peretz, M. (2012). Accountability vs teacher autonomy: An issue of balance. In C. Day (Ed.), *The Routledge international handbook of teacher and school development* (pp. 57–66). Routledge. https://doi.org/10.4324/9780203815564.ch4

Berkovich, I. (2019). Process implementation perspective on neoliberal regulation: A comparative analysis of national curricula and standards-based reforms in the USA and Australia. *Globalisation, Societies and Education, 17*(5), 593–609. https://doi.org/10.1080/14767724.2018.1559042

Bradford, C., & Braaten, M. (2018). Teacher evaluation and the demoralization of teachers. *Teaching and Teacher Education*, 75, 49–59. https://doi.org/10.1016/j.tate.2018.05.017

Bronzini, M., & Spina, E. (2018). Italian teachers: A profession in transition? *Cambio. Rivista sulle Trasformazioni Sociali, 8*(16), 83–98. https://doi.org/10.13128/cambio-23255

Buisson-Fenet, H., & Pons, X. (2019). Responsable, mais pas redevable? Gouvernance par les résultats et relations d'"accountability" dans les établissements scolaires en France. *Éducation et sociétés, 1*, 41–56. https://doi.org/10.3917/es.043.0041

Bunar, N., & Ambrose, A. (2016). Schools, choice and reputation: Local school markets and the distribution of symbolic capital in segregated cities. *Research in Comparative and International Education, 11*(1), 34–51. https://doi.org/10.1177/1745499916631064

Camphuijsen, M. K. (2021). Coping with performance expectations: Towards a deeper understanding of variation in school principals' responses to accountability demands. *Educational Assessment, Evaluation and Accountability*, 1–27. https://doi.org/10.1007/s11092-020-09344-6

Capano, G., & Terenzi, P. (2019). I gruppi di interesse e la legge sulla «Buona Scuola». *Rivista Italiana di Politiche Pubbliche, 14*(2), 247–276.

Da Silva, A. L., & Mølstad, C. E. (2020). Teacher autonomy and teacher agency: A comparative study in Brazilian and Norwegian lower secondary education. *The Curriculum Journal, 31*(1), 115–131. https://doi.org/10.1002/curj.3

Day, C. (2002). School reform and transitions in teacher professionalism and identity. *International Journal of Educational Research, 37*(8), 677–692. https://doi.org/10.1016/s0883-0355(03)00065-x
Evans, L. (2008). Professionalism, professionality and the development of education professionals. *British Journal of Educational Studies, 56*(1), 20–38. https://doi.org/10.1111/j.1467-8527.2007.00392.x
Evetts, J. (2009). New professionalism and new public management: Changes, continuities and consequences. *Comparative Sociology, 8*(2), 247–266. https://doi.org/10.1163/156913309x421655
Falabella, A. (2020). The ethics of competition: Accountability policy enactment in Chilean schools' everyday life. *Journal of Education Policy, 35*(1), 23–45. https://doi.org/10.1080/02680939.2019.1635272
Farvis, J., & Hay, S. (2020). Undermining teaching: How education consultants view the impact of high-stakes test preparation on teaching. *Policy Futures in Education, 18*(8), 1058–1074. https://doi.org/10.1177/1478210320919541
Flores, M. A. (2018). Teacher evaluation in Portugal: Persisting challenges and perceived effects. *Teachers and Teaching, 24*(3), 223–245. https://doi.org/10.1080/13540602.2018.1425677
Flores, M. A., & Ferreira, F. I. (2019). Leading learning in schools in challenging times: Findings from research in Portugal. In T. Townsend (Ed.), *Instructional leadership and leadership for learning in schools* (pp. 133–162). Palgrave Macmillan. https://doi.org/10.1007/978-3-030-23736-3_6
Fujishiro, K., Farley, A. N., Kellemen, M., & Swoboda, C. M. (2017). Exploring associations between state education initiatives and teachers' sleep: A social-ecological approach. *Social Science & Medicine, 191*, 151–159. https://doi.org/10.1016/j.socscimed.2017.09.019
Goodson, I., & Hargreaves, A. (1996). *Teachers' professional lives*. Falmer Press.
Gunnulfsen, A. E., & Roe, A. (2018). Investigating teachers' and school principals' enactments of national testing policies: A Norwegian study. *Journal of Educational Administration, 56*(3), 332–349. https://doi.org/10.1108/jea-04-2017-0035
Hamilton, L. S., Stecher, B. M., & Klein, S. P. (2002). *Making sense of test-based accountability in education*. Rand Corporation.
Hardy, I. (2019). The quandary of quantification: Data, numbers and teachers' learning. *Journal of Education Policy, 36*(1), 44–63. https://doi.org/10.1080/02680939.2019.1672211
Hardy, I. J., Reyes, V., & Hamid, M. O. (2019). Performative practices and 'authentic accountabilities': Targeting students, targeting learning? *International Education Journal: Comparative Perspectives, 18*(1), 20–33.

Högberg, B., & Lindgren, J. (2021). Outcome-based accountability regimes in OECD countries: A global policy model? *Comparative Education, 57*(3), 301–321. https://doi.org/10.1080/03050068.2020.1849614

Holloway, J. (2019). Risky teachers: Mitigating risk through high-stakes teacher evaluation in the USA. *Discourse: Studies in the Cultural Politics of Education, 40*(3), 399–411. https://doi.org/10.1080/01596306.2017.1322938

Ingersoll, R. M., & Collins, G. J. (2017). Accountability and control in American schools. *Journal of Curriculum Studies, 49*(1), 75–95. https://doi.org/10.1080/00220272.2016.1205142

Kaynak, N. E. (2020). A close look at teachers' lives: Caring for the well-being of elementary teachers in the US. *International Journal of Emotional Education, 12*(1), 19–34.

Keddie, A. (2018). Supporting disadvantaged students in an English primary school: Matters of entrepreneurial and traditional professionalism. *Cambridge Journal of Education, 48*(2), 197–212. https://doi.org/10.1080/0305764x.2016.1270257

Kelly, P., Andreasen, K. E., Kousholt, K., McNess, E., & Ydesen, C. (2018). Education governance and standardised tests in Denmark and England. *Journal of Education Policy, 33*(6), 739–758. https://doi.org/10.1080/02680939.2017.1360518

Landri, P. (2021). To resist, or to align? The enactment of data-based school governance in Italy. *Educational Assessment, Evaluation and Accountability, 33*(3), 563–580. https://doi.org/10.1007/s11092-021-09367-7

Lee, T. T. L., Kwan, P., & Li, B. Y. M. (2020). Neoliberal challenges in context: A case of Hong Kong. *International Journal of Educational Management, 34*(4), 641–652. https://doi.org/10.1108/ijem-06-2019-0220

Lewis, S., & Hardy, I. (2017). Tracking the topological: The effects of standardised data upon teachers' practice. *British Journal of Educational Studies, 65*(2), 219–238. https://doi.org/10.1080/00071005.2016.1254157

Maroy, C., & Pons, X. (2019). *Accountability policies in education. A comparative and multilevel analysis in France and Quebec*. Springer. https://doi.org/10.1007/978-3-030-01285-4

Maroy, C., Dupriez, V., & Pons, X. (2021). Accountability and datafication in francophone contexts: A reinforcing cognitive state still challenged by local actors. In S. Grek, C. Maroy, & A. Verger (Eds.), *World yearbook in education 2021: Accountability and datafication in education* (pp. 130–146). Routledge. https://doi.org/10.4324/9781003014164-10

Mausethagen, S., Prøitz, T. S., & Skedsmo, G. (2020). Redefining public values: Data use and value dilemmas in education. *Education Inquiry, 12*(1), 1–16. https://doi.org/10.1080/20004508.2020.1733744

Mincu, M. E. (2018). Overcoming fragmented professionalism? Accountability for improvement in teacher preparation in Italy. In R. Normand, M. Liu, L. M. Carvalho, D. A. Oliveira, & L. LeVasseur (Eds.), *Education policies and the restructuring of the educational profession* (pp. 235–244). Springer. https://doi.org/10.1007/978-981-10-8279-5_16

Molina-Pérez, J., & Lunego, J. (2020). Reconstrucciones "resilientes" de la identidad profesional del profesorado: Endoprivatización y cultura performativa en Andalucía (España). *REICE: Revista Iberoamericana sobre Calidad, Eficacia y Cambio en Educación, 18*(2), 57–75. https://doi.org/10.15366/reice2020.18.2.003

Monarca, H., & Fernández-Agüero, M. (2018). Opinión del profesorado sobre las fortalezas y debilidades de las evaluaciones externas de aprendizaje en España. *Educación XX1, 21*(2), 249–273. https://doi.org/10.5944/educxx1.19416

Ozga, J., & Lawn, M. (1981). *Teachers, professionalism and class: A study of organised teachers*. The Falmer Press.

Paletta, A. (2019). How do school leaders respond to the growing intrusiveness of accountability policies? Evidence from Italy. *Journal of Educational Administration and History, 51*(4), 381–401. https://doi.org/10.1080/00220620.2019.1607266

Paletta, A., Basyte Ferrari, E., & Alimehmeti, G. (2020). How principals use a new accountability system to promote change in teacher practices: Evidence from Italy. *Educational Administration Quarterly, 56*(1), 123–173. https://doi.org/10.1177/0013161x19840398

Parding, K., Abrahamsson, L., & Berg-Jansson, A. (2012). New conditions for identities, cultures and governance of welfare sector professionals: The teaching profession. *Ephemera: Theory & Politics in Organization, 12*(3), 294–308.

Paufler, N. A., King, K. M., & Zhu, P. (2020). Promoting professional growth in new teacher evaluation systems: Practitioners' lived experiences in changing policy contexts. *Studies in Educational Evaluation*, 65, 1-9. https://doi.org/10.1016/j.stueduc.2020.100873

Petticrew, M., & Roberts, H. (2006). *Systematic reviews in the social sciences: A practical guide*. Blackwell Publishing.

Ro, J. (2019). Seeking the meaning of the job: Korean novice secondary teachers' professional identity. *Asia Pacific Education Review, 20*(1), 135–146. https://doi.org/10.1007/s12564-018-9573-2

Ro, J. (2020). Curriculum, standards and professionalisation: The policy discourse on teacher professionalism in Singapore. *Teaching and Teacher Education, 91*, 1–10. https://doi.org/10.1016/j.tate.2020.103056

Simpson, A. (2017). Teachers negotiating professional agency through literature-based assessment. *Literacy, 51*(2), 111–119. https://doi.org/10.1111/lit.12114

Tan, C. (2018). *Comparing high-performing education systems: Understanding Singapore, Shanghai, and Hong Kong*. Routledge. https://doi.org/10.4324/9781351238724

Thiel, C., Schweizer, S., & Bellmann, J. (2017). Rethinking side effects of accountability in education: Insights from a multiple methods study in four German school systems. *Education Policy Analysis Archives, 25*(93), 1–32. https://doi.org/10.14507/epaa.25.2662

Thompson, G., & Cook, I. (2017). The politics of teaching time in disciplinary and control societies. *British Journal of Sociology of Education, 38*(1), 26–37. https://doi.org/10.1080/01425692.2016.1234365

Tsang, K. K., & Kwong, T. L. (2017). Teachers' emotions in the context of education reform: Labor process theory and social constructionism. *British Journal of Sociology of Education, 38*(6), 841–855. https://doi.org/10.1080/01425692.2016.1182007

Verger, A., & Pagès, M. (2018). New public management and its effects in the teaching profession: Recent trends in Spain and Catalonia. In R. Normand, M. Liu, L. M. Carvalho, D. A. Oliveira, & L. LeVasseur (Eds.), *Education policies and the restructuring of the educational profession* (pp. 119–135). Springer. https://doi.org/10.1007/978-981-10-8279-5_9

Verger, A., & Parcerisa, L. (2017). A difficult relationship: Accountability policies and teachers—International evidence and premises for future research. In M. Akiba & G. LeTendre (Eds.), *International handbook of teacher quality and policy* (pp. 241–254). Routledge. https://doi.org/10.4324/9781315710068-16

Verger, A., Fontdevila, C., & Parcerisa, L. (2019a). Reforming governance through policy instruments: How and to what extent standards, tests and accountability in education spread worldwide. *Discourse: Studies in the Cultural Politics of Education, 40*(2), 248–270. https://doi.org/10.1080/01596306.2019.1569882

Verger, A., Parcerisa, L., & Fontdevila, C. (2019b). The growth and spread of large-scale assessments and test-based accountabilities: A political sociology of global education reforms. *Educational Review, 71*(1), 5–30. https://doi.org/10.1080/00131911.2019.1522045

Voisin, A., & Dumay, X. (2020). How do educational systems regulate the teaching profession and teachers' work? A typological approach to institutional foundations and models of regulation. *Teaching and Teacher Education, 96*, 1–16. https://doi.org/10.1016/j.tate.2020.103144

Warren, A., & Ward, N. (2021). 'How do you get the courage to stand up?' Teachers constructions of activism in response to education policy reform. *Discourse: Studies in the Cultural Politics of Education, 42*(4), 544–558. https://doi.org/10.1080/01596306.2020.1716689

Werler, T., & Færevaag, M. K. (2017). National testing data in Norwegian classrooms: A tool to improve pupil performance? *Nordic Journal of Studies in Educational Policy, 3*(1), 67–81. https://doi.org/10.1080/20020317.2017.1320188

Wronowski, M. L. (2020). De-professionalized and demoralized: A framework for understanding teacher turnover in the accountability policy ERA. *Leadership and Policy in Schools*, 1–31. https://doi.org/10.1080/15700763.2020.1734209

10

Inequalities in Neo-mutualistic Professional Organisations: The Boundary Work of Creative Workers in Italy

Silvia Lucciarini and Valeria Pulignano

1 Introduction

The multiple transformations that have occurred in the labour market in recent decades have radically changed the skills sought by employers (McAfee & Brynjolfsson, 2017). A significant outcome of such changes has been an increase in the number of skilled professionals who are primarily self-employed workers and freelancers (Gallie, 2013), working in a variety of production sectors. The occupational landscape has thus been

The original version of this chapter was previously published non-open access. A correction to this chapter is available at https://doi.org/10.1007/978-3-031-31278-6_15

S. Lucciarini (✉)
Department of Social and Economic Sciences (DISSE), Sapienza University of Rome, Rome, Italy
e-mail: silvia.lucciarini@uniroma1.it

V. Pulignano
Centre for Sociological Research, KU Leuven University, Leuven, Belgium
e-mail: valeria.pulignano@Kuleuven.be

© The Author(s) 2023, corrected publication 2024
L. Maestripieri, A. Bellini (eds.), *Professionalism and Social Change*,
https://doi.org/10.1007/978-3-031-31278-6_10

altered, with many 'emerging' professions being added to it. The growing demand for 'new' skills, inside and outside organisations (Evetts, 2011; Noordegraaf, 2011; Liu, 2006), has led to different repertoires of actions emerging that identify and legitimise workers as 'professionals'.

According to the analytical dichotomy of *professionalism* versus *organisation* (Freidson, 2001), the strategies of *occupational professionalism* (Evetts, 2013), based on workers' self-directed practices and specific competencies (Gieryn, 1983), are understood as distinct from 'controlled' strategies (Noordegraaf, 2015) that are governed by managerial principles, standardised routines and protocols, and are organised 'from above' (Evetts, 2011). More recently, scholars have identified a 'hybrid' model of professionalism, namely *organising professionalism* (Noordegraaf, 2015), in which organisations and professionals are mutually connected in ways that serve to continuously redefine their work and tasks.

These workers enact strategies that bring about change in organisations. This change gives rise to new actions on the part of professionals (Noordegraaf, 2009) in a dynamic of 'co-evolution'. Indeed, these actions are driven by two fleshed-out logics: *professionalism* and *managerialism* (Noordegraaf, 2015). As such, they are hybrid by nature and are widespread in new forms of organisations, the very kinds of collective entities that are shaping organising professionalism (Alvehus et al., 2021).

Far from being neutral groupings of workers, these organisations, which are frequently 'multi-professional', bring about a 'division of labour' amongst professionals while responding to higher standards of competitiveness. The mechanisms they put into place come to segment workers, dividing them into 'elite' workers, on the one hand, and 'rank-and-file' workers, on the other (Waring & Bishop, 2013; Alacevich et al., 2017).

This is especially true in specific productive sectors, such as the creative industries that are characterised by emerging professional jobs. Many creative workers have joined multi-professional organisations to find legitimacy or effective forms of protection. These organisations pursue multiple aims: they operate as labour-market intermediaries and also act as agents of professionalism by defining the work their members do based on their specific skills and expertise and by consolidating their legitimacy (Franzini

& Lucciarini, 2022). This role related to skills and expertise is especially important for sectors that do not have established training systems (Evetts, 2013).

Some studies have focused on the strategies enacted by the organisations that govern emerging professions, examining the implications of their activities in compensating for market pressures and meeting workers' needs in times of crisis (Maestripieri & Cucca, 2018). Others have pointed out the problematic aspects of these strategies, such as the tendency to stratify workers in a way that might lead to forming professional elites (Waring, 2014). However, few of them have addressed both the positive and the negative aspects. The study presented here aims to fill this gap.

The underlying idea is that analysing the actions of individuals and organisations and how they influence each other is key for understanding their implications in terms of *differentiation* 'within' and 'between' professions (see the introduction to this volume; see also Bellini & Maestripieri, 2018; Parding et al., 2021), in the dual sense of the growing division of labour and rising inequalities amongst workers operating in the same occupational ecosystem—creative labour—but in different professional fields. Drawing on Lamont and Molnar's (2002) concept of 'boundary work', which is already used in the sociology of professions (see Bucher et al., 2016; for an overview, see Heusinkveld et al., 2018), we seek to uncover and explain the relational dynamics characterising the 'professional closure regimes' (Boussard, 2018) assembled in creative industries as a result of the activities of cooperatives of creative workers and of these workers themselves.

Our work is grounded in a case study of a creative workers' cooperative based in Italy (hereafter, also 'CWC'), employing approximately 8000 workers with different professional profiles. Of these, the ones discussed in the analysis are *photographers*, *video makers*, and *lighting and sound technicians*.

The chapter is divided into three parts. In the first part, we lay out the theoretical framework. In the second, we present the research methods and empirical findings. Finally, we discuss the results of the analysis in light of our theoretical framework and suggest lines for future research.

2 Boundary Work in Multi-professional Mutual Aid Organisations

In creative industries, organisations inspired by the principles of new mutualism (Horowitz, 2021) have set out to create new market players from the bottom up, based on a combination of cooperation and protection mechanisms. These organisations bring together workers who pursue careers in which periods of work under employment contracts alternate or overlap with periods of self-employment. Moreover, it is common for creative workers to be 'multiple job holders'.

The multifaceted nature of workers' identities (Pernicka, 2006) translates into two intertwined needs: to increase their market opportunities and to improve their levels of protection. Joining a neo-mutualist professional organisation gives self-employed workers access to the benefits and safeguards usually reserved for employees.

According to Murgia and de Heusch (2020) and Franzini and Lucciarini (2022), these organisations present themselves as 'cooperatives of self-employed salaried workers'. They make the workers eligible for social protection by 'hiring' them, transforming self-employed workers into salaried ones, who are entitled to wider welfare provisions. These organisational actions try to compensate for the lack of protection suffered by self-employed workers, but do not lead to equal treatment for all the different categories of workers within these organisations. Moreover, CWCs foster increased job opportunities both inside and outside the organisation by giving value to workers' skills and cultivating professional networks. For instance, these organisations provide training courses on health and safety at work, as well as other professionalisation strategies. Workers can earn a safety certification, a mandatory requirement in high-level assignments, and foster their professional positions, both material and immaterial (i.e. public perceptions). However, this system of job opportunities is produced and reproduced along definite demarcation lines, namely, 'symbolic boundaries': conceptual tools by which individuals separate people into groups and generate feelings of similarity and belonging and, in so doing, make sense of social reality (Lamont, 2017).

Symbolic boundaries become *social* boundaries in cases where access to both material and immaterial resources and power is determined by the differential positions of actors in the system of inequalities built along these symbolic dividing lines. As such, social boundaries are symbolic boundaries that have been 'objectified' based on specific combinations of class, gender, age, race, and other possible differentiating factors. Symbolic discrimination, then, manifests as a social disadvantage because it conditions how resources are redistributed amongst and within social groups. These mechanisms whereby resources are allocated also regulate the perceived legitimacy of professions, in that they define the degree of social recognition granted to a given occupational group and its specific expertise (Gieryn, 1983); they do this through dynamics of 'boundary-setting' diversification and 'boundary-crossing' integration (Heite, 2012) between workers who inhabit the same occupational ecosystem. These processes of occupational group-building are crucial when discussing the so-called emerging professions, in which workers consider themselves professionals, but lack public regulation and recognition (Maestripieri & Cucca, 2018). In addition, the construction of boundaries is strategic both for defensive actions (against workers of similar occupational ecosystems: 'boundary-setting') and expansive actions (between workers in similar occupational contexts: 'boundary-crossing').

Cooperatives of emerging professionals play a crucial role in constructing professional groups and their public legitimacy. Moreover, they face a series of organisational dilemmas due to their specific nature. On the one hand, they adopt inclusive practices to strengthen their ranks, maximise job opportunities, and improve their ability to influence the market (Cucca & Maestripieri, 2016). On the other hand, they activate stratification mechanisms that form a professional elite with a relatively advantaged position over others.

If we analyse the stratification processes in these formally horizontal organisations, we find an example of enactment of symbolic and social boundaries. These boundaries draw lines dividing workers based on objective characteristics (e.g. gender and age). The reproduction of these forms of discrimination has been defined as 'boundary maintenance' (Giullari & Lucciarini, 2023; Smith & Ward, 2015). In addition, the analysis of stratification processes has also revealed 'boundary blurring' practices (Smith & Ward, 2015), through which the boundaries between occupational groups are redefined. These practices aim to maximise job opportunities by mixing professional skills.

In this chapter, we investigate the dialectic between symbolic and social boundaries leading to discrimination against workers in terms of access to the resources provided by the organisation to its members; we also study the organisational boundaries that the cooperative sets up in pursuing advantageous business models, in order to understand what—if any—forms of inequality these models produce. To analyse these instances of boundary work, we focus on the recruitment, training, and career advancement mechanisms that operate in the organisation in question.

3 Case Study and Methods

The cooperative under analysis was created at the beginning of the 1990s by musicians and live performers looking for a way to reduce the precariousness and intermittent nature of certain creative occupations. Over the years, this first unit of professionals has been supplemented by further sub-divisions aimed at organising other types of creative workers, such as educators, journalists, and photographers. Today, the cooperative is made up of eight organisational units representing different professional areas. The organisation has grown stronger by creating a complex network of services that it supplies to its members (from legal and tax assistance and training courses to a travel agency). This array of services aims to reduce transaction costs and maximise the incomes of worker-members and the organisation, as the cooperative collects a share of the worker's payment for a given 'gig' (short-term contract), namely, 9–12 per cent of the established fee (for an overview of how these organisations work, see Franzini & Lucciarini, 2022). The cooperative has over 8000 members and in 2019 had a turnover of approximately 60 million euros.

We carried out the fieldwork between September 2018 and October 2019, conducting in-depth interviews with the CEO, the management, and the managers of the three professional areas being researched: *photographers*, *video makers*, and *lighting and sound technicians*. We selected these three groups of professionals based on how many members they have and their relative importance within the cooperative. Lighting and sound technicians make up approximately 70 per cent of the total number of members. In contrast, photographers and video makers account for 5 and 10 per cent, respectively.

Preliminary interviews with the management allowed us to identify the most significant groups of professionals within the cooperative and organise a series of focus groups, each with a high number of participants and heterogeneous composition.

We decided to use the focus group method because this tool allows researchers to understand the dynamics of interaction within the group (Kitzinger, 1995) while uncovering the opinions and conditions of minority groups (Smithson, 2000), albeit in the context of a 'peer group conversation' (Gamson, 1992). We conducted the focus groups according to a discursive scheme based on five main narrative parameters: profession, employment and working conditions (i.e. type of employment, hours worked and work organisation, income), interest representation, associational identity, and unmet needs (i.e. in terms of social protection and job quality).

Four focus groups were held: the first two were addressed to lighting and sound technicians (with 20 participants in each group, making a total of 40), the third was addressed to photographers (15 participants), and the fourth involved video makers (15 participants). We selected the participants based on their profession, age (20–55 years old), gender (except for lighting and sound technicians, because of the lack of women amongst them), and seniority (see Tables 10.1 and 10.2).

We analysed the data we had collected using the standard multi-stage approach (Conover et al., 1991) commonly used for focus groups. This

Table 10.1 Interviewees and participants in focus groups

	Video makers		Photographers		Lighting and sound technicians	
Age class	M	F	M	F	M	F
20–34	7	5	4	2	30	–
35–60	3	–	6	3	10	–

Table 10.2 Key informants

Cooperative CEO (1)
Cooperative managers by professional field (3)
Communications office manager (1)
Research office manager (1)

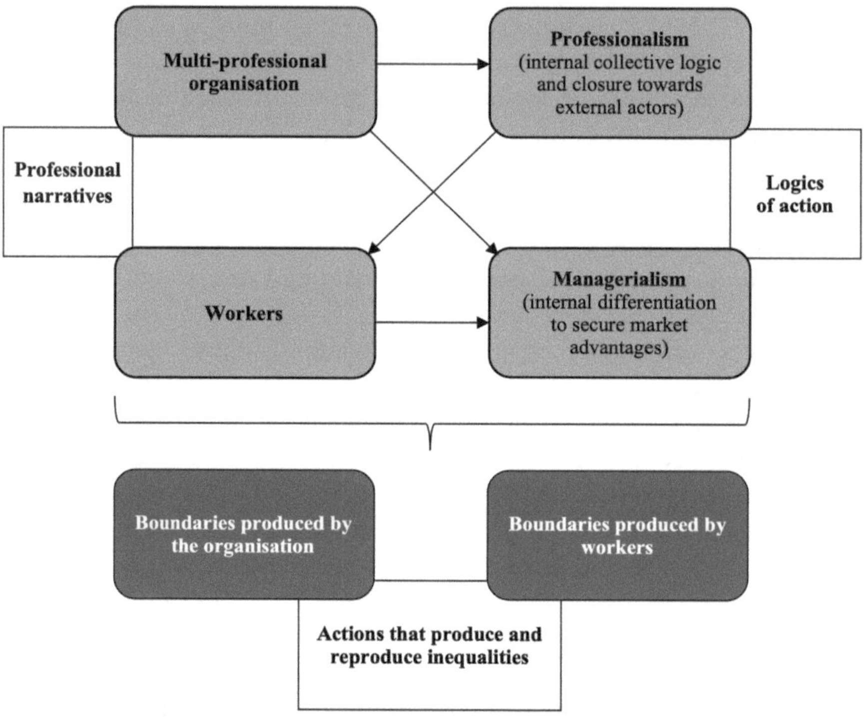

Fig. 10.1 Principles and actions that produce inequalities in the multi-professional organisation

approach involves classifying the interviewees' statements by using a coding process to identify themes and concepts. We based our analysis on two narratives, *professionalism* and *managerialism*, and observed how they were segmented (for the processing of the qualitative model, see Fig. 10.1) to identify the boundary line(s).

4 Main Research Results

To understand the relationship between the strategies of the organisation and those of the workers, we focussed on three dimensions: the mission and vision of the organisation, job quality as perceived by the workers, and the market opportunities to which they have access. The CWC was created by artists for artists in the form of a social enterprise cooperative. In its over 30 years in existence, the organisation has built a collaborative network that offers two main lines of services. The first aims to professionalise workers through a method of soft coordination in which the cooperative 'recommends' a minimum fee for each job. The workers are also helped to update their skill sets through a system of training courses run each year on occupational safety regulations and the use of technical equipment. The membership system also encourages members to share job opportunities, increasing the cooperative's volume of jobs available. Interviews with the management clarified the spirit of the cooperative.

> You can live off the arts. The goal of (the CWC) is to connect workers and employers, professionals, and practitioners and to help everyone understand that the arts should be considered a job like any other. Stop thinking of it as a passion: passion does not buy you dinner, and talent must be nurtured through hard work, dedication, and money. That's why art must be paid for. (Int_management1)

The second line of service aims to lower transaction costs (Williamson, 1979), maximise income, and guide the workers through the tortuous maze of tax deduction regulations by providing them with tax and social security assistance.

> We focus on building and having our members follow a system that leads them to increase their income and 'deduct' as much as possible on each job order through contracts that also provide protection. We take care of them, so they make thoughtful decisions and don't rush into choices for a few dirty bucks. We invite them to collaborate and not just compete with each other, passing on jobs and projects. If the cooperative grows, they grow too. (Int_management1)

The CWC offers similar activities to the various professions. The common starting point is the awareness of the transformation of the overall sector and the new skills required by clients. In this regard, the cooperative supports professional specialisation through training. However, access to specialisation courses is selective and not open to all workers, with different access criteria for the three professions under analysis.

4.1 Photographers

Conversations in the focus groups revealed new market needs, specifically a heightened demand for images, both to be used online and in print. This has contributed to a fall in the quality of such work.

> Do you see this picture? [showing a magazine] It's all wrong; it's a bad picture. But now, many newspapers and web pages are asking only for quantity, not quality… In some reports, you can see that they used a smartphone [camera], not professional equipment. (FGs_photographers_1A)

At the same time, participants identified the employment niches that are more 'professionalising'.

> I took a [photography] post-production course because that's the industry where they pay the most because you have to know how to use the camera and software. I had to invest money and take the course, but it was worth it. I send [the photos] to Bangladesh for contouring [isolating the photographed object from the background] as we all do, even Australian colleagues send them there, because it's lengthy work but not particularly skilled. For one euro per photo, they contour it, and then I can work on post-production, and it's worth it in terms of both time and money. (FGs_photographers_1)

That said, workers can access these market niches if they have completed specific training courses and obtained certifications. The worker pays for the professional courses; based on this training, the participants can secure their first assignments and thereby begin to develop a portfolio. Courses such as these involve a significant commitment for workers in terms of time and money, and as such are more accessible to young people who receive financial help from their families:

> Post-production courses are mostly taken by young people who can afford to pay for them and the equipment. You can't fit in the course time if you already have a job. I have a salaried job and set work hours that are incompatible. I only keep doing work related to small public and private events. (FGs_photographers_1C)

4.2 Video Makers

Of the three sectors examined, video making has experienced the steepest increase in demand. This growth has specific implications in terms of job quality and fair pay.

> The demand for content has increased, particularly on the web. So, many people lured by this opportunity have suddenly set themselves up as video makers. But you must know how things work to make even low-quality videos. If you don't have any training, not only do you offer poor quality work but you also get paid very little, [thus] putting your colleagues in a difficult position. The market demands low-quality products, but you can't charge too little for making them because it's not good for you or others and, most importantly, you must learn how to do it. It's a job not a hobby. (Int_managment_videomaker_2)

Although the volume of work has increased, the quality of job opportunities remains relatively low unless workers manage to make their way into the higher standard networks of independent productions made for both public and private broadcasters.

> Doing a lot of small jobs for websites or feeding your own site and earning through advertisement is very tiring and tends to flatten you onto a single mode of communication, in addition to not ensuring a stable income. I have chosen to work for a private client who provides me with a reliable economic base, and then I invest in independent projects that I sell to other private clients. This way, I keep my reputation for quality work and have an easier time selling subsequent projects. (Int_managment_videomaker_1)

Access to high-quality collaboration networks is a strategy that leads to high-quality jobs and professional advancement, but it is not for everyone.

> You have to invest a lot in networks, participate in festivals, and convince well-known personalities to participate in your projects to make them more appealing and get a bigger audience. This costs money and time, even for international collaborations. If you have a family, it's very difficult: you're away from home a lot, and in order to cut the costs of filming, you have to concentrate all your work, which has a very tight schedule.

4.3 Lighting and Sound Technicians

Again, the first theme that emerged in the focus groups with lighting and sound technicians was their awareness of changes in the job market and technical equipment and the need to develop a high degree of professionalism and specialisation.

> Before, you used to do everything; you loaded the trucks, drove them, unloaded the trunks and assembled the sound and lighting system. Now, I only work as a technician; whoever hires me has to hire a driver and porter as well because working times have shortened. You don't go on tours that last months anymore; with the materials you have, you set up a stage in a day, work the event in the evening and take it down the next day. You can't do anything else. Before, they would even ask you to sleep in the truck. Now, to work, they ask for safety certificates, and if you work for the CWC, they call you because everyone in the sector knows that the cooperative offers basic courses to its members. (FGs_technicians_1)

This market sector has proven to be highly polarised in terms of the content and quality of the work.

> […] the creative market is like a curve that plunges downwards. There is a lot of demand for low-quality work and very little demand for really good work. It's not just your skills that get you to the end of the curve; it depends a lot on your networks, both clients and colleagues. You get some jobs only if you've got into certain circuits, and the people in them don't want to let you in. (FGs_technicians_2)

Workers secure better quality jobs not only because of their technical skills but also because they have access to elite networks.

> In Italy, there are two services [the companies that deal with organising and managing artistic events]. The big ones that work for large public and private events. They've always been the same, and they belong to two families that have always worked in this industry. If you get to work with them, you've made it. (FGs_technicians_2)

However, working conditions remain physically challenging in both higher quality and lower quality networks.

> I'm 24 years old, and I'm on pain medication constantly because you're hanging from a rope for hours. That's why you only see young people doing this part of the job; older people can't do it anymore. (FGs_technicians_5)

All three professions are largely affected by a polarisation process and have a *core* populated by work for larger companies with ties to important public and private contractors and a *periphery* of fragmented and occasional jobs. In creative industries, the clients vary significantly in terms of scale, and 'good' clients are mostly large public or private companies; the rest of the field is taken up by a plethora of smaller private clients, which are more likely to have trouble paying on time or to offer less favourable conditions.

5 'Dual' Boundary Work: The Fit Between the Organisation's Strategies and the Workers' Strategies

Thanks to our multi-stage approach, we developed two lines of interpretation for analysing the strategies pursued by the cooperative and the professionals and the inequalities these strategies produce. The people interviewed described the cooperative's approach to *professional* work as reinforcing collaborative mechanisms amongst worker-members and setting up closure against external workers. At the same time, a set of *managerial* practices stimulated competition inside and outside the cooperative. Both logics, professionalism and managerialism, were enacted through a system of practices and a repertoire of actions that work to include or exclude workers based on certain boundaries. These inclusion and exclusion mechanisms generate inequalities amongst workers (see Fig. 10.1).

5.1 Boundary Work as Part of the Cooperative's Strategies

We identified a repertoire of actions performed in the CWC to organise work and manage worker-members internally. This repertoire includes boundary maintenance strategies that unfold through three segmentation mechanisms implemented by the cooperative: recruitment, training, and career development (see Table 10.3).

Recruitment follows the historical boundaries reproduced in these professions. In particular, the profession of lighting and sound technician continues to be male-dominated and involves primarily young people. The exclusion of women and older workers is justified on the basis of two elements. On the one hand, equipment and working methods have used technological innovations to improve quality, thereby decreasing the time required. These improvements have not eliminated the need for physical strength and agility, so these traits continue to be essential for performing such tasks. On the other hand, the work of lighting and sound technicians is organised in such a way as to prioritise the client's need to minimise working time as their primary strategy for cutting costs. The result is a system that is irreconcilable with family commitments and caring responsibilities, which in Italy still falls primarily to women. This profession is thus characterised by a stark gender and age asymmetry.

Training likewise addresses two sets of needs. On the one hand, it creates and sustains the organisation's reputation for promoting workplace safety and for spearheading the provision of safety certifications. This grants the cooperative an important place in a market characterised by high competition and makes it attractive to the public and private actors that produce both local and national cultural events. The organisation

Table 10.3 The cooperative's boundary strategies

CWC's strategies	Photographers	Video makers	Lighting and sound technicians
Recruitment	Open, inclusive boundary	Open, inclusive boundary	Age-based and gender-based boundary: an area in which the concept of physical strength reproduces inequalities
Training	Selective boundary, based on the individual professional's economic capital		
Career development	Selective boundary, based on training and networking		

offers this type of training free of charge to all its members. This service is instrumental for maintaining high-quality standards or, at least, fair pay. On the other hand, the cooperative also offers second-level training focused on learning how to use technical equipment. These are optional courses paid for by the workers themselves. This business model reproduces inequalities based on the socio-economic resources availability, favouring workers who can self-finance specialised training, which in turn opens the door to higher level jobs and better pay. This two-track training system is a factor that contributes towards creating divisions amongst professionals, which leads to groups forming that have a competitive disadvantage inside the same organisation.

Career development follows the boundaries constructed through the managerial strategies pursued in the previous steps, reinforcing segmentation inside and outside the organisation. For example, the cooperative has an organisational practice that involves buying expensive, technologically advanced equipment to be shared amongst workers, especially in the case of video makers and photographers. This practice meets individual workers' needs to keep production costs down by taking advantage of possible economies of scale; nevertheless, it exacerbates the differentiation *between* professional groups based on the equipment needed. It also reproduces the segmentation created in training. Since access to this training depends on workers' economic resources, this practice prevents some of them from developing the skills needed to use complex technologies.

Generally, the tendency to adapt to market demands—such as hiring young men in technical roles—reproduces inequalities inside the cooperative while reinforcing discrimination outside it.

5.2 Boundary Work in Workers' Strategies

As for workers, the empirical evidence pointed to the logics of high and low professionalisation (see Table 10.4). Creative work is often teamwork. The mechanisms triggering collaboration amongst workers involve a selection process that is based on boundaries. Since this sector lacks formal boundaries drawn by legal regulations or rules that establish specific training requirements for certain roles, boundary work is primarily based on each worker's characteristics. In some professional areas, workers tend to give more value to characteristics that are traditionally considered appropriate for the sector. Boundary making is thus based on age and professional experience in addition to gender, with the profession of lighting and sound technician being especially male-dominated. Indeed, age and experience affect the types of jobs to which workers have access. Moreover, the workers who do secure jobs tend to share them with those they see as 'similar', that is, workers with 'standard' characteristics (i.e. young, male, and experienced).

Like other studies (Liu, 2006, 2015, 2018), we found that the size of networks is crucial in counteracting boundary mechanisms. Professionals fight to maintain their jurisdictions while building networks to create distinctive teams and to expand their skill sets in order to provide specialised services. Our focus groups showed that the ability to meet a wide range of professionals makes it easier to have access to more and better jobs. In these processes, technological innovation offers an important space for renegotiation, especially for younger professionals with less social capital who have up-to-date technical skills.

The cooperative is committed to consolidating its reputation—internally and externally—as a response to the boundary-making and boundary-blurring processes enacted by workers. Internally, by maintaining boundaries, it retains its ability to attract new members, confirming the competitive advantage of a managerial choice that is open to different

Table 10.4 Workers' boundary strategies

Workers' strategies	Photographers	Video makers	Lighting and sound technicians
High trajectory	Involving professionals who are recognised as the best fit for the reference market: young men with specialised skills and technical expertise but a limited portfolio, which decreases their chances to compete for legitimacy and reputation in the market	Involving flexible professionals that accept difficult working conditions: young men, excluding older workers and women with caregiving responsibilities	Involving professionals who are recognised as the best fit for the reference market: young men, excluding older workers and women
Low trajectory	Offering low-quality jobs Favouring the selection of workers outside the networks, with limited training, whose careers are stuck at the bottom of the ladder		

types of professionals. The mechanisms for bringing professionals together and fostering collaboration ensure a high engagement amongst worker-members, especially the highly qualified professionals that had been excluded from high-quality networks before joining the organisation. Externally, both mechanisms reinforce the cooperative's leadership position in the market, securing a range of professional services that are highly diversified in terms of quantity and quality.

As the fieldwork revealed, many workers conveyed a positive narrative about being members of the CWC. They acknowledged that membership brought them instrumental benefits, particularly in consolidating their professional legitimacy. This legitimacy is fostered, for instance, by the practice of setting 'recommended' minimum fees or giving worker-members the chance to attend training courses and earn the certification stipulated by occupational safety regulations. As a matter of fact, by establishing formal parameters for accessing the market, this kind of certification distinguishes professionals from non-professionals. In so doing, the CWC protects its members against 'similar' workers leading 'invasions' of the market (Noordegraaf, 2015). To this end, it acts through professional closure regimes (Boussard, 2018).

6 Conclusions

The analysis carried out in the previous pages has brought to light the strategies that the cooperative and its worker-members, namely creative workers, use to produce and reproduce boundaries. Moreover, it has shown that one of the purposes of maintaining these boundaries is to ensure the organisation's survival. The segmentation of the internal labour supply prevents the accumulation of a 'reserve army of labour' that is stuck in less-skilled jobs and forced to accept precarious employment terms based on number of clients rather than job quality. At the same time, it produces professional elites.

A counterintuitive result is that, although the organisation claims to be 'inclusive' and to be guided by 'horizontal' principles in structuring the relationship between the management and the membership, its activities produce and reproduce mechanisms of internal differentiation. These mechanisms act as boundaries that draw lines of discrimination that divide workers based on objective characteristics such as gender and age.

Although symbolic and social boundaries are factors that exacerbate inequalities in all three of the professional areas analysed, we found that the intensity of boundary work varies by profession. For video makers and photographers, the falling cost of equipment has reduced the push to engage in boundary work, encouraging a progressive increase in the number of low-capital workers in these professions. Conversely, the importance of physical strength means that the lighting and sound technician profession remains a persistently male-dominated group.

This case study has outlined how multi-professional organisations, such as mutual aid cooperatives of creative workers, operate as agents of differentiation within and between professions. Furthermore, it has emphasised the intersecting character of these two dimensions of differentiation processes. The *between* dimension is inherent to the multi-professional nature of such organisations. Indeed, the professional groups have differential weights in the organisation, which in turn exacerbates differentiation, for example, when expensive technical equipment is bought and shared to support specific categories of workers. This mechanism also produces differentiation *between* those operating inside and outside the organisation, but *within* the same professional group. Other mechanisms based on managerial and professional strategies operate to differentiate workers *within* their professional group. Further reflection would nevertheless be needed on how organisations with a 'mutual' character, which have the purpose of counterbalancing the deficiencies of welfare states, contribute to building collective narratives in competitive occupational ecosystems, such as creative labour (see Bellini & Lucciarini, 2019), and reconstructing solidarity in an individualised society: the vision that in this book is referred to as the *beyond* dimension.

Acknowledgements We would like to thank Dr Antonio Corasaniti and Prof. Luisa De Vita for collaborating in conducting the focus groups. Prof. De Vita also made worthwhile contributions to discussions about the research results, particularly concerning boundary-making and boundary-blurring dynamics. This chapter has been developed within the framework of the *Researching Precariousness across the Paid-Unpaid Work Continuum* ERC Advanced Grant, funded by the European Research Council under the Horizon 2020 programme (Grant Agreement No. 833577), with Valeria Pulignano as principal investigator.

References

Alacevich, F., Bellini, A., & Tonarelli, A. (2017). *Una professione plurale: il caso dell'avvocatura fiorentina*. Firenze University Press.

Alvehus, J., Eklund, S., & Kastberg, G. (2021). To strengthen or to shatter? On the effects of stratification on professions as systems. *Public Administration, 99*(2), 371–386. https://doi.org/10.1111/padm.12695

Bellini, A., & Lucciarini, S. (2019). Not only riders: The uncertain boundaries of digital creative work as a frontier for emerging actors in interest representation. *PACO, 12*(3), 845–870.

Bellini, A., & Maestripieri, L. (2018). Professions within, between and beyond. Varieties of professionalism in a globalising world. *Cambio. Rivista sulle Trasformazioni Sociali, 8*(16), 5–14. https://doi.org/10.13128/cambio-24947

Boussard, V. (2018). Professional closure regimes in the global age: The boundary work of professional services specializing in mergers and acquisitions. *Journal of Professions and Organization, 5*(3), 279–296. https://doi.org/10.1093/jpo/joy013

Bucher, S. V., Chreim, S., Langley, A., & Reay, T. (2016). Contestation about collaboration: Discursive boundary work among professionals. *Organization Studies, 37*(4), 497–522.

Conover, P., Crewe, I., & Searing, D. (1991). The nature of citizenship in the United States and Great Britain: Empirical comments on theoretical themes. *Journal of Politics, 53*(3), 800–832. https://doi.org/10.2307/2131580

Cucca, R., & Maestripieri, L. (2016). Architects and consultants between formal regulation and organised professionalism. *Cambio. Rivista sulle Trasformazioni Sociali, 4*(7), 25–39. https://doi.org/10.13128/cambio-19231

Evetts, J. (2011). A new professionalism? Challenges and opportunities. *Current Sociology, 59*(4), 406–422. https://doi.org/10.1177/0011392111402585

Evetts, J. (2013). Professionalism: value and ideology. *Current Sociology, 61*(5–6), 778–796. https://doi.org/10.1177/0011392113479316

Franzini, M., & Lucciarini, S. (2022). The social costs of the gig economy and institutional responses. Forms of institutional bricolage in Italy, France and The Netherlands. In E. Armano, M. Briziarelli, & E. Risi (Eds.), *Digital platforms and algorithmic subjectivities* (pp. 227–239). University of Westminster Press.

Freidson, E. (2001). *Professionalism, the third logic: On the practice of knowledge.* University of Chicago Press.

Gallie, D. (Ed.). (2013). *Economic crisis, quality of work, and social integration: The European experience.* Oxford University Press.

Gamson, W. A. (1992). The social psychology of collective action. In A. D. Morris & C. M. Mueller (Eds.), *Frontiers in social movement theory* (pp. 53–76). Yale University Press.

Gieryn, T. F. (1983). Boundary-work and the demarcation of science from non-science: Strains and interests in professional ideologies of scientists. *American Sociological Review, 48*(6), 781–795.

Giullari, B., & Lucciarini, S. (2023). Same job, different conditions. Comparing direct and indirect employment via procurement in public services in Italy, Rassegna Italiana di Sociologia, Mulino, Bologna.

Heite, C. (2012). Setting and crossing boundaries: Professionalization of social work and social work professionalism. *Social Work and Society, 10*(2)., online. https://doi.org/10.5167/uzh-85442

Heusinkveld, S., Gabbioneta, C., Werr, A., & Sturdy, A. (2018). Professions and (new) management occupations as a contested terrain: Redefining jurisdictional claims. *Journal of Professions and Organization, 5*(3), 248–261.

Horowitz, S. (2021). *Mutualism: Building the next economy from the ground up.* Random House.

Kitzinger, J. (1995). Qualitative research: Introducing focus groups. *British Medical Journal, 311*, 299–302. https://doi.org/10.1136/bmj.311.7000.299

Lamont, M. (2017). *Prisms of inequality: Moral boundaries, exclusion, and academic evaluation*. Praemium Erasmianum Essay.

Lamont, M., & Molnar, V. (2002). The study of boundaries in the social sciences. *Annual Review of Sociology, 28*, 167–195. https://doi.org/10.1146/annurev.soc.28.110601.141107

Liu, S. (2006). Client influence and the contingency of professionalism: The work of elite corporate lawyers in China. *Law & Society Review, 40*(4), 751–781. https://doi.org/10.1111/j.1540-5893.2006.00280.x

Liu, S. (2015). Boundary work and exchange: The formation of a professional service market. *Symbolic Interaction, 38*(1), 1–21. https://doi.org/10.1002/symb.137

Liu, S. (2018). Boundaries and professions: Toward a processual theory of action. *Journal of Professions and Organization, 5*(1), 45–57. https://doi.org/10.1093/jpo/jox012

Maestripieri, L., & Cucca, R. (2018). Small is beautiful? Emerging organizational strategies among Italian professionals. *Canadian Review of Sociology, 55*(3), 362–384. https://doi.org/10.1111/cars.12208

McAfee, A., & Brynjolfsson, E. (2017). *Machine, platform, crowd: Harnessing our digital future*. W. W. Norton.

Murgia, A., & de Heusch, S. (2020). It started with the artists and now it concerns everyone: The case of Smart, a cooperative of "salaried autonomous workers". In S. Taylor & S. Luckman (Eds.), *Pathways into creative working lives* (pp. 211–230). Palgrave Macmillan.

Noordegraaf, M. (2009). Dynamic conservatism: The rise and evolution of public management reforms in The Netherlands. In S. Goldfinch & J. Wallis (Eds.), *International handbook of public management reform* (pp. 262–278). Edward Elgar.

Noordegraaf, M. (2011). Risky business: How professionals and professional fields (must) deal with organizational issues. *Organization Studies, 32*(10), 1349–1371. https://doi.org/10.1177/0170840611416748

Noordegraaf, M. (2015). Hybrid professionalism and beyond: (New) Forms of public professionalism in changing organizational and societal contexts. *Journal of Professions and Organization, 2*(2), 187–206. https://doi.org/10.1093/jpo/jov002

Parding, K., Bellini, A., & Maestripieri, L. (2021). Heterogeneity among professions and professionals. *Professions and Professionalism, 11*(1), e4398. https://doi.org/10.7577/pp.4398

Pernicka, S. (2006). Organizing the self-employed: Theoretical considerations and empirical findings. *European Journal of Industrial Relations, 12*(2), 123–140. https://doi.org/10.1177/0959680106065024

Smith, S., & Ward, V. (2015). The role of boundary maintenance and blurring in a UK collaborative research project: How researchers and health service managers made sense of new ways of working. *Social Science & Medicine, 130*, 225–233. https://doi.org/10.1016/j.socscimed.2015.02.023

Smithson, J. (2000). Using and analysing focus groups: Limitations and possibilities. *International Journal of Social Research Methodology, 3*(2), 103–119. https://doi.org/10.1080/136455700405172

Waring, J. (2014). Restratification, hybridity and professional elites: Questions of power, identity and relational contingency at the points of "professional–organisational intersection". *Sociology Compass, 8*(6), 688–704. https://doi.org/10.1111/soc4.12178

Waring, J., & Bishop, S. (2013). McDonaldization or commercial re-stratification: Corporatization and the multimodal organization of English doctors. *Social Science & Medicine, 82*, 147–155. https://doi.org/10.1016/j.socscimed.2012.12.023

Williamson, O. E. (1979). Transaction-cost economics: The governance of contractual relations. *Journal of Law and Economics, 22*(2), 233–261.

Open Access This chapter is licensed under the terms of the Creative Commons Attribution 4.0 International License (http://creativecommons.org/licenses/by/4.0/), which permits use, sharing, adaptation, distribution and reproduction in any medium or format, as long as you give appropriate credit to the original author(s) and the source, provide a link to the Creative Commons license and indicate if changes were made.

The images or other third party material in this chapter are included in the chapter's Creative Commons license, unless indicated otherwise in a credit line to the material. If material is not included in the chapter's Creative Commons license and your intended use is not permitted by statutory regulation or exceeds the permitted use, you will need to obtain permission directly from the copyright holder.

Part III

Beyond

11

The Changing Nature of Profession-State Relations in Canada: The Persistence of Self-Regulation in the Context of Reform, 1960–2010

Tracey L. Adams

1 Introduction

In the west, traditional meanings and structures of professionalism have been contested over the last 50 years and professionals' roles in society are being redefined. Professional authority and autonomy have been challenged by a wide range of societal stakeholders, including politicians and other state actors, consumers, managers and other leaders in professional workplaces, as well as lower-status workers seeking to increase their social influence and market position (see also Chaps. 6 and 8). Professionals' claims to apply their knowledge and expertise in the service of the public interest have been regarded sceptically, and dramatic scandals have provided periodic evidence of their failure to meet their public interest obligations (Saks, 2015; Eyal, 2019).

T. L. Adams (✉)
University of Western Ontario, London, ON, Canada
e-mail: tladams@uwo.ca

© The Author(s), under exclusive license to Springer Nature Switzerland AG 2023

L. Maestripieri, A. Bellini (eds.), *Professionalism and Social Change*,
https://doi.org/10.1007/978-3-031-31278-6_11

At the same time, expertise remains crucial to western economies, and regulating professional work in the public interest continues to be essential. Experts who are engaged in practices that carry potential risks to the public and society—especially in fields like health, law, engineering, and several others—continue to be governed by state legislation and legislated bodies charged with monitoring professionals' work to ensure it is conducted competently and ethically in the public interest. Despite calls for deregulation in some locales, professional regulation persists, since completely unregulated markets are believed to carry risks that endanger the public (Freidson, 2001). In this sense professional regulation remains an important contested social practice that extends 'beyond professionalism' and reflects the continuing importance of professional expertise and practice within western societies.

There is little agreement, however, about how expert work is best regulated. Structures of professional regulation vary cross-nationally—and in some locales cross-regionally—and across professions. In Anglo-American countries, self-regulation was historically the norm. Bodies composed predominantly of professionals made key decisions about entry into practice and the conduct of practice, also overseeing complaints and discipline. Self-regulation was highly contested in the late twentieth and early twenty-first centuries, leading to legislative change that has reduced, although not entirely eliminated, professionals' ability to have a voice in their regulation. The trend appears to be towards systems of co-regulation where state leaders and lay members play predominant roles (Leslie et al., 2018). Still, regulatory best practices continue to be debated.

This chapter explores professional regulation in Canada, where self-regulation has taken a different form than in some other countries and where it has persisted longer. More specifically, I explore regulatory change in two provinces, Ontario and British Columbia, over a 50-year span of time (1960–2010). Patterns of professional regulation extend 'beyond professionalism' and specifically reflect professions' relations with society. These relations are being redefined as social values and the interests of various stakeholders—including professionals, the state, and consumers—are changing in a context of declining public trust.

2 Theorising Professions and Professional Regulation

Within sociological research on professions, it has become the norm to focus on experts and expertise rather than professionals (Eyal, 2019). Nonetheless, only some experts are regulated by statute in a manner that allows them a voice over their own affairs, and these—in Canada at least—are commonly called professions. This chapter treats professions as occupations requiring advanced education, training, and expertise that are regulated by state legislation establishing bodies to govern their practice. Self-regulating professions are those that have a voice in their own regulation: bodies comprised of professionals (and members of the public) make key decisions about professional governance, guided by legislation and state (or state-sanctioned) oversight bodies. In Canada, professions have enjoyed a particular form of self-regulation wherein all practitioners are incorporated into a 'college' or association that is governed by a council/board comprised of professionals and members of the public. Regulation varies cross-regionally in the country, but historically professionals made up the majority of board members, and most of these professionals were elected by their peers. Such structures aimed to establish democratic processes and avoid the pitfalls of nepotism (Adams, 2018), but they are increasingly viewed as outdated (Cayton, 2018).

Scholars seeking to understand professional regulation—both past and present—have drawn on a variety of theories, with neo-Weberian approaches being the most influential. Professional privileges, generally, and regulatory privileges, specifically, are the product of social closure processes whereby professionals succeed in cutting off access to education, training, and entry into practice. To achieve social closure, professionals organise and appeal to the state for legislation that allows them to limit access to skills and opportunities and to enhance market privileges (Saks, 2015). Historically, several professions like medicine and law succeeded in achieving social closure and benefitted accordingly.

While the concept of social closure provides a description of a set of processes that are important to the creation of professions, it cannot effectively explain how these processes played out historically. Several accounts either have the state simply acceding to professionals' requests for power unquestioningly, or negotiating a 'regulative bargain', whereby legislators granted professionals power in exchange for the promise that they would use their powers in the public interest (Macdonald, 1995). Although there was certainly an expectation that self-regulating professions would govern in the public interest, regulatory outcomes were a great deal more controversial and fraught than such accounts imply (Adams, 2018). To understand these processes better, some scholars have returned to Weber, this time to draw on his theories of social action (Adams & Saks, 2018). Weber has argued that much of social action is rational, in that it is goal-oriented (Weber, 1968). The most common types of goal-oriented actions are instrumentally rational actions—aimed at achieving calculated ends that are generally material in nature—and value-rational actions, focused on achieving more intrinsic and less material goals or that act in accordance with values (Weber, 1968). Research drawing on this theory has explored the complex and changing reasons why state actors delegate regulatory authority to certain professions at specific points in time and what political, economic goals, and social values have shaped their activity. A neo-Weberian action approach also sheds light on the complexity of professionals' efforts, acknowledging that professionals' drive for self-regulation is not simply about enhancing their power, but is shaped by social values including the public interest (Adams & Saks, 2018; Bonnin, 2019), as well as the intersection of class, gender, and race (Adams, 2018).

Weber's concepts of social action and social closure help to shed light on regulatory processes and outcomes, but they are predominantly focused at the micro level. To understand the macro-level contexts in which these processes occur, it is helpful to draw on Abbott's (1988; 2005) ecological approach. Abbott (1988) has argued that professions exist in an ecology or system, within which they jockey for jurisdiction; that is, they battle for control over a scope of practice or field of activity by appealing to a variety of audiences, including the state, the public, workplaces, and others. For Abbott, developments within the ecology of professions are driven by interprofessional conflicts (Abbott, 1988), as well as by the interplay between activities in that ecology and ecologies linked to it, such as the state, or education and healthcare systems (Abbott, 2005). Later writers have emphasised that collaboration and alliances within and across ecologies are also important (Adams, 2007, 2018). Indeed, Abbott (2005) has argued that when it comes to regulation, it is at those moments where regulatory solutions address concerns within both state and professional ecologies that change is most likely to occur.

Combining neo-Weberian and ecological theory enables us to understand the broader contexts in which social action and social closure processes occur. Nevertheless, Abbott does not fully illuminate how linked ecologies have changed over time, and how they differ across social and historical contexts. Here it is helpful to bring in Light's (1995) concept of *countervailing powers*—the idea that once a party accumulates sufficient power, other parties will mobilise to counter them and diminish their influence. Light (1995) has applied this concept to understanding changes in healthcare, and especially the declining influence of dominant professions such as medicine in the late twentieth century, brought about by a constellation of actors: politicians, consumer and occupational groups, managers, and others. Light's concept draws our attention to a wide range of actors that shape professional and regulatory change and to the increasingly important role of consumers and other stakeholders in shaping regulatory processes. It is not simply professionals, state actors, and their linked ecologies that determine regulatory outcomes, but a wide variety of goal-oriented individuals and groups, influenced by changing social values. Many of the latter are decidedly reform-minded, seeking to reduce professional power, with some groups endeavouring to advance their own claims to power and influence.

This combined theory helps illuminate processes of professional regulation and regulatory change—shedding light on the actors and motivations that shape regulation, as well as the contexts in which it occurs. It highlights the roles of actors and social-historical context, as well as the centrality of relationships to regulation. Professions are embedded within institutions and ecologies. It is the relationships between and among professional groups, state actors, consumers, within and across these institutions (within, between, and beyond professionalism), which shape processes of change and power inequalities. Even as their collective power declines, professions remain important societal institutions, and professional practice continues to be a key focus of state and social oversight.

3 Professional Regulation and Change in Canada

As noted above, in Canada most professions are regulated at the provincial level; who is regulated and how varies from one province to another. In several provinces, regulatory legislation recognises *colleges* (especially in the area of health) or *associations/societies*. All registered/licenced practitioners belong to one of these organisational entities, which are each governed by a council (or board). Members of these regulatory councils may be elected or appointed, but it has been common for professionals to elect at least some of their number to the boards that govern them, in line with the principles of democracy which guided early profession formation in Canada (Adams, 2018). Traditional professions were truly self-regulating in this respect. Since it was the state that delegated these powers of self-regulation to the professions, they were accountable to it, but the degree of oversight was variable, and not typically high.

Although these structures have always had their critics, professional regulatory bodies were often regarded as valued social institutions that enabled professionals to govern in both their own interests and the public's interests, with state actors and the public occasionally reining professionals in to remind them of their public responsibilities. The establishment of professions was important in Canada's early days as a country. With a small population spread across a large territory, a small nascent state, and government that only sat for a few weeks a year, professions helped to extend governance and order at no cost to the state, since they were self-funding (Adams, 2018).

This system of professional regulation was regularly tweaked throughout the late nineteenth and early twentieth centuries, but its fundamental essence did not change. It came up against its first strong challenges in Canada, as well as in other countries (Saks, 2015), beginning in the 1960s and over subsequent decades. At this time, forces outside professions—from counter-culture and civil rights movements, changes to the health sector wrought by the emergence of publicly funded healthcare and other changes, increasing specialisation and the rise of new healthcare occupations and professions, and consumer-advocacy movements—combined with trends within professions to generate winds of change.

In the remainder of this chapter, I focus on the nature of these changes, paying particular attention to trends in professional self-regulation in Canada, through a focus on two provinces—Ontario and British Columbia (BC). I examine how social change, tensions within the ecology of the professions, and various stakeholders (professions, the state, and consumers) shaped regulatory change. Research questions include the following:

1. How did professional regulation in these two Canadian provinces change in the 50-year period between 1960 and 2010?
2. How did attitudes (and values) surrounding professional self-regulation alter during this period?

4 A Brief Note on Methodology and Sources

To address these research questions and shed light on processes of change in professional regulation I use historical methods, analysing historical documents including legislation and government-commissioned reports on professional regulation, as well as relevant legislative debates in British Columbia and Ontario between 1960 and 2010. These historical documents not only reveal what was regulated and when, but the values and concerns that drove regulation and regulatory change in the past. This analysis sheds light on shifting social values and countervailing powers and looks 'beyond professionalism' to explore professions' relationships with the state and other social institutions.

Initially, all (477) acts passed in the two provinces respecting professional regulation between 1960 and 2010 were identified and reviewed, as were the debates surrounding this legislation; legislative trends over time were also mapped. Subsequently, the findings of six policy commissions in the two provinces were analysed. Analysis of documents was both descriptive and thematic. The thematic analyses revealed the changing nature of professionalism and the changing role of expertise in society in the late twentieth and early twenty-first centuries.

The findings, presented in the following sections, highlight trends by era.

5 Findings

5.1 The 1960s and 1970s

In Canada, as elsewhere, the 1960s represented a time of significant social change where a wide variety of voices questioned prevailing social institutions and the systems of social inequality they reproduced and upheld. Professions were one of the dominant social institutions challenged by the civil rights movement, which raised questions about professional powers, limited access to professional careers, and uneven access to professional services. State actors faced rising costs and were challenged by grassroots movements demanding change. The decision to implement a publicly funded healthcare system in Canada generated concerns about costs and inefficiencies, at least some of which were blamed on professionals and the prevailing system of professional regulation which was not designed with efficiency as an overarching goal. These trends (and others) collided to generate considerable debate in the 1970s and in subsequent decades, and in some instances led to regulatory change.

With respect to professional regulation, by 1960 the pattern of regulation in Canada was well-established. A list of self-regulating professions in both provinces in 1960 is provided in Table 11.1, along with the dates these professions first became self-regulating. Early professions established in the late nineteenth century included law, medicine, dentistry, pharmacy, and land surveying. As European settlers moved into British Columbia later than Ontario, BC established self-regulating professions later on. In the early twentieth century, the number of self-regulating professions in each province expanded to include a variety of building and resource professions, as well as other allied and alternative health occupations. The latter were initially granted only limited powers of self-regulation. In the period immediately following the Second World War, a variety of new professions were established, not only in healthcare but in accounting, forestry, and agrology. Some new professions provided support for, or worked in tandem with, earlier professions including dental technicians and licenced/registered practical nurses.

Table 11.1 Self-regulating professions (closed and reserved title) to 1960

Profession	BC	Ontario
Lawyers	1874	1797
Medical Doctors	1886	(1839) 1869
Dentists	1886	1868
Pharmacists	1891	1871
Land Surveyors	1891	1892
Architects	1920	1890
Chartered Accountants	1905	1882
Engineers	1918	1922
Veterinary Medicine	1901	1920
Optometrists	1920	1919
Nurses	1918	1922
Drugless Practitioners	(Naturopathy)	1925
Osteopaths	(Med Act 1909)	(under DP Act)
Chiropractors	1934	(DP Act), 1991
Chiropodists/Podiatrists	1929	(DP Act), 1944
Naturopaths	1936	(DP Act), 2007
Funeral Directors & Embalmers		1928
Miscellaneous other accountants	1945, 1951	1926, 1941
Physiotherapy (& Massage Therapy)	1946	DP
Music Teachers	1947	1946
Professional Foresters	1947	1957
Agrology	1947	1960
Dental Technicians	1958	1946
Teachers	1987	1968
Psychiatric Nursing	1951	n/a
Practical Nurses	1951 (1964)	1947 (1963)
Notaries	1956	n/a
Interior decorators/designers	n/a	1956
Dieticians	2002	1958

The first seven rows of Table 11.2 show the new professions created between 1960 and 1979—a very small number. Only psychologists and radiological technicians were first regulated in both provinces during this two-decade period. Opticians, landscape architects, denturists, and social workers began to be regulated in one province, with legislation following in the other province several decades later. Although a number of acts regulating professions were passed in this era, they typically only tweaked the regulation of existing professions, rather than regulating new professions. This was a period of reflection and debate about the purposes and

Table 11.2 New self-regulating professions, 1960–1979

Profession	British Columbia	Ontario
Psychologists	1977	1960
Opticians	1994	1961
Radiological Technicians	1966	1963
Landscape Architecture	1968	1984
Denturists	1995	1974
Social workers	1968	1998
Interior decorators/designers	n/a	1984
Engineering Technicians and Technologists	1985	1984
Midwifery	1998	1991
Audiology & Speech Pathology	2008	1991
Massage Therapists	1994	1991
Occupational Therapists	1998	1991
Dental Hygienists	1995	1991
Respiratory Therapists	n/a	1991
Geoscientists	1993	2000
Traditional Chinese Medicine & Acupuncture	2000/1996	2006
Applied Biology	2003	n/a

goals of professional regulation and of systematic reviews being made of existing regulatory policy. These reviews informed subsequent regulatory change. It is worth looking at these reviews and the issues they raised in more detail to get a sense of the values, conflicts, and concerns of this period.

There were several major commissions that produced reports during this period, including the federal *Royal Commission on Health Services* (1961 to 1964), the detailed investigations conducted by Ontario's *Committee on the Healing Arts* (1966–1970), BC's *Foulkes Commission into Health Security for British Columbians* (1972–1973), and Ontario's *Royal Commission Inquiry into Civil Rights* (1964–1971). These reports were the results of considerable research and consultation with a variety of stakeholders, and hence reflect prevailing thought about self-regulation in this era. Their recommendations shaped regulatory legislation moving forward. The federal Royal Commission on Health Services report was primarily important for its impact on the other health commissions and the rise of Medicare in Canada, generally. This Commission (also known as the Hall Commission) examined healthcare services, facilities, supply and demand of professionals in Canada, with particular attention to issues including costs and financing, system improvements, training, and the best use of health services personnel (Hall, 1965). A variety of health professional practices were reviewed, and in some cases recommendations for expansion and licencing were advanced. Not only did this Commission lead to publicly funded healthcare in Canada, but its in-depth look at health services encouraged provinces like Ontario and British Columbia to take a closer look at the healthcare system and the professions working within it.

Ontario's *McRuer Commission Inquiry into Civil Rights* examined all the laws and statutes of the province, so its scope was not limited to professional regulation; however, McRuer did conduct a full review of regulatory legislation and published a detailed and influential evaluation of self-regulating professions in the early 1960s (there were 22 such professions at the time). McRuer confirmed that professional self-regulation was "a delegation of legislative and judicial functions" from the state to professional bodies, and there was only one justification for this delegation—that these powers were exercised in "the public interest" (McRuer, 1968, p. 1162). McRuer was critical of professional self-regulation in some respects. He identified discriminatory practices within professions, and he found that laws, structures, and state oversight were variable and inconsistent. He had great concerns about disciplinary mechanisms, questioning why "extensive judicial powers" were placed in "the hands of persons who have little to no judicial experience" (1184). Nonetheless, he ultimately supported self-regulation with more oversight and public participation. McRuer opposed the extension of self-regulation to what he called 'technical occupations'; however, he supported the continuing independence of existing self-regulating professions, as long as public members were appointed to governing councils, and the government supervised regulatory activities. The latter changes would ensure that regulators prioritised the public interest. At the same time, he recommended that disciplinary powers be removed from individual regulators, and that instead, these should be centralised in a Professions Disciplinary Tribunal, comprised of representatives of the professions.

These recommendations reflect the dissatisfaction of many stakeholders—and especially of the public—with the existing systems of self-regulation. Further, they reflect a desire to alter the prevailing relationships between professions and society. At the same time, these reports continued to endorse self-regulation, with increased accountability to government and the public. Only some of McRuer's recommendations were adopted: specifically, changes to add public members to regulatory boards and increased state oversight. Various other changes (deregulating technical occupations, centralised discipline) are still being discussed in some corners, over half a century later. The McRuer report is important in signalling the principle that professional regulation should be guided by principles of fairness, equity, and accountability, as well as the public interest, and that regulation should become more standardised so that each profession is on a similar footing.

Ontario's Committee on the Healing Arts (1970, p. 29) also underscored that professional self-government was "a delegation from the state" and that it "imposes on the profession … a corresponding trust to see that the right is exercised in the public interest". This latter point was emphasised: "It cannot be overemphasised that *primacy of the public interest* must be the cornerstone of any regulatory structure". The Committee also stressed that self-regulating professions should remain autonomous and not micro-managed by government. Nonetheless, state oversight was needed: "society can no longer afford to tolerate a total abdication by government of the right to guide, direct, and in some areas, become directly involved in the affairs of the professions" (Ibid.). The Committee also emphasised the need for more inter-professional collaboration, signalling that conflict within the professional ecology had become a problem for the state ecology, prompting reform. Although the Committee endorsed continuing self-regulation, it cautioned against the creation of new self-regulating professions, arguing that new professions should only be created if "it is clearly established that the public interest demands it" (p. 45). Moreover, it was recommended that many occupations linked to health (from dental hygienists and pharmacy assistants, to opticians, physiotherapists, chiropractors, and others) be regulated under one amalgamated board (the Health Disciplines Regulation Board). With respect to other changes, the Committee recommended more public membership on regulatory boards and more standardisation. Finally, they asserted that professions needed to recognise that their interests and those of the public might differ, and their overriding consideration needed to be the public interest.

Reflecting widespread attitudes at the time, the Committee on the Healing Arts was critical of both the government and professions, but ultimately endorsed professional self-regulation, especially for long-established professions, with an alternative structure for regulating other practices.

Finally, British Columbia's Foulkes Commission had a slightly different mandate as it focused on health services, with the goal of enhancing co-ordination and efficiency. Controversially, the report recommended "a complete re-organization of services including integration of all levels of Health and Human Resources" (Foulkes, 1973, p. III-5-3). Moreover, Foulkes recommended a redistribution of power, which he saw as being too centralised in "the hands of politicians, bureaucrats, professionals (especially the medical profession), and businessmen [sic]" (p. 3). His recommendations included diminishing the role of dominant professions and increasing the voice of subordinate professionals and consumers, in part through establishing a Health Disciplines Regulation board to oversee the professional regulators, as professions had been left to operate with too little oversight. Nonetheless, Foulkes continued to endorse self-regulation. For him, "the key task … is to establish a framework … under which the professions … accept public regulation & accountability … without crushing professional autonomy and pride" and without lowering service quality (Foulkes, 1973 p. III-5–8).

Combined, these various reports provided a clear blueprint with respect to regulation for state actors, but the response from politicians was half-hearted at best. On one extreme, the Foulkes report was highly criticised and its controversial suggestions largely buried in the face of medical opposition and government resistance. In Ontario, only some recommendations from The Committee on the Healing Arts and the McRuer Commission were eventually adopted, including the enhancement of state oversight and the participation of lay members on regulatory boards.

Ontario's *Health Disciplines Act* (1974) brought several professions under one legislative umbrella (medicine, dentistry, pharmacy, nursing, and optometry), introduced lay members to regulatory councils and committees, and subjected these professional groups to tighter oversight by the Minister of Health. Legislation was also passed to create a Health Disciplines Board to oversee cases and hear appeals concerning complaints, discipline, and registration at the colleges. Professionals protested about this diminishing their self-regulation (CMAJ, 1974), but they continued to manage their own affairs despite additional layers of oversight. Parallel changes to professional regulation were not made in BC following Foulkes' recommendations.

5.2 The 1980s–1990s

Many of the trends shaping regulatory debates in the 1960s and 1970s were carried into the following decades. Consumer movements challenged professional authority. The emergence of new specialisations, including technicians and assistants, some of whom sought professional status, combined with existing inter-professional tensions to spur inter-professional conflict. Legislators continued to grapple with how to reform professional regulation in a manner that increased fairness and effectiveness but that satisfied multiple stakeholders within and across ecologies that were seeking regulatory change. Although the recommendations of McRuer, Foulkes, and the Committee on the Healing Arts were relatively recent, governments established additional commissions to guide further change. In Ontario, a Professional Organizations Committee was established in 1976 by the Attorney General's office and the Ontario Law Reform Commission to review professional regulation in accountancy, architecture, engineering, and the law (Trebilcock et al., 1979). This Committee's recommendations shaped regulatory discussions in the 1980s. Ontario also established the *Health Professions Legislative Review* whose 1989 report was the foundation for redrawing legislation regarding the regulation of health professions in the province in the early 1990s under the umbrella of the *Regulated Health Professions Act* (RHPA, 1991). This legislation expanded who was regulated, standardised how they were regulated by bringing them under one piece of legislation, and partly shifted the focus, regulating the activities performed rather than the practitioner. In British Columbia, the Health Professions Council was established by legislation to determine which new health professions should become self-regulating, and subsequently "to review the scopes of practice of 15 regulated health professions and to review the legislation under which 10 of them were self-regulating" (HPC, 2002). Despite the evident appetite for reform, legislators and policymakers continued to endorse professional self-regulation, arguing that it was consistent with the public interest.

Table 11.2 summarises new professions regulated in Ontario and British Columbia from 1970 to the early 2000s. Few new professions were established in the 1980s: those that were newly legislated (engineering technicians and technologists, interior designers) were granted restricted titles only.

More sweeping change occurred in the 1990s with an expansion of regulated healthcare professions—including midwifery, audiology, speech-language pathology, occupational therapy, traditional Chinese medicine, and acupuncture. Massage therapy and dental hygiene had previously been regulated under other acts but acquired their own legislation and the right to self-regulate. The significant expansion of health professions in this era is perhaps ironic given the advice given by several commissions against creating new self-regulating professions. Governments in both provinces, however, were open to expanding professional self-regulation in the early 1990s, influenced by professional and consumer lobbying.

Regulating more health professions served at least four aims during this period. First, it addressed inter-professional conflict in the ecology of professions and the lobbying activities of a variety of groups seeking regulated status. Second, it addressed consumer concerns about choice, allowing them "a range of safe options" when choosing health providers (HPLR, 1989, p. 2). Third, it addressed lingering concerns about fairness. For example, the regulation of midwifery and the removal of dental hygienists' regulation from the regulatory control of dentists were both viewed as enhancing gender equity. Fourth, a shift in how regulation was accomplished—through regulations under general legislation in British

Columbia and through umbrella legislation focused on controlled acts in Ontario (and later British Columbia)—provided an opportunity for expansion. The shift to controlled acts was an innovation adopted in several Canadian provinces, beginning with Ontario. A number of "controlled acts" (specific activities undertaken by health professionals such as making a diagnosis or conducting a procedure below the dermis) were identified, to be shared by a variety of professions, instead of granting groups exclusive scopes of practice. As legislation shifted to cover a wide range of practitioners who might engage in such acts during the course of their work, there was opportunity to extend regulation. The latter shift was intended to facilitate "flexibility" in order to ensure that "health services are delivered with maximum efficiency" (HPLR, 1989, p. 2).

In British Columbia, after a review by a government-appointed body, the Health Professions Council, the *Health Professions Act* (1990) provided a mechanism "to establish self-governing powers for a variety of health professions" that had up until then been unregulated. Legislators argued that the act would allow "more efficient" means of regulation and improve standardisation and government oversight (BC Hansard, 1990). Such legislation reflects continuing emphasis on efficiency within social and government discourse. In subsequent years the act was expanded to bring existing professions that had previously had separate acts under the legislation.

The Regulated Health Professions Act recognised and regulated 22 health professions in Ontario and was the result of extensive consultation with a wide variety of stakeholders. All regulatory councils had public members and were subject to oversight from the Ministry of Health and a Health Professions Review and Appeal Board, which monitors complaints and discipline, as well as other processes. Mechanisms were set in place for groups that might seek professional status in the future. In Ontario the Health Professions Regulatory Advisory Committee (HPRAC) was established to conduct investigations and advise the Ministry (it was disbanded in 2021). HPRAC served a similar function to British Columbia's Health Professions Council (1991–2002)—investigating aspiring professional groups' requests for self-regulation and advising the Minister of Health.

This was a period of considerable reform, in which the entire regulatory system was up for review, in response to inter-professional conflict and dissatisfaction with prevailing practices. Regulatory changes impacted not only inter-professional relations (between professionalism) but also the place of professions in society (beyond professionalism). However, key stakeholders continued to support principles of self-regulation. For instance, the HPLR (1989, p. 13) report stated that "The complex and specialised nature of professional work demands that professionals play a role in their own regulation. … Self-regulation is the regulatory system of choice for Ontario." At the same time the review asserted—like many of those that preceded it—that oversight was required to "safeguard the public interest". The Professions Organization Committee (1979) arrived at a similar conclusion, but cautioned that self-regulation should be rare and "justified only by the most compelling circumstances" (Trebilcock et al., 1979, p. 20). The Health Professions Council (2002), and British Columbia legislators (Hansard, 1990) also affirmed their commitment to self-regulation, while arguing that changes to traditional structures and enhanced oversight were necessary.

5.3 The Early 2000s

After decades of reviews and legislative reform, including a complete restructuring and expansion of health profession regulation in Ontario and British Columbia, there were very few new professions regulated during the early 2000s. In British Columbia, applied biology acquired a restricted title, as did human resources professionals in Ontario in 2011. Nonetheless, there has been meaningful legislative change. First, there has been a trend towards regulatory reform, only nascent in the early 2000s, but picking up speed at the time of writing. British Columbia expanded the coverage of the *Health Professions Act* to encompass all self-regulating health professions, including a focus on controlled acts. These changes continued the practice of self-regulation, but regulatory failures in the teaching profession in British Columbia led to the removal of self-regulation from that profession in 2011 (Glegg, 2013). Teacher regulation came to be handled by a government-appointed council (which does include teachers), within the Ministry of Education and subject to its oversight. Ontario (2006) passed the *Fair Access to Regulated Professions Act* in 2006, which established the Office of the Fairness Commissioner, originally reporting to the Minister of Citizenship and Immigration, to oversee the registration practices of all regulated professions, occupations, and skilled trades, and to ensure that entry-to-practice is "transparent, objective, impartial and fair"—especially towards the internationally educated (for more on entry into professions among the internationally educated, see Chap. 7). Under the act, all regulators are required to regularly review their registration practices for fairness and efficiency and report to the Fairness Commissioner (and the public) regarding their practices; they are also subject to periodic audits.

Second, there has been evidence of enhanced amalgamation and co-ordination. Umbrella legislation in health care has brought the various regulators into more regular communication with each other, and there are signs of enhanced co-operation between them. Groups such as BC Health Regulators and, in Ontario, HPRO (Health Profession Regulators of Ontario) provide forums for discussion, exchange of best practices, and information-sharing, encouraging collaboration. Such collaboration may facilitate regulator amalgamation occurring in several provinces. The accounting professions experienced their own amalgamation, with the national associations merging in 2013–2014, and regulatory legislation establishing a single Chartered Professional Accountant (CPA) profession, bringing previously distinct accounting professionals together in British Columbia between 2013 and 2015 and in Ontario between 2012 and 2017 (CPA Ontario, 2017). The rationales for such mergers include public protection, reduction of market confusion, facilitation of inter-professional mobility, and global trends in the profession (CPAA, 2021).

All these trends have recently intensified, with the expansion of regulator amalgamation especially in British Columbia, an increased emphasis both on oversight and on collaboration among professionals (collaboration with state leaders is variable). The trend until recently, however, has been for self-regulation to persist, along with more oversight and checks and balances (for more on closer oversight of professionals, see Chap. 6). Regulatory change increases apace.

6 Conclusion

Professional regulation both reflects and shapes relations between professions and society (beyond professionalism), as well as relations between and among professionals (within and between professionalism). In the fifty-year period between 1960 and 2010, professional regulation was revised, but not transformed, in the Canadian provinces of Ontario and British Columbia, as states and professions redefined their relationships with each other. Regulatory change was shaped by multiple stakeholders—consumers, state actors, employers, and other experts—seeking to redefine the place of professionals in society. Guiding regulatory change was the overarching principle of the public interest. By the mid- to late twentieth century in Canada, as elsewhere, consumers and other stakeholders were becoming cynical about professions, seeing them as elitist and self-interested. Professions' claims to serve the public interest were viewed with scepticism. However, despite rising distrust, state actors and the commissioners they appointed to inform policy-making in this area continued to endorse self-regulation for professions in the two provinces. Their recommended reforms sought to increase regulatory bodies' accountability to the state and the public, but not to change them fundamentally.

Reform in the two provinces was gradual during this period. Changes reflected not only declining public trust in professionals but also the emergence of new values guiding regulation, including fairness, accountability, and a continuing commitment to the public interest. Less common initially, but mentioned more often over time were principles of transparency, efficiency, standardisation, and collaboration. By the end of the period, professionals were pursuing additional reforms to win back public trust and forge a new relationship with society. Regulators were forced to demonstrate that they were working to serve the public or they otherwise risked deregulation.

Theoretically, this chapter finds evidence of the countervailing powers identified by Light (1995). Inter-professional conflict within the ecology of professions shaped regulatory change, as legislators expanded the number of professions and tried to put them on equal footing—despite recommendations by commissions that the privileges of self-regulation should not be extended too far. Principles of fairness encouraged this expansion. The number of commissions set up throughout this era and the sheer volume of legislation passed regarding professional regulation provide evidence of the importance of professions and regulation for Canadian states and society. States and professions are overlapping ecologies, and the interplay between these ecologies continues to have important implications for individuals and organisations. Regulatory change continues to occur in Canada, and there are signs that it is intensifying. Regulated professions remain an important force in Canadian society, but their relationship with the state, consumers, and other stakeholders continues to evolve. What is clear, however, is that the impact of Canadian professions extends *beyond professionalism*, to society and social institutions more generally.

Acknowledgement This research was funded by a grant from the Social Science and Humanities Research Council of Canada.

References

Abbott, A. (1988). *The system of professions: An essay on the division of expert labor*. University of Chicago Press.

Abbott, A. (2005). Linked ecologies: States and universities as environments for professions. *Sociological Theory, 23*(3), 245–274.

Adams, T. L. (2007). Inter-professional relations and the emergence of a new profession: Software engineering in Canada, the U.S. and the UK. *The Sociological Quarterly, 48*(3), 507–532.

Adams, T. L. (2018). *Regulating professions: The emergence of professional self-regulation in four Canadian provinces*. University of Toronto Press.

Adams, T. L., & Saks, M. (2018). Neo-Weberianism and changing state-profession relations: The case of Canadian health care. *Sociologia Problemas e Práticas, 88*(fall), 61–77.

An act to provide for fair registration practices in Ontario's regulated professions, c31 Ontario (2006). Queen's Printer.

BC Hansard. (1990). Legislative debates on bill 31. https://www.leg.bc.ca/documents-data/debate-transcripts/34th-parliament/4th-session.

Bonnin, D. (2019). Striking a regulatory bargain: The legal profession, associations and the state in South Africa. Professions & Professionalism, 9(3), e3113. https://doi.org/https://doi.org/10.7577/pp.3113.

Cayton, H. (2018). An Inquiry into the performance of the College of Dental Surgeons of British Columbia and the Health Professions Act. Retrieved from https://www2.gov.bc.ca/assets/gov/health/practitioner-pro/professional-regulation/cayton-report-college-of-dental-surgeons-2018.pdf

CMAJ (Canadian Medical Association Journal). (1974). Ontario's new Health Disciplines Act will put laymen on professional governing bodies, *110*(May 4), 1099–1101.

CPA Ontario. (2017). Ontario government passes the Chartered Professional Accountants of Ontario Act, 2017. Retrieved from https://www.cpaontario.ca/newsroom/ontario-government-passes-the-chartered-professional-accountants-of-ontario-act-2017

CPAA. (2021). Reasons for Unification. Retrieved from https://www.cpaalberta.ca/About-Us/History/Reasons-for-Unification

Eyal, G. (2019). *The crisis of expertise*. Polity Press.

Freidson, E. (2001). *Professionalism: The third logic*. University of Chicago Press.

Foulkes, R. G. (1973). *Health Security for British Columbians*, Report. Queen's Printer.

Glegg, A. (2013). The British Columbia College of Teachers: An obituary. *Historical Studies in Education, 24*(2), 45–64.

Hall, E. M. (1965). *Report of the Royal Commission on health services*. Queen's Printer.

Health Disciplines Act, c27 Ontario. (1974). Queens Printer.

Health Professions Council. (2002). *Safe Choices: A new model for Regulating Health Professions in British Columbia*. Retrieved from https://www2.gov.bc.ca/assets/gov/government/ministries-organizations/ministries/health/safe-choices-a-new-model-for-regulating-health-professions-in-british-columbia.pdf

Health Professions Legislation Review. (1989). *Striking a new Balance: A blueprint for the regulation of Ontario's health professions*. Queen's Printer.

Leslie, K., Nelson, S., Deber, R., & Gilmour, J. (2018). Policy tensions in regulatory reform: Changes to regulation of health professions in Australia, the United Kingdom, and Ontario, Canada. *Journal of Nursing Regulation, 8*(4), 32–42.

Light, D. (1995). Countervailing powers: A framework for professions in transition. In T. Johnson, G. Larkin, & M. Saks (Eds.), *Health professions and the state in Europe* (pp. 25–41). Routledge.

Macdonald, K. (1995). *The sociology of the professions*. SAGE.
McRuer, J. C. (1968). *Royal Commission Inquiry into Civil Rights, Report 1, Volume 3*. Queen's Printer
Regulated health professions act, c18 Ontario. (1991). Queens Printer.
Saks, M. (2015). *Professions, State and the Market: Medicine in Britain, the United States and Russia*. Routledge.
Trebilcock, M. J., Tuohy, C. J., & Wolfson, A. D. (1979). *Professional regulation: A staff study of accountancy, architecture, engineering and law in Ontario prepared for the professional organizations committee*. Queen's Printer.
Weber, M. (1968). *Economy and society* (Vol. 1). Bedminster Press.

12

Expand or Translate?: Theorising Work in Professionals' Activism

Joris Gjata, Matthew S. Rowe, and Shawhin Roudbari

1 Professions and Social Problems

"Refuse together" and "confront the inhumane": these phrases captured two architects' positions towards President Trump's proposal for a wall on the U.S.-Mexico border. The former summarised a strategy for architects to withhold their labour in an effort to slow down or halt the machinery of a system that "benefits the entrenched elite through division". The

J. Gjata (✉)
C Space, Boston, MA, USA

University of Colorado, Boulder, CO, USA

M. S. Rowe
Department of Sociology, San Diego State University, San Diego, CA, USA
e-mail: msrowe@sdsu.edu

S. Roudbari
Center for Community Engaged Design and Research (CEDaR),
University of Colorado, Boulder, CO, USA
e-mail: shawhin@colorado.edu

© The Author(s), under exclusive license to Springer Nature Switzerland AG 2023

L. Maestripieri, A. Bellini (eds.), *Professionalism and Social Change*,
https://doi.org/10.1007/978-3-031-31278-6_12

latter challenged designers to "subvert attempts to dehumanise migrants" by "[encouraging] the government to house immigrant families" in humane and dignified conditions.

How one engages with efforts to address social problems raises important sociological questions about the meaning of professional work and its future transformation. Professionals benefit from extensive material and symbolic resources such as high levels of expertise, skills, and social status. However, their decisions about how to leverage these resources require navigating dilemmas around professional identity and the role of professions in society. Debates among architects—such as the one highlighted above—show the different perspectives professionals can adopt in addressing social issues and, importantly, the different practices through which they enact such perspectives.

Previous studies have highlighted two main pathways through which professionals contribute to addressing social issues. The first path involves applying the abstract knowledge that distinguishes one's profession, that is, providing professional services for a lower fee or no fee at all to a disadvantaged section of the public (Amadei and Wallace, 2009 on engineers; Hoffman, 1989 and Fox, 2014 on doctors; Boutcher, 2013 on lawyers). The second path entails leveraging one's status and power to support and legitimise broad processes of social change, which are typically led by the efforts of groups outside one's profession, such as social movements or advocacy organisations (Gendron et al., 2006; Goodrick & Reay, 2011; Bell, 2014; Cornfield et al., 2018; Saks, 1995; Frickel & Gross, 2005). However, focusing on these paths assumes that professionals deliberately aim to change society and does not examine how professionals organise around social problems within their professions (Muzio et al., 2013; Perrucci, 1972; Riley, 2008 and Wisnioski, 2012 on engineers; Minow, 1996, Gobe & Salaymeh, 2016, and Powell, 1979 on lawyers, Reisch & Andrews, 2014 on social work, Bell & Wakeford, 2008 and Karim, 2018 on architects). Here there exists a gap in our sociological knowledge of professions and social change, which stems from an incomplete understanding of professional work (Ross, 1976; Saks, 1995; Timmermans, 2008). In their practice, professionals do not only use the skill sets for which they are primarily known—design in the case of architects. Sometimes they primarily employ additional relational and organisational skill sets that they develop as part of exchanges with other sectors, through borrowing and even translating new practices from other fields.

Existing scholarship considers professional action as either being in the service of a state or another powerful formal organisation such as a corporation, and neglects the variety of practices that professionals use to navigate their environments through both formal and informal organising. Consequently, scholars tend to ignore the public service role of professions, making assumptions rather than empirically examining professionals' contributions. A multi-institutional politics model of social movements indicates that the profession is another form of power that movement actors can challenge (Van Dyke et al., 2004; Levitsky & Banaszak-Holl, 2010). This premise also highlights the need to examine professionals' mobilisation and organising practices regarding social issues to better understand their public service contributions.

Our research asks the following questions: How do professionals organise around social justice issues? And what role does professional work—the application of abstract knowledge specific to and distinguishing one profession from another—play in mobilising in pursuit of social change? Scholars have an incomplete picture of how professionals engage and organise around social problems, leading them to lack a clear understanding of whether, and if so, how, professionals use their extensive resources, especially their professional work, to serve the public, and what the implications of this are.

Examining the involvement of professionals in addressing social justice issues—what we call "professional activism"—is both timely and important given the rise of new social movements involving professionals, such as Me Too, Black Lives Matter, and the March for Science. Previous research treats the activities of professionals organising around social problems as symbolic: principally aimed at legitimising the right of professions to self-regulate and practice with some autonomy from the state. Few researchers have paid attention to more contemporary forms of professional activism and their role in shaping professions and society (see Lee, 2017; Liu & Halliday, 2019; Liu et al., 2019; Wang & Liu, 2020; Howard-Grenville et al., 2017).

In this chapter, we present a novel typology of professional activism based upon an empirical study of architects mobilising around social issues. We theorise professional work as a form of professional action implicated in professionals' engagements both within and beyond their fields of practice and examine it as a complex web of institutional arrangements and relationships. This approach draws attention to forms of professional practice beyond an architect's core skill set—practices which may be considered peripheral yet are essential in everyday work. Our framework stands in contrast to the trend of framing professional work in terms of knowledge and expertise (Gorman & Sandefur, 2011) and of studying its application within formal organisations (Leicht & Fennell, 2001). We connect Liu's (2018) processual theory of professional action and Abbott's (2005) linked ecologies approach to Lichterman and Eliasoph's (2014) conception of civic action to devise a novel typology of professional activism, defined as any form of action that professionals use to address social problems. After outlining our data and methods, we present our analysis of architects' diverse ways of mobilising for social change and identify two patterns of professional activism: expansion and translation. We conclude with our contributions and a research agenda on professional activism as a mechanism for social change.

2 Professionals for Social Change: Revisiting Professional Action and Work

Our study contributes to existing conversations on the role of professionals as agents of social change by examining professionals' mobilisations as distinct forms of work. Professionals who work to address social issues challenge current conceptualisations of professional action. Scott (2008) highlights that professions offer cultural-cognitive, normative, and regulative resources that support other institutional actors; however, these resources may not be available to, or be used by, all professionals. Professionals' roles in building, maintaining, and shaping relations beyond their professions cannot be considered in isolation from their professional work nor from their involvement in institutional change processes within the profession.

Building on the interactionist approach of the Chicago School of sociology, Liu (2018) centres the sociology of professions on professional action rather than order or change. His processual theory of action calls for studying formal and informal professional practices to understand changes in professional fields over time. Liu underlines the importance of examining exchange processes: practices in which professionals engage with actors within and across professional boundaries. These include practitioners of the same profession, of different professions, clients, and the state (see Table 1 in Liu, 2018: 47). Bringing exchange to the forefront of professional action recognises "more cooperative and interdependent social processes that shape professional life", something which had been overshadowed by the dynamics of competition in Abbott's canonical work (Liu, 2018: 54). Liu (2018) identifies two additional forms of action: "boundary work", employed in the formation of professional jurisdictions, and "diagnosis", involved in the social construction of expertise. The exchange form of action, however, is not seen as involved in shaping either boundary work or diagnosis but in maintaining social networks. Liu (2018: 54) explains:

Professionals develop expertise and fight for jurisdictions in the social space of work, but they also build networks to consolidate the profession and facilitate their everyday work. … [Exchange] does not demarcate or blur jurisdictional boundaries but facilitates the flow of power, capital, and other resources between two or more actors.

However, studies of activist professionals such as cause lawyers and social movement lawyers (Sarat & Scheingold, 2006), activist lawyers in China and Hong Kong (Liu et al., 2019), human rights lawyers in China (Pils, 2014), lawyers who do pro bono work (Boutcher, 2013), and studies of social movements and healthcare professions in the United States (Levitsky & Banaszak-Holl, 2010) indicate that such exchanges do not simply maintain the boundaries of professions, but can challenge and reshape both professionals' boundary work and diagnosis practices. Histories of activism show that professionals often mobilise their considerable material and symbolic resources even without any obvious threat being posed to these resources (see Chiarello, 2011; Goldstein, 2010; Moore, 2008; Wisnioski, 2012).

While this perspective of institutional logics draws attention to professionals' behaviour, it does not aim to examine the manner in or the extent to which professional practices maintain or transform the "constellations guiding behaviour" (Goodrick & Reay, 2011: 399). This implicit view of logics as ideologies that guide behaviour through the internalisation and diffusion of values echoes functionalist approaches to professions, which define professions in terms of the public service role itself. Freidson (2001: 122) writes: "[t]he professional ideology of service goes beyond serving others' choices. Rather, it claims devotion to a transcendent value which infuses its specialisation with a larger and putatively higher goal which may reach beyond that of those they are supposed to serve." We adopt a relational approach by highlighting the practices and relationships that constitute public service logics. This relational approach is productive and generative, in that instead of assuming that some professionals are carriers of a given logic and others are not, it empirically examines how the logic of professional action is constituted in relationship with other actors (e.g. Eyal et al., 2010). An open question is whether the public service logic is shared by members of a profession who work in diverse environments or if it can actually become a source of conflict in itself.

Abbott's (2005) ecological approach to professions provides important insights into understanding the exchange practices articulated by Liu (2018). Abbott uses the concepts of "hinge" and "avatar" to highlight the practices of professionals who move across institutional contexts and introduce new forms of work and practices into the professional ecology. Put simply, hinges are "issues or strategies that 'work'" in two ecologies at once, while avatars are "attempts to institutionalise in one ecology a copy or colony of an actor in another" (Abbott, 2005: 245). These concepts play a central role in the proposed framework, as they place the analytical focus on how professionals navigate across institutional contexts and how they apply resources to address social problems. While Abbott's primary examples of hinges and avatars illustrate linkages between professions, higher education, and the state, we adapt the concepts in order to understand the linkages that professionals construct between professional ecologies and social movement ecologies.

These concepts provide useful guidance for studies of activist professionals who inhabit multi-institutional contexts that use multiple institutional logics. In addition to the conceptualisation of exchanges and linkages, respectively, Liu's (2018) and Abbott's (2005) theories are also amenable to interactionist analyses that draw attention to actors who skilfully navigate these contexts. Just as professional work can take a practitioner outside their usual scope of work and into new institutional environments, professionals' activism does not only take place in large-scale, formal social movement organisations but also include the more informal and transitory practices that people use to formulate and respond to social problems (Walker & Martin, 2018). As Lichterman and Eliasoph (2014) point out, action in the public interest is best conceptualised not as a separate field or social domain but rather as an emergent feature of small groups. Their interactionist concept of "civic action" pairs well with Abbott's ecological model of professions and Liu's processual theory of action. As Abbott (2005) writes, social interaction constitutes "social locations", such as jurisdiction over specific tasks where professional work takes place. Therefore, we propose a typology of professional activism that focuses on the different forms of mobilisation of professionals in pursuit of social issues. This approach allows us to capture both formal and informal practices that professionals employ to service the public and to identify a variety of activist practices: humanistic, expressive, policy-making, and exemplary activist actions.

3 Data and Methods

In the United States, architecture—one of the main domains of expertise and authority regarding the design and construction of the built environment—has evolved to develop its own distinct professional culture and institutions. In the nineteenth and twentieth centuries, the profession's leading organisation, the American Institute of Architects (AIA), consolidated power and fended off challengers; state-mandated licensure was established; and large, corporate architectural firms emerged as the dominant model of practice. The contemporary period of the profession's history begins with the subsequent "postmodern" period (1970s–1990s), as architects and their clients began to reject Modernism's formal rigidity and idealism and to embrace more pragmatic, site-specific, and community-sensitive approaches to design (Bell & Wakeford, 2008).

American architecture displays significant levels of intra-professional contention around social justice issues. Modernism (1920s–1960s in American architecture) brought social engagement to the forefront of architectural discourse by embracing industrial technology for the sake of social improvement through design. As the civil rights, women's rights, and anti-war movements developed in the 1960s, architects responded by forcing change within the profession and its institutions (Karim, 2018). Today, some of the issues around which socially engaged architects organise are: racial and gender-based bias within the profession; ameliorating economic inequality by advocating for and designing sustainable, affordable housing; advancing environmentally friendly standards throughout the building process; and addressing economic justice within this traditionally hierarchical profession (Bell & Wakeford, 2008; Karim, 2018). Given the unique location of architecture at the intersection of artistic and technical domains of practice, the efforts of architects to address the potential harms caused by their work provide a useful case for developing knowledge about the contentious dynamics within professions and their implications for and beyond work and public service.

To examine how professionals organise around social problems, we collect and analyse qualitative data from multiple sources. We examine transcripts of in-depth interviews with individuals and written ethnographic field notes from events and interactions between groups and individuals that we have observed and experienced (Emerson et al. 2011). This form of "interpretative analysis" uncovers what Luker (2008): 167) calls "mental maps" of "some aspect of social life". This approach enables us to understand how architects understand civic engagement and social justice and how they view their role and agency in shaping professional and social change.

In line with our wider project, we collected three principal sources of data: (1) written documents reflecting communications made by architects and architectural organisations/associations on issues of professional change; (2) participant observations of professional architects' social mobilisations and gatherings, organised formally or informally, in small or large groups; and (3) in-depth interviews with architects involved in organising around social problems to challenge the status quo. While all these sources inform our analysis, this chapter draws mainly from participant observations and in-depth interviews.

Team members conducted 30 in-depth interviews with professionals who are involved in activist or humanitarian work in architecture in the United States. We also observed 14 events in which activist professionals are planning to mobilise or are already doing so, mainly organised in West Coast and East Coast cities. These include conferences and events sponsored by the primary member organisations in the field, such as the American Institute of Architects (AIA) and their regional affiliates. In addition, team members regularly observed a series of meetings of selected organisations, including equity and social justice organisations such as The Architecture Lobby (TAL), Black in Design (BiD), and Architects, Designers, and Planners for Social Responsibility (ADPSR).

Our analysis examines: (1) detailed field notes taken during and immediately after professional events; (2) analytic memos synthesising field notes, with feedback given by team members; and (3) team discussions on synthesising observed findings across observation events. The study's findings are the product of this inductive process in which concepts emerge during the process of comparative observation of professional activists in situ.

The findings shared in this chapter come from team members' analysis of interview transcripts, field notes, and memos written about first-hand observations of professional events. The team developed a thematic coding scheme to analyse data systematically. We refined this coding scheme through analytical memo writing, paying attention to definitions of key concepts, inclusion and exclusion criteria for codes, identifying relationships between codes, and highlighting themes and representative examples. To compose mental maps and reconstruct landscapes of meaning, we used analytical strategies such as focusing on individuals' meaning-laden examples and self-contradictions, identifying evidence of changing cultural meanings and codes, as well as highlighting moments of emotional labour (Pugh, 2013). We paid special attention to "the gaps within and between institutional orders" (Lizardo & Strand, 2010: 21), when different understandings of social engagement had competing demands for the professionals and professional groups and when these tensions needed to be managed.

4 Two Modes of Professional Activism

In this section, we develop our typology of professional activism by creating a dialogue between what we learned from our ethnographic fieldwork on architects mobilising and organising to address social issues and existing theoretical developments in the sociology of professions. First, we present two sets of cases that exemplify two distinct forms of architects' activism emerging in our data. Then we expand upon the key features of each mode of professional activism.

4.1 Examples of Professional Activism in Architecture

This section provides several cases that highlight the activism of architects. Our data analysis led us to identify two-way architects engaged with social problems to challenge the status quo in their profession. While all these activist architects organise around social justice issues with the more or less deliberate goal of changing the status quo, they do so in many different ways. One group of architects might engage with social problems to assert the core expertise of their profession, employing their technical skills in design in order to support broader social movements. In turn, another group of architects might employ non-technical skills that are not traditionally considered to be typical "professional work" in architecture in order to change the profession. Below we present examples to showcase each mode of professional activism that emerged from our analysis.

The first group of architects exemplifies how professionals expand their architectural work to support social movements. Professionals draw upon material and symbolic resources to address social issues and to advocate for professional and social change. Professional work is one of the most important tools they have at their disposal, in that their professional expertise defines them as members of an elite occupation with the skills to address particular kinds of complex problems. Our fieldwork indicates that not all professionals who address social issues employ their professional work in their efforts to promote change. Architects organise around building-related topics that range from criminal justice reform to building industry reform, around social issues that range from unjust immigration policies to racism in the built environment, and around fundamental economic and political aspects of labour and democracy. These engagements span formal and informal modes of addressing social problems, and their tactics involve the cooperation of local communities and various stakeholders. The following mobilisation efforts carried out by architects exemplify how professionals use their professional work to support social issues advanced by groups outside their profession.

Historically, architects have often provided services to underprivileged communities in order to address social issues and injustices, particularly in cities. Recounting the work of Black architects in Washington, D.C., in the aftermath of the 1968 urban uprisings, architect Harry Robinson III recalled how "for the first time, communities had a front-row-seat say at what was going to happen" in their city (architecture and race symposium, September 2018). Addressing a symposium on activism in the design professions at the National Museum of African American History and Culture, Robinson explained how architects embraced community-engaged design by saying: "What we did is we went to the communities and became their architects" (ibid.). At the same time, white architects were reluctant to cede their effective monopoly on architectural work to the first cohorts of young, minority architects that emerged in the 1960s. Robinson's explanation shows the influence of the social movements of the time in the creation of innovative, community-based practices: "Whenever there was pushback against our doing this, we invoked 'power to the people'" (ibid.).

Architects like Robinson in D.C. and J. Max Bond, Jr. in New York City used their professional work as a tool for broader social reform. They partnered with community leaders to advocate, design, plan, and construct projects, including housing, cultural facilities, and public spaces. Bond led the Architects' Renewal Committee in Harlem (ARCH), an organisation that became renowned for its work defending Harlem's diverse communities from Columbia University's perceived "land grab" tactics (Sutton, 2017). ARCH and other organisations established an ethos of practice in the service of the community that was fuelled by the era's civil rights activism (Sutton, 2017; architecture and race symposium, September 2018).

The civil rights era ethos of using commitment to the community to inform professional practice finds new modes of expression in contemporary design practices. A recent example emerged in response to the 2017 Take 'em Down movement, which saw the removal of Confederate monuments such as a notable Robert E. Lee statue in New Orleans. Colloqate—a small, local architecture practice—became involved in organising community participation to reconstruct their city's narratives (architecture conference, October 2018). The firm's Paper Monuments project asks its audience to "consider decolonising the individual and consider what communities are actually being served". The firm's founder, Brian C. Lee, explained to participants at the National Organization for Minority Architects 2018 annual meeting: "It's not just about an individual to be put back up on top of a pillar, but it's actually about what are the movements that shaped this city and how were those movements distributed across our city" (ibid.). Through projects like Paper Monuments, architects connect their work to aspirations for social change and social justice. As another long-time architectural activist noted: "In this moment where we're questioning what democracy is, and how we can sustain or save our democracy, I think architecture should be engaged in those questions. We don't only work and advocate in architecture. Those of us who practice, we have a much broader mission, and there are very many ways we fulfil that." Cy Richardson of the National Urban League told another gathering commemorating 50 years of activism in architecture to "Embed yourself in the work, the technical skills that you have. That is Civil Rights today" (architecture symposium, September 2018). At major branches of professional associations, we observed examples of this kind of professional activism for issues concerning infrastructure, environmental justice, and housing, as well as issues of representation for women and other minorities (various meetings and gatherings; interview, May 2019).

The second group of architects exemplifies how professionals mobilise around social problems by translating practices borrowed from broader social movements into the domain of architecture, questioning what counts as architecture work. Activists in this group apply their efforts to reforming professional practice by targeting the member associations that set rules and guidelines (Greenwood et al., 2002), relying on practices beyond the ones considered typical professional work. In doing so, these activist professionals treat professional work as part of the target of their efforts in pursuit of social change. This quest for reform may be guided by a belief that the profession's current leaders no longer represent the group's interests in changing times (Evetts, 2011). For example, a group of activists organised the Equity by Design (EQxD) symposium series to showcase the enduring presence of gender inequality in architecture firms. This work began with a small group of architects organising to bring attention to "the missing 32%" of women who obtain degrees in architecture but never seek licensure. The group carried out a large-scale survey of the architectural profession, leading to many respondents addressing topics such as discrimination in the workplace, family leave policies, and wage differences by gender. EQxD's 2018 symposium in San Francisco brought together architects from around the country for three days of tours to firms, workshops, group activities, panel discussions, and receptions (architecture conference, November 2018).

At one EQxD training workshop, Emily Grandstaff-Rice reminded the twenty architects in attendance that "equity" meant "meeting people's specific needs". She noted that an "irony" of presenting the AIA's Guides for Equitable Practice at the session was that the issues the guide discussed—including cultural competence, workplace diversity, and inclusion—were already in line with the architects' work. "[W]e should not do this only for our client", she added, presenting the pursuit of equity as a broad social problem that was in line with professionalism in architecture, and therefore to be revisited as a professional problem. Grandstaff-Rice made the business case for justice, equity, diversity, and inclusion (or JEDI) by referencing management consultants and studies in the Harvard Business Review. Another organiser assisting with data analysis for the EQxD 2018 survey interrupted Grandstaff-Rice's presentation, wanting to prioritise participants' stories regarding JEDI issues in their workplaces and their plans for future action that had been shared during previous small group activities (ibid). These examples show that many architects consider the social problems defined as JEDI to be synonymous with the field's mandate and ethos. In addition, advocates believe that addressing such problems demands that architects view their professional work in terms that are broader than usual, encompassing sources of information and guides to practice from outside the profession.

As a final example, a storytelling event organised as part of EQxD 2018 revealed how architects leveraged symbolic resources that allowed them to intersect the "intimate and personal" aspects of everyday life with participants' identities as design professionals. The session began by reaffirming the expertise and competence of architects as core values by seeing the adaptations and professional change necessary "to sustain our work" and make "good design". As with subsequent EQxD 2018 events, participants cited their motivation and capacity to pursue social equity as architects.

By merging a range of diversity and inclusiveness frames and practices—from barriers to advancement in large firms to the MeToo movement—the event aimed to expand the collective consciousness around feminist workplace issues. In addition, the EQxD events leveraged members' insider status within the AIA and other major professional organisations to fund a large-scale, long-term survey of architects that addressed diversity and inequalities, and then presented results from the latest survey in a high-tech presentation at the EQxD 2018 meeting.

4.2 Towards a Typology of Professional Activism

Two kinds of professional activism emerge from our analysis that are linked to contemporary theories on professional action and work: expanding and translating activism.

Expanding professional activism encompasses cases when professionals use their professional work—their expertise, skills, and practices—to address social issues, maintain their positions in social networks, and expand their relationships with other ecologies. Expanding activist professionals are involved in increasing the range of social issues that other professionals (peers) engage with and aim to have more professionals offering their professional work/services in support of broader efforts to address social problems. They use individualistic or outward-directed strategies, that is, attempting to use existing identities simply to reimagine the public they serve. These professionals rely extensively on hinges:

addressing issues by becoming allies or supporters of them in other ecologies. The debates they engage in offer rewards in different ecologies. However, these engagements do not question the degree to which professionals are agents or leaders in addressing such issues. Expanding professional activism overlaps mainly with value-centred occupational activism, including humanistic, expressive, and exemplary forms of occupational activism as defined by Cornfield et al. (2018).

The examples above show that architects address the needs of African-American and other minority communities through design projects. They employ their skills as designers to give a voice and visibility to these groups' experiences. They design, though with an expanded view of who they are serving: their "client" now encompasses one or more communities. Projects like Colloqate's Paper Monuments use design work in innovative ways, but they do not challenge the design practices of fellow architects. By extending the tradition of Black Power social reform into work that interacts with the urban landscape and its residents in new ways, the project effectively takes long-standing social critiques about racial justice from a social movement ecology and incorporates them into a professional designer's approach. The project itself, then, by addressing the issue of representation in monuments, attempts to create a linkage between two ecologies—in Abbott's terms, a hinge—between the design professions and contemporary Black empowerment movements' ecologies. The issue, however, does not extensively challenge existing social networks and professional identities.

The creation of hinges is also pursued through individual professional action and outward-directed efforts to find "new" clients or public to be served. Community-informed design then represents a novel space of professional work guided by a new constellation of logics. The way these architects engage with a social issue involves informing their practice by applying a public service or care/civic logic that would normally be considered outside an architect's work. While public service is a common feature of professional work, the ways that activist professionals understand this responsibility is distinct from the usual duty to serve paying clients ethically. While Colloqate's designers are undoubtedly also informed by these requirements, the new logic of public service that they enact in their work responds to a different responsibility: building a better-informed community of citizens and architects. The social issues they address vary, but they all revolve around the development needs of communities mostly outside the United States.

Translating professional activism includes cases when professionals do not rely on their professional work to engage with social issues, but use other forms of work that are borrowed or adapted from their social networks. Translating activist professionals attempt to shape and transform their positions in these networks by transforming social problems into professional problems. They do not simply borrow practices and values from other ecologies, but they also translate and transform them for their professional ecology. They employ inward-directed collective and organisational strategies to shape existing professional identities. These professionals rely extensively on creating avatars—kinds of professional actors involved in other ecologies and mobilise to institutionalise the issues they address. They engage in debates that raise questions about professional agency: the leadership of professionals and their impact in shaping social change. Translating professional activism overlaps mainly with peer-centred occupational activism, including policymaking, exemplary, and humanistic forms of occupational activism as defined by Cornfield et al. (2018).

Instead of using the particular form of expertise that defines them as an occupational group, the professionals in these examples use a set of cultural, bureaucratic, and political skills to advocate for reform within organisations that represent the profession's interests. EQxD member engagements show the inward-directed collective and organisational strategy these architects used to engage with several social issues. They involve employing tactics to transform the existing identities of professionals and even mention the rise of a new kind of identity: the JEDI architect. These activist architects, therefore, have been invested in translating social issues, such as gender equity, into professional issues, such as licensure and the pay gap. The target-based activist professionals have aimed to create and institutionalise diversity and equity issues in the form of a specific kind of architect at the intersection of several ecologies: the state/policymaking ecology, the higher education ecology, and that of the broader public. This reliance on avatars, in Abbott's terms, has been somewhat successful, as a similar project has been set up that is inspired by the EQxD group. This is in the field of structural engineering and is called Structural Engineering, Equity, and Engagement (SE3). These events have opened conversations about reimagining architects as service providers, oscillating between reaffirming their expertise, distinguishing practices, and problem-solving skills to a call for trying to build alliances across professional and organisational boundaries.

The diversity of positions held in these groups has also created space for multiple interpretations of the civic/care/public service logic and has raised questions about professional agency. At an event of the New York branch of the AIA entitled "Call to Action", the chair of the Civic Leadership programme there shared that fully employing her agency as an architect was a recent development and that she encouraged everybody to get involved with the programmes they offered, including the one on policy advocacy led by a non-architect there. We have observed similar debates about the nature of professional agency in other target-based activist engagements in architecture that challenge existing beliefs about architects' ability to shape social change. The Black in Design conference series—founded at Harvard University's Graduate School of Design in 2017—is another example where architects explore "the agency of the design profession to address and dismantle the institutional barriers faced by our communities" (Table 12.1).

Table 12.1 Typology of professional activism

Kind of professional action	Processes involved	Type of professional activism
Use of professional work in social networks	Expanding the range of social issues professionals engage with Strategies: Individualistic and outward-directed, identity-maintaining, by reimagining the public served Reliance on hinges	Expanding
Use of other forms of work from social networks	Translating social issues into professional issues Strategies: Collective and organisational and inward-directed, identity-transforming, by reimagining the service providers Reliance on avatars	Translating

5 Conclusion

Prevailing depictions of professionals in sociology are ones of elite, privileged workers who use their expertise and skills to serve well-paying clients, or ones that act radically to promote a broader cause. When they organise collectively, it is mostly to counter external threats to their autonomy at work and their jurisdiction or to support social movements. However, we observed professionals acting in influential ways that do not fit neatly into these polarised institutional roles: not only expanding their typical professional work into social movements but also translating social justice issues and incorporating them into their professional work. They operate in extended social networks and develop many relationships across institutional boundaries—with other professions, with state agencies, with industry actors, as well as with grassroots mobilisation communities and formally organised social movements. The exchanges of symbolic and material resources that take place through these networks shape professionals' practices in important ways, leading to professionals engaging in efforts to address broad social problems, such as through humanitarian projects or advocacy with fellow professionals for racial and gender equity and other social justice goals. While previous work has highlighted the different roles that professionals play in supporting or resisting institutional change, mostly assuming their contribution to the public interest, sociologists have not developed a conceptual framework to account for the work done by professionals who engage in addressing social justice issues. This is a phenomenon that it is important to understand, given the proliferation of examples of these practices amid shifts in the structures of professional work. Therefore, we have offered a conceptual framework to make sense of the different ways professionals organise around social problems to challenge the status quo. In our typology of professional activism, professional work represents one kind of professional action that is used in navigating relationships with other actors within and beyond the professional ecology. In their activism, some professionals rely on expanding their typical professional work into other professional ecologies, while others rely on translating skills and expertise from other professional ecologies into their own profession.

Our contribution to the sociology of professions is twofold: first, to empirically examine, rather than assume, how professionals serve the public, and second, to better understand professional work and its implications for inequality. Relying on relational and processual approaches to professions (Liu, 2018; Abbott, 2005) and the institutional logics perspective (Goodrick & Reay, 2011), we advance a research agenda that studies the engagement of professionals with social justice issues as a way of gauging profession-society relations and what public service means to professionals. Our study highlights how exchanges between actors of the profession and other ecologies can build linkages—hinges and avatars—to shape professional work. We follow Goodrick and Reay's (2011) premise that professional work reflects the influence of multiple institutional and societal logics and helps clarify one of the mechanisms through which these logics are translated into professional work: professional activism.

By examining the activism of professional workers, our study follows new developments in the sociology of work that focus on the agency of workers in workplaces and their occupational roles. It gives weight to professionals' and their representative organisations' roles as agents that are not just affected by institutional logics, but who translate and even bring them to life in powerful ways through their practices (Cornfield et al., 2018). We draw attention to when and how professionals' institutional innovations can be manifestations of professional work. Our typology complements the typology of occupational activism that Cornfield et al. (2018) proposed, by highlighting when the flow and employment of resources in professional ecologies may support professionals' identities and engagements as workers within and beyond their fields of practice. As a form of organising, the activism and advocacy of professionals appear to play a key role in shaping professional work (Gorman, 2017), orienting advocates to new publics and purposes, or positioning their engagements as ways of expanding the micro-level jurisdiction of each individual's tasks.

Additional research on such engagements can reveal more about the past and future of the many manifestations of professional work and clarify the rise of a "care" or "civic" logic guiding professional work in certain parts of professional ecologies (Dunn & Jones, 2010). Rather than assuming that professionals act in ways that are necessarily self-serving (in that they seek to serve paying clients) or altruistic (in that they seek to serve the broader public), our work calls for more research that considers public service and the care logic as 'civic action', an emergent property of professionals' involvement in micro-level organising (Lichterman & Eliasoph, 2014). This approach towards professionals and their practices may also help sociologists understand the relationship between the institutional logics of professionalism and the practices that are characteristic of "caring capitalism" (Barman, 2016).

The framework presented here is intended to instruct our continuing research and that of other scholars whose work examines inter-ecology linkages. Scholarship comparing different professions (e.g. Hoffman, 1989) and their dynamics in different countries (e.g. Harris, 2017) and cities (e.g. Liu et al., 2019) would help further these conversations and advance the research agenda implied in our work. While identifying the trends in the American context is important, in order to better understand the meaning of "professional mobilisation" (Liu & Halliday, 2019) and "professional movement" (Harris, 2017), our proposed framework also needs to be applied to studies of other professions, those that reflect national particularities (e.g. doctors in Brazil, Thailand, and South Africa in Harris' research) as well as ones with a more transnational reach (examples in Seabrooke & Henriksen, 2017). More research is also needed to examine the way professionals mobilising around social justice and their engagement in movements impact professional work and inequality in contexts that feature meritocratic and hierarchical professional cultures (see Sommerlad & Ashley, 2015; Seron et al., 2018). Our approach to professional activism may be adapted for use in studies of how professionals from socially disadvantaged backgrounds shape politically resonant identities within the institutional configurations of professional work and contribute to informal or "unobtrusive" forms of collective mobilisation (Katzenstein, 1990).

References

Abbott, A. (2005). Linked ecologies: States and universities as environments for professions. *Sociological Theory, 23*(3), 245–274. https://doi.org/10.1111/j.0735-2751.2005.00253.x

Amadei, B., & Wallace, W. A. (2009). "Engineering for humanitarian development." In *IEEE Technology and Society Magazine, 28*(4), 6–15. https://doi.org/10.1109/MTS.2009.934940

Barman, E. (2016). *Caring capitalism: The meaning and measure of social value.* Cambridge University Press.

Bell, J. M. (2014). *The black power movement and American social work.* Columbia University Press.

Bell, B., & Wakeford, K. (2008). *Expanding architecture: Design as activism.* Metropolis Books.

Boutcher, S. A. (2013). Lawyering for social change: Pro Bono Publico, cause lawyering, and the social movement society. *Mobilization (San Diego, Calif.), 18*(2), 179–196. https://doi.org/10.17813/maiq.18.2.p8213u5715181441

Chiarello, E. (2011). Challenging professional self-regulation. *Work and Occupations, 38*(3), 303–339. https://doi.org/10.1177/0730888411400700

Cornfield, D., Coley, J., Isaac, L., & Dickerson, D. (2018). Occupational activism and racial desegregation at work: Activist careers after the nonviolent Nashville civil rights movement. *Research in the Sociology of Work, 32*, 217–248. https://doi.org/10.1108/S0277-283320180000032014

Dunn, M. B., & Jones, C. (2010). Institutional logics and institutional pluralism: The contestation of care and science logics in medical education, 1967–2005. *Administrative Science Quarterly, 55*(1), 114–149. https://doi.org/10.2189/asqu.2010.55.1.114

Emerson, R. M., Fretz, R. I., & Shaw, L. L. (2011). *Writing ethnographic fieldnotes.* 2nd ed. Chicago: The University of Chicago Press.

Evetts, J. (2011). A new professionalism? Challenges and opportunities. *Current Sociology, 59*(4), 406–422. https://doi.org/10.1177/0011392111402585

Eyal, G., Hart, B., Onculer, E., Oren, N., & Rossi, N. (2010). *The autism matrix: The social origins of the autism epidemic.* Polity Press.

Fox, R. C. (2014). *Doctors without borders: Humanitarian quests, impossible dreams of Médecins Sans Frontières.* Johns Hopkins University Press.

Freidson, E. (2001). *Professionalism: The third logic.* University of Chicago Press.

Frickel, S., & Gross, N. (2005). A general theory of scientific/intellectual movements. *American Sociological Review, 70*(2), 204–232. https://doi.org/10.1177/000312240507000202

Gendron, Y., Suddaby, R., & Lam, H. (2006). An examination of the ethical commitment of professional accountants to auditor independence. *Journal of Business Ethics, 64*(2), 169–193. https://doi.org/10.1007/s10551-005-3095-7

Gobe, E., & Salaymeh, L. (2016). Tunisia's "revolutionary" lawyers: From professional autonomy to political mobilization. *Law & Social Inquiry, 41*(2), 311–345. https://doi.org/10.1111/lsi.12154

Goldstein, M. (2010). Complementary and integrative medicine in medical education: The birth of an organized movement. In J. Banaszak-Holl, S. R. Levitsky, & M. N. Zald (Eds.), *Social movements and the transformation of American health care* (pp. 210–227). Oxford University Press.

Goodrick, E., & Reay, T. (2011). Constellations of institutional logics. *Work and Occupations, 38*(3), 372–416. https://doi.org/10.1177/0730888411406824\

Gorman, E. (2017). The Oxford handbook of professional service firms [Review of the Oxford handbook of professional service firms]. *Work and occupations, 44*(2), 233–235. Sage.. https://doi.org/10.1177/0730888416675483

Gorman, E. H. & Sandefur, R L. (2011). "Golden Age," Quiescence, and Revival. Work and Occupations, 38(3), 275–302. https://doi.org/10.1177/0730888411417565

Greenwood, R., Hinings, C. R., & Suddaby, R. (2002). Theorizing change: The role of professional associations in the transformation of institutionalized fields. *Academy of Management Journal, 45*(1), 58–80. https://doi.org/10.2307/3069285

Harris, J. (2017). *Achieving access: Professional movements in the politics of health universalism.* Cornell University Press.

Hoffman, L. M. (1989). *The politics of knowledge: Activist movements in medicine and planning.* State University of New York Press.

Howard-Grenville, J., Nelson, A. J., Earle, A. G., Haack, J. A., & Young, D. M. (2017). "If chemists don't do it, who is going to?" peer-driven occupational change and the emergence of green chemistry. *Administrative Science Quarterly, 62*(3), 524–560. https://doi.org/10.1177/0001839217690530

Karim, F. (Ed.). (2018). *Routledge companion to architecture and social engagement.* Routledge.

Katzenstein, M. F. (1990). Feminism within American institutions: Unobtrusive mobilization in the 1980s. *Signs: Journal of Women in Culture and Society, 16*(1), 27–54. https://doi.org/10.1086/494644

Lee, M. Y. K. (2017). Beyond the 'professional project': The political positioning of Hong Kong lawyers. *International Journal of Law, Crime and Justice, 50*, 1–11. https://doi.org/10.1016/j.ijlcj.2017.01.003

Leicht, K. T., & Fennell, M. L. (2001). *Professional work: A sociological approach* (1st ed.). Wiley-Blackwell.

Levitsky, S. R., & Banaszak-Holl, J. (2010). Social movements and the transformation of U.S. health institutions: Introduction. In J. Banaszak-Holl, S. R. Levitsky, & M. N. Zald (Eds.), *Social movements and the transformation of American health care* (pp. 3–18). Oxford University Press.

Lichterman, P., & Eliasoph, N. (2014). Civic action. *American Journal of Sociology, 120*(3), 798–863. https://doi.org/10.1086/679189

Liu, S. (2018). Boundaries and professions: Toward a processual theory of action. *Journal of Professions and Organization, 5*(1), 45–57. https://doi.org/10.1093/jpo/jox012

Liu, S., & Halliday, T. C. (2019). The ecology of activism: Professional mobilization as a spatial process. *The Canadian Review of Sociology, 56*(4), 452–471. https://doi.org/10.1111/cars.12258

Liu, S., Hsu, C.-F., & Halliday, T. C. (2019). Law as a sword, law as a shield. China. *Perspectives, 2019*(1 (116)), 65–74. https://doi.org/10.4000/chinaperspectives.8798

Lizardo, O., & Strand, M. (2010). Skills, toolkits, contexts and institutions: Clarifying the relationship between different approaches to cognition in cultural sociology. *Poetics (Amsterdam), 38*(2), 205–228. https://doi.org/10.1016/j.poetic.2009.11.003

Luker, K. (2008). *Salsa Dancing Into the Social Sciences: Research in an Age of Info-glut*. Cambridge MA: Harvard University Press.

Minow, M. (1996). Political lawyering: An introduction. *Harvard Civil Rights-Civil Liberties Law Review, 31*(2), 287.

Moore, K. (2008). *Disrupting science: Social movements, American scientists, and the politics of the military, 1945–1975*. Princeton University Press.

Muzio, D., Brock, D. M., & Suddaby, R. (2013). Professions and institutional change: Towards an institutionalist sociology of the professions. *Journal of Management Studies, 50*(5), 699–721. https://doi.org/10.1111/joms.12030

Perrucci, R. (1972). In the service of man: Radical movements in the professions. *The Sociological Review, 20*(1 suppl), 179–194. https://doi.org/10.1111/j.1467-954X.1972.tb03216.x

Pils, E. (2014). *China's human rights lawyers: Advocacy and resistance*. Routledge.

Powell, M. (1979). Anatomy of a counter-Bar association: The Chicago Council of Lawyers. *American Bar Foundation Research Journal, 4*(3), 501–541. https://doi.org/10.1111/j.1747-4469.1979.tb01027.x

Pugh, A. (2013). What good are interviews for thinking about culture? Demystifying interpretive analysis. *American Journal of Cultural Sociology, 1*(1), 42–68. https://doi.org/10.1057/ajcs.2012.4

Reisch, M., & Andrews, J. (2014). *The road not taken: A history of radical social work in the United States*. Routledge.

Riley, D. M. (2008). *Engineering and social justice* [Morgan & Claypool Publishers online document]. doi:https://doi.org/10.2200/S00117ED1V01Y200805ETS007.

Ross, R. J. S. (1976). The impact of social movements on a profession in process: Advocacy in urban planning. *Sociology of Work and Occupations, 3*(4), 429–454.

Saks, M. (1995). *Professions and the public interest: Medical power, altruism and alternative medicine*. Routledge.

Sarat, A., & Scheingold, S. A. (Eds.). (2006). *Cause lawyers and social movements*. Stanford University Press.

Scott, W. R. (2008). Lords of the dance: Professionals as institutional agents. *Organization Studies, 29*(2), 219–238. https://doi.org/10.1177/0170840607088151

Seabrooke, L., & Henriksen, L. F. (2017). *Professional networks in transnational governance*. Cambridge University Press.

Seron, C., Silbey, S., Cech, E., & Rubineau, B. (2018). "I am not a feminist, but. …": Hegemony of a meritocratic ideology and the limits of critique among women in engineering. *Work and Occupations, 45*(2), 131–167. https://doi.org/10.1177/0730888418759774

Sommerlad, H., & Ashley, L. (2015). Diversity and inclusion in professional service firms. In L. Empson, D. Muzio, J. P. Broschak, & B. Hinings (Eds.), *Oxford handbook of professional service firms*. Oxford University Press.

Sutton, S. (2017). *When ivory towers were black: A story about race in America's cities and universities*. Oxford University Press.

Timmermans, S. (2008). Professions and their work. *Work and Occupations, 35*(2), 164–188. https://doi.org/10.1177/0730888407313032

Van Dyke, N., Soule, S. A., & Taylor, V. A. (2004). The targets of social movements: Beyond a focus on the STATE. In D. J. Myers & D. M. Cress (Eds.), *Authority in contention (research in social movements, conflicts and change)* (Vol. 25, pp. 27–51). Emerald Group Publishing Limited. https://doi.org/10.1016/S0163-786X(04)25002-9

Walker, E. T., & Martin, A. W. (2018). Social movement organizations. In D. A. Snow, S. A. Soule, H. Kriesi, & H. J. McCammon (Eds.), *Wiley-Blackwell companion to social movements* (pp. 167–184). Wiley-Blackwell.

Wang, D., & Liu, S. (2020). Performing Artivism: Feminists, lawyers, and online legal mobilization in China. *Law & Social Inquiry, 45*(3), 678–705. https://doi.org/10.1017/lsi.2019.64

Wisnioski, M. (2012). *Engineers for change: Competing visions of technology in 1960s America*. MIT Press.

13

Social Media Influencers: A New Hybrid Professionalism in the Age of Platform Capitalism?

Paola Sedda and Oihana Husson

1 Introduction

Changes in professions seem to follow a contradictory logic: a tendency to de-professionalise and proletarianise classic professions goes hand in hand with the emergence of new hybrid forms of professionalism (Noordegraaf, 2007), mostly pushed by digitalisation and market mechanisms. The importance of new technologies in the evolution of capitalism is already well documented by different works that point to the preeminent role played by digital platforms in the extraction and capture of value (Casilli, 2019). Platforms mediate between supply and demand,

P. Sedda (✉)
GERiiCO Laboratory, Information and Communication Sciences, University of Lille, Lille, France
e-mail: paola.sedda@univ-lille.fr

O. Husson
CIMEOS Laboratory, Information and Communication Sciences, University of Burgundy, CIMEOS Lab, Dijon, France
e-mail: oihana.husson@u-bourgogne.fr

© The Author(s), under exclusive license to Springer Nature Switzerland AG 2023

L. Maestripieri, A. Bellini (eds.), *Professionalism and Social Change*,
https://doi.org/10.1007/978-3-031-31278-6_13

between any informational good and a social group likely to be interested in it. The concept of "platform capitalism" refers then to the "outsourcing of workers and the displacement of the boundaries of work, but also to the creation of value and its unequal sharing between, on the one hand, the owners of the algorithms, sites and applications that are the platforms and, on the other hand, the workers who are present on them" (Abdelnour & Méda, 2019, p. 10).

In this context, labels for new occupations are emerging, such as YouTubers, Instagrammers, and TikTokers. These stem from the names of digital platforms and represent hybrid professional identities situated between profane and expert activities, leisure and work (Conley, 2010). As their participation in corporate and marketing communication relies on their capacity to manage and engage a digital community, we can refer to them as "social media influencers", or SMIs (Freberg et al., 2011; Campbell & Farrell, 2020). While they do not constitute a "pure profession"—the individualisation of their activities and the high heterogeneity of their practices, fields, remuneration received, and negotiating power constitute a major obstacle to the recognition of the profession—we posit that they can be studied as a specific form of hybrid professionalism. Hybridised images of professionalism help us to establish a "reflexive control" over what is considered "professional" (Noordegraaf, 2007) in order to form meaningful connections between online communities of practices, influence on digital platforms, and organised action.

We conceive professionalism as "a conceptual tool that can be used to analyse and interpret social change" (Bellini & Maestripieri, 2018, p. 8). It designates both a "discourse", conveying norms, values, and specific competencies and a "practice" that allows workers to be identified and recognised within their community. In communities of practices, relations are created around activities that are performed by the members so that skills and knowledge are recognised by the community and transmitted to the new participants. Practice is then considered a situated and collective social activity that allows one to learn, organise, and acquire knowledge. Practices are said to be "professional" when they are based on a set of skills, resources, and capacities mobilised by specialised actors in a certain field.

We thus analyse the way SMIs, acting in the context of communities of practice, participate in redefining professionalism and professional practices in the marketing and communications fields while promoting social values or advocating for a cause of public interest. By expanding the modes of making their experiences and acquired knowledge more visible, SMIs are engaged in the construction of new social problems in the public sphere (Sedda & Botero, 2022). The struggle for new forms of visibility (Voirol, 2005) is rooted in a process of reconfiguring practices of political engagement and their hybridisation with professional practices in managing social media. Activism that relies on the use of digital platforms is carried out by networks of individuals that are ready to act at specific moments within a framework that remains weakly or differently organised, favouring an individual approach that is freed from institutional rigidities (Sedda, 2022). In this sense, the digital sphere offers both an expressive and an organisational dimension, providing a framework where citizens can publicise their needs and give them a political dimension. The actions and strategies of making oneself visible on social media may result in a connection between the registers and repertoires of communication campaigns and those of social struggles.

We can thus formulate the hypothesis of how the hybridisation processes in professionalism are linked to the emergence of online communities of practices which may in turn lead to new individualised forms of political activism.

2 Influencers: An Emblematic Professional Identity within Platform Capitalism

Capitalism has appropriated "individualism" and the demand for authenticity and diversity that began to be expressed in the 1960s. The use of social media is rooted in aspirations for authenticity and autonomy which are the pillars of the "artistic critique" (Boltanski & Chiapello, 2011). From the moment when the idea of this individual autonomy became paramount, it seemed essential to manage the imaginary, desires, and beliefs of it adequately through marketing techniques.

In a context in which professional identities are challenged by individualisation, hybridisation, and marketisation processes, influencers participate in the production of new informational and "experiential goods" (Moeglin, 2007) transferred to specific communities of interest. If expertise, independence, and professionalism continue to be valued, their legitimacy rests above all on a "regime of proximity" (Coavoux & Roques, 2020). The latter also constitutes a form of adaptation to the formalisation of cultural exchanges that, on the one hand, involve a strong diversification of the supply and, on the other hand, a degradation of working and employment conditions dominated by uncertainty. Highlighting proximity thus guarantees content producers a place in the logic of supply through the creation of market niches.

As part of the production relationship, in line with the capitalist chain of value, the influencer's activity can be considered "digital labour": "networked social work" in which the relational aspect of the tasks of content production, shared among affective communities, contributes to "reversing the respective roles of autonomy and subordination, choice and constraint [...]" (Casilli, 2019, p. 163). Unlike on-demand work or micro-work, the user-producer is not formally subordinated to the platform, although he or she is subject to incentives, which are sometimes symbolic (through reputational rewards), and sometimes economic (in the form of monetary compensation or commercial advantages), for performing in a connected social environment. Social platforms sell the promise that users can become their own media, giving them the power to influence the behaviour or thinking of other individuals. At the same time, the contribution of the user-producer is eminently social, as it is based on content circulating between individuals and being evaluated. This "free labour" is part of the structure of the cultural economy of late capitalism, which mobilises labour by confining it to an "underpaid activity" (Terranova, 2000). In this regard, the tendency towards the autonomy of labour comes into conflict with the attempt to subordinate the totality of social time to the heterogeneous logic of the valorisation of capital (Vercellone 2011).

The essence of these new figures, whose endeavours are the product of a tension between the construction of digital identity and the deployment of marketing and platform strategies, is that they manage and rely on a community over which they claim to have influence. Their "practice" should therefore be understood as "knowledgeable doing", since practical knowledge emerges from it being produced, and is anchored in material supports, objects, and technologies that achieve agency through their performative connections (Gherardi, 2018).

By fitting into the beyond perspective, our chapter emphasises the role of professionals as actors of change. Differentiation in professionalism is actually the result of two processes: on the one hand, professional practices and discourse are increasingly defined by political challenges, social movements, and socio-technical changes and, on the other hand, professionals contribute to the evolution of organisations, both in terms of strategies and narratives, to the point of ensuring a new activist posture. In order to question SMIs as a specific form of hybrid professionalism, we need to shift the focus beyond the academic discourse on professionalism, in a way that includes the relationships between professionals, technology, and society. SMIs' professionalism is actually built through the recognition of their social and political functions. Their action evokes the figure of "artistic critique" (Boltanski & Chiapello, 2011), while also questioning reticular models of cooperation as providing new modular repertoires (Tarrow & Tilly, 2008) that are part of the professionalisation dynamic.

3 Methodological Approach

Our study is made up of two parts. The first part concerns mainstream communications and marketing professionals' perceptions of social media influencers and, more generally, their conceptions of professionalism. This part relies on an ethnographic observation of the "Com' en Nord Day 2022",[1] a French event bringing together communications and marketing professionals to reflect on corporate social responsibility approaches to tackling the environmental crisis (the professionals' speeches have been recorded), as well as a series of semi-directed

[1] "La journée de la Com' en Nord de France", Lille Grand Palais, March 2022: https://comenorday.com/ledition-2022/

interviews conducted with representatives from agencies specialising in influence marketing. This part of the study is complemented with a discourse analysis conducted on a corpus of four practitioner handbooks presenting the best practices to adopt in the context of influence marketing and of 20 articles published on the website of the COM-ENT professional association communications[2] between April 2020 and March 2021, stemming from the "DirCom (Re)confined" section. This section was created during the pandemic, it adopted an interview format and aimed to identify the way communication directors defined and perceived changes in their profession during the health emergency.

The second part aims at better understanding the professionalisation processes visible in the evolution of self-presentation practices of health and lifestyle social media influencers. In order to do this, we have conducted an online ethnography of five Instagram accounts of users diagnosed with congenital melanocytic nevus. The selected accounts match the description of an influencer, in that they gather communities around them, with the power to impact their opinions and actions, both small (micro and nano-influencers) and large ones (macro-influencers).

By adopting a diachronic approach, we have analysed a total of 777 posts, uploaded to the platform between February 2013 and July 2021. The analysis of this corpus mobilises both the discourse analysis and the qualitative content analysis approaches. We categorised the publications of each profile as either health-related posts, commitments to a cause, self-promotional, brand-endorsement, motivational (self-confidence, body-positive messages) or lifestyle-oriented posts. The weight of each category reveals the account's editorial policy that enables the owners to specialise in one domain, cater to their audience's expectations, and therefore secure their follower base, as well as the resulting opportunities. Since these actors are engaged in raising awareness around body stigma and providing online support for building self-esteem, this part also enables us to further understand the links between digital hybrid professionalism and collective action frames.

[2] https://www.com-ent.fr

4 Social Influence at the Core of the Communications and Marketing Professions

The differentiation processes of professions related to digital communication are evident in the growing number of titles and functions (community manager, social media manager, multimedia project manager, etc.). For all of them, skill in mansaging social media to influence online communities is key for claiming legitimacy and recognition (Coutant & Millette, 2021). However, professions related to digital communication are part of contemporary "knowledge work" that is not characterised by strong epistemological formalisation or state-backed regulation (Butler et al., 2012). The lack of formalisation encourages professionals to engage in reflective and discursive activity aiming at (re)framing "professionalism" through a rhetorical process in which their identity and status are perceived to be precarious (Cheney & Ashcraft, 2007). As such, professionalism is conceived both as a "disciplinary" mechanism, aimed at controlling professional practice within organisations, and as a mechanism of "occupational mobilisation" (Evetts 2006). Based on the reconceptualisation of the notion of "professionalism" in terms of "discursive resources" (CH 1: 5), this section aims to explore professionals' framing activities and their links to the mechanisms of social influence and political engagement.

4.1 The Social Function of Professionals in a World of Crises

External pressures exerted by social movements and audiences regarding environmental and health emergencies are shaping the professional identities of people who now wish to redefine their professionalism based on political and societal demands. Entitled "Towards an ethical and responsible communication", the 2022 edition of the "Com' en Nord" day allowed us to observe the way professionals are adapting their discourses and practices to face the climate emergency.

> *The impacts of marketing on overconsumption, on the accumulation of waste in the oceans, on global pollution, pushed me to deconstruct what I was doing and what I was teaching.* (Florence Touzé-Rieu, Associate Professor at Audencia Business School, member of "Responsables! by Adetem"; from an intervention in the "Com' en Nord de France" conference, March 2022)

They then re-frame their discourses on professionalism by asserting their capacity to influence society. In the first instance, influence is mentioned as a field in its own right, involving all types of professionals in the communications sector. In this case, SMIs are considered as new partners/providers with whom professionals establish ethical relationships. In the second instance, it is considered as a function that cuts across all communications and marketing professions. In the end, taking into consideration their impact on major environmental and social issues, it also appears that the status of professionals as producers of new narratives to transform society is restored. From this perspective, "influence" refers to:

> *The responsibility of professionals in building a collective imaginary with the aim of accompanying and propelling the promotion of another society.* (Valérie Martin, Head of the Citizen Mobilisation and Media Department at ADEME, from an intervention in the "Com' en Nord de France" conference, March 2022)

Professionalism is thus linked to the ability to interpret and encourage social change. The practice of influence is often considered, in a pejorative way, as a manipulative activity. These professionals are trying to re-signify it in order to build the legitimacy of the profession:

> *Let's stop seeing it* [referring to influence in communications professions] *as a constraint and see it as an opportunity to support the transformation of society and to re-legitimise our profession. [...] We have a responsibility because we have enormous power to influence society.* (Valérie Martin, Head of the Citizen Mobilisation and Media Department at ADEME, from an intervention in the "Com' en Nord de France" conference, March 2022)

The context of the climate crisis can thus be seized as an opportunity to establish the legitimacy of the profession: corporate social responsibility mechanisms are strengthened as part of a transformation perspective that aims to mobilise actors,

> *[...] to shape new consumption and production practices and to integrate them into the company's global strategy.* (Adeline Ochs, Professor at Audencia Business School, Founder of Topoye, from an intervention in the "Com' en Nord de France" conference, March 2022)

Acting inside and outside organisations, communicators see themselves as key actors in the socio-ecological transition. Their role becomes one of accompanying the change in consumer practices through the creation of new narratives, which are linked to the aspirations and demands of civil society. Involving customers as co-creators of value adds complexity, in that it introduces tension between professionals' identities (defined by organisational hierarchies, professional legitimacy, specialised knowledge, professional competence, work ethic, etc.) and an imagined customer with expertise and who has a critical eye on the business and consumer world. This tension opens up a space for reflexive professional action (Echeverri, 2022), where practitioners, focused on creative and discursive processes, constantly interact with the public and consider their links with the outside world as a key element of their professionalism. The reflexive posture of communications professionals was particularly intense during the COVID-19 pandemic:

> *Today's consumers expect companies to provide values as well as products, meaning as well as services. And the crisis* [referring to COVID-19] *has only accelerated the phenomenon.* (Domitille Fafin, Director of External Communications, L'Oréal Group, from an interview published on the COM-ENT website on 8 August 2020)

In particular, this will involve re-framing the task of professionals on the basis of their ability to influence and bring about change within organisations and in society. The discourse around corporate social responsibility also feeds into the audience's political demands. This stimulates the professionals to look at and adopt a committed attitude towards the causes held dear by the consumers with which they wish both to build a relationship and to address their corporate communication:

> *[...]People will want to consume better, and more in favour of positive, honest brands that are concerned with the collective interest. There is every reason to believe that consumption will become a political and cultural act in its own right.* (Caroline Tiquet, Director of Communications and Marketing at Le Slip Français, from an interview published on the COM-ENT website on 4 May 2020).

While accentuating the "committed" approach of professionals, this discourse has both a "legitimising" and an "integrating" function (Ricoeur, 1978), in that it actually seeks to reduce conflict and develop a desirable system through cooperation and belief in its legitimacy. The discourse that can be traced back to the categories of critique actually model the reformulations and rearrangements of "artistic critique" and "social critique" (Boltanski & Chiapello, 2011) within the framework of the devices of new responsible communications, aiming to influence and engage people in the promotion of a sustainable society.

In addition to the responsibilities traditionally associated with professionals and driven by the ideology of communications—to create links, produce meaning and values, mobilise and unite people around a common project—professionalism is also seen and experienced as a political commitment to the ecological transition.

This first part highlights professionals' contributions to the process of change, both inside and outside organisations (Chap. 1: 12). It shows the way they are constantly re-framing their perceptions and conceptions of "professionalism" on the basis of social change and due to the emergence of new political and societal causes embraced by the public and which they are trying to engage with and promote.

4.2 Social Media Influencer: A Specific Form of Hybrid Professionalism that Challenges Marketing Strategies

With the growth of the SMI phenomenon, influencer marketing is on the rise. Experts expect the market to reach a value of 16.4 billion dollars in 2022.[3] For online marketing professionals, influencers are gradually becoming new content providers and professional partners capable of influencing marketing practices and changing relationships with clients:

> *You don't need to appreciate influencer content to know that it works, because influencers know how to talk to their communities. [...] What does work is peer-to-peer communication... and you are not a peer. [...] influence marketing must become one of your key communication levers because [...] the results are really there and measurable.* (Bouillet, 2020, p. 28)

The work of influencers is recognised here for its measurable profitability, something that does not necessarily include expertise. SMIs' ability to be perceived as insiders by the community adds value. These statements suggest an ambiguity regarding the status of influencers as professionals. Theoretically, anyone can become an influencer, without any training or educational prerequisites. Unlike the craft consumers of pre-Internet capitalism, influencers are not already endowed with significant social or cultural capital (Casilli, 2019). They use these platforms to create both the product and the community that can appreciate their content and on whom they can exert influence.

The emergence of new platforms, such as Kolsquare or Hivency, allows sponsors to access performance metrics and choose influencers accordingly. This shows that the field of influence is not exempt from commissioned work, platform work, and the digital labour logic. Moreover, according to some of the influencer marketing agency professionals we

[3] Geyser, W. (2022 January 24). The State of Influencer Marketing 2022. Benchmark Report. *Influencer Marketing Hub.*
https://influencermarketinghub.com/influencer-marketing-benchmark-report/

interviewed, being an influencer requires expertise in a specific domain that it is recognised by a community:

> *In my opinion, an influencer is an opinion leader who specialises in a subject and who, with time, has acquired notoriety and credibility, without any exterior media.* (Christophe P., strategic planner, Agency #1)

> *Expertise is what makes influencers legitimate in speaking out.* (Laura P. marketing manager, Agency #3)

In this sense, influencers act as opinion leaders (Katz & Lazarsfeld, 1955), and social media acts as "alternative media", as opposed to more mainstream media, such as television. However, social media influencers have responsibilities that require skills that can be acquired through their repeated use of social media. Some professionals clearly contribute to the construction of an emergent discourse on the "professionalism" of SMIs (Bellini & Maestripieri, 2018), one that conveys specific values, competencies, and practices that allow them to be identified and recognised within both professional groups and online communities:

> *Clearly, it is a new profession. I see a lot of people making a living out of it. It's very new. Five years ago, it was not a profession. People had followers because they were interesting and posted nice content, but now it is a real profession. In the future, maybe there will be some kind of training to teach people how to make good, interesting content, good descriptions, and how to film videos and take good pictures, all of that. These are skills that take practice.* (Laura P., marketing manager, Agency #3)

One of the main things pointed out by the interviewees was the central role played by the expertise of the "talent" in the influencer marketing strategies. Rather than being considered as walking billboards with no say regarding their content, they themselves are the creative minds initiating it:

> *The talents themselves are the creatives. They have the most control over their careers. [...] On the creative side, in terms of content and what they're saying*

and their opinions, that's all down to the talent, that doesn't come from us. (Emma W., marketing manager of Agency #2)

The use of the word "creative" when referring to the SMIs demonstrates the hybrid status of the profession of influencers, who deal with platform, market, and professional logics, as well as creative and collective ones. Creativity and professionalism are two elements that can go hand in hand. The connection between them can be guaranteed by both professional associations and more informal communities that are committed to promoting individual competencies and social capital (Dorigatti et al., 2019). Unlike other professional groups, what is really important for influencers is not having standards, values, and knowledge recognised by intermediate bodies, but the social meaning of their knowledge, and the fact that they are recognised as experts by social media users who share the same interests and commitments. This can be traced back to the "beyond" issue that refers to the marketisation process that makes professionals much more dependent on clients' choices in a context characterised by the democratisation of expert knowledge and public distrust of institutional actors.

But the market dimension creates tension both within followers' communities and professional groups that bemoan that the shift from volunteer work to contractual work involves a loss of authenticity:

I find that this monetisation distorts things a little. (…) Nowadays, when an influencer charges money, you can tell it's what motivates them. Loving the brand takes a back seat. I think it distorts what influencers were, originally. (Lucie P., marketing manager of Agency #3)

Nevertheless, practitioner handbooks state that it is now becoming customary to pay influencers and identify them as new members of professional marketing groups:

If brands are using influencers as part of their marketing strategy, those influencers are an extension of the brand's marketing team. They deserve to be compensated for their time, energy, and the finished product. In this respect,

> *influencers are more like freelance marketers than celebrity endorsers.* (Sammis et al., 2016, p. 62)

Within the framework of collaborations, contracts are drawn up, setting out the commitment of both parties, highlighting the professional nature of the relationship and setting out ground rules that leave no ambiguity about the expected deliverables or the compensation to be paid for them. In addition, due to its exponential growth, influencer marketing is now subjected to regulations. This means that, despite the reticence of some marketing agencies and professionals, the work of influencers is recognised as valuable, and it is increasingly regulated by the professional group itself (Wood, 2022; Kuhlmann, 2021). Once again, in order to understand this new form of hybrid professionalism and its integration into marketing strategies, we must go beyond the traditional framework of professions and focus on external dynamics in terms of their meaning and power relations in society (Klegon, 1978).

This study thus shows the tension dominating the status of influencers. They face a double challenge: they benefit from being seen as peers by their audience, but it is also advantageous for them to promote their professional status in community management and online content creation. They involve communities of interest and practices by building on social awareness and recognition.

As the latest avatar of advertising ideologies, social media influencers also fit into the legitimation and transformation processes by responding to a search for profitability and authenticity in the face of increased public mistrust. In the end, external dynamics—influencing social change—are perceived as the main source of their professionalism, as well as being a way to legitimise the profession and its claim for social recognition in a context where deregulation is eroding the capacity of professionals to secure their status (Butler et al., 2012). Influencers make the great heterogeneity of professionalisation processes visible, via their link to the wider dynamics of social change and the increasingly reflexive, negotiated, and essentially "discursive" dimension (Chap. 1: 5) that professionalism takes on in contemporary society.

5 Professionalism and Collective Action: The Case of Health Influencers

Health and lifestyle influencers can be viewed through the analytical category of "hybridised professionalism" (Noordegraaf, 2007), which refers to new ways of controlling or "standardising" practices, new mechanisms for legitimating work, fresh searches for occupational identities and novel links between individual demands, professional claims, and organised action. This section studies the online self-presentation strategies developed by health influencers with congenital nevus, a stigma-inducing dermatological condition manifested by the presence of visible pigmented proliferations in the skin (called nevi).

The analysis shows that influencers' practices involve "mechanisms for legitimating their work" (see Table 13.1), expressed through the willingness to conform to the aesthetic standards of the platform by moving to a business account, developing an editorial policy and publishing quality content. We also noticed an improvement in the quality of the content over time: captions became longer and more optimised and the picture quality improved significantly. Overall, we saw that more attention was paid to details in order to engage the audience with pleasant, consistent, and curated content, bringing the practices of influencers closer to those of digital communications professionals.

The quest for legitimacy is also reflected in the "search for occupational identities" illustrated by the choice of a job title in the Instagram account, which aims to justify their position as professionals (Maestripieri, 2016) in their own field of expertise. Even though marketing agency professionals, by virtue of their strategic potential and ability to reach and influence an audience, consider them as influencers, the SMIs themselves do not emphasise this label. Instead, they highlight their occupation as entrepreneurs, bloggers, artists, or digital creators, thus demonstrating a desire to build their identity around these activities rather than the "influencer" identity. But even if it is not exclusive or declared, their occupation as social media influencers appears to be relevant to developing a personal brand that allows them to promote other projects or to obtain access to more professional opportunities.

Table 13.1 SMIs hybrid professionalism inspired by the "From Pure to Hybrid Professionalism" table presented by Noordegraaf (2007, p. 779)

Name	Followers/posts/domain of expertise	Hybrid approaches	Mechanisms for legitimating work	Searches for occupational identity[a]	Linkages with collective action
@luna.love.hope	289 k 150 posts Daily life with a rare disease	Professional/committed	Business account Editorial policy	Blogger	Advocacy hashtags Fundraising Mutual endorsement
@yulianna.yussef	121 k 253 posts Fashion and lifestyle	Professional/committed	Business account Self-promotion Professional photos Editorial policy	Entrepreneur Sponsorships	Association Advocacy hashtags Fundraising Mutual endorsement
@lovingmydots	16.2 k 220 posts Body positive	Professional/committed	Business account Editorial policy	Digital creator Motivational speaker Sponsorship	Advocacy Hashtags Mutual endorsement
@robiarcuri	3149 47 posts Daily life	Professional/personal	Business account Self-promotion Professional photos Editorial policy	Artist	Association Mutual endorsement
@_bw_boy	833 107 posts Sport	Personal	Self-promotion		Association Hashtags Mutual endorsement

[a]Occupational identity refers to how the account is described by its owner as well as other sources of income

We also found a hybridisation dynamic bringing together different approaches: professional (posts aiming at promoting one's work and product placement); personal (focusing on self-narrative and sharing stories of life with the disease); and committed (aiming at raising awareness and influencing other people's views on stigma issues). By fitting into the analytical model of hybrid professionalism, the rise in professionalism here is closely linked to the other two approaches, personal and committed, enabling influencers to reach out to the public and build their reputation as a person who provides resources and whose expertise is derived from direct experience of the disease and stigma (see Table 13.1 "Hybrid approaches").

As interest for their content grows, new customs emerge and lead to influencers being considered professionals, and their work requires supervision and assessment. The recognition by the professional sector is then complemented by peer-to-peer recognition mechanisms. Professionalism is thus shaped and performed in a relational and reputational way, from links to political and social phenomena that are external to the professional sphere of reference. Throughout our study, we have observed the implementation of a rationale of reciprocity, with influencers showing mutual support by sharing each other's content and endorsing one other, rather than taking on competitive positions. Influencers with nevus are part of the same online community of practice, sharing the same commitments and registers, all building knowledge and harmonising self-representation practices by using consistent visual branding as a vehicle of professionalism. This is not surprising as recent studies show indeed that the sharing and the collective construction of harmonised professional practices apply to a large number of influencers' communities, such as expert readers—who talk about their reading practices (Siguier, 2020)—and independent videographers (Coavoux & Roques, 2020).

This "practical knowledge" (Gherardi, 2018), anchored in the platform registers and metrics, achieves a performative dimension. Beyond the self-exposure practices and the rise in professionalism, these strategies are also part of a logic of collective action: the images and content posted contribute to creating a collective framework of action (Benford & Snow, 2000) and reflect the desire for the user to take action, whether it is a change in the way they perceive body differences in society or to act for a cause, such as taking part in a fundraiser (@luna.love.hope). This is where we find the reference to the third variable that identifies hybrid forms of professionalism: the links between work and organised action:

> [....] *I want people to know that this disease (Congenital Giant Nevus) exists. I also hope that my activity on the networks can somehow help and encourage adults and children affected by CGN. I have found many new members and directed them to our support page on Facebook [speaking about a patients' association]. Basically, everything I say and do on Instagram is related to my experience with CGN, my choices and responsibilities*!!
> *#perfectionofmyskin #bareyourbirthmark #inmyskiniwin #nevus* (Published in April 2018 on Yulianna Yussef's Instagram profile @yulianna.yussef)

When these influencers are involved in traditional forms of collective action such as patients' associations, which work to build expert and experiential knowledge to fight body stigma, their commitment is primarily deployed through the logic of "connective action" (Bennett & Segerberg, 2012). In this new pattern, political demands are often shared in very personalised accounts on social networking platforms. These individualised orientations include the propensity to develop flexible and ephemeral political identifications based on personal aspirations and lifestyles rather than strong ideological identifications. Health influencers advocate for a cause, promote self-esteem, and try to raise awareness about body difference discrimination, in particular through the use of hashtags as new collective action repertories (#nevuslove, #inmyskiniwin or #bareyourbirthmark). While showing themselves as unique, they each preserve the harmony and coherence encouraged by the increasingly professional application of Instagram's aesthetic standards and by conveying the same message. In line with the neoliberal ethos, their discourse revolves around personal development, self-mastery, and the resilience capacity of the individual.

> *Beauty is being comfortable in your own skin. It's about knowing and accepting who you are. #wearebeautiful #selfesteem #selflove #mentalhealthchallenge @ bbcbodypotitive @dove* (Published on 9 May 2019 on Natalia Freitas' Instagram profile @lovingmydots)

The online ethnography shows that the role of SMIs goes beyond generating income through promoting content and products on their social media accounts. Through the professionalisation and the optimisation of their presence on online platforms, influencers can be seen as "infomediaries" (Frau-Meigs, 2017): not only do they share their narratives and opinions online, they become intermediaries and providers of resources. Moreover, we can see they use their voices and celebrity capital (Driessens, 2013) in order to give visibility to causes such as diversity and representation of bodily differences. From this angle, professionalisation can be understood as a contentious performance (Tarrow & Tilly, 2008) that can be seized by dominated groups in order to define new norms or needs.

Hiring SMIs appears to be an opportunity to re-enchant the corporate world by responding to a search for authenticity and by performing, through the biographical narrative, the "real talk" which was actually conceived by traditional advertisers. Social media influencers share a common range of competencies and a common objective with marketing and communications professionals: they both claim community management skills and expertise and produce creative content in order to influence their audience's representations and practices; they both conceive professionalism as a tool to interpret and answer real social needs and aspirations for change.

6 Conclusion

Digitalisation and platformisation processes contribute to blurring boundaries between expert and non-expert actors and to accelerating the dynamics of differentiation of professions and perceptions of professionalism, leading to a wide heterogeneity of occupational identities and professional practices. Platforms reinforce inequalities and accentuate processes of flexibility, precariousness, and outsourcing while also opening up new opportunities for employment or professional integration.

Becoming a professional influencer constitutes an opportunity for claiming remuneration to be paid for a social activity that is extremely productive and profitable for both platforms and traditional companies. SMIs fit into the analytical frame of this book, as a part of increasingly precarious expert labour group that is working outside acknowledged professional models and traditional partnerships and that has taken on board the market logic as something natural (Maestripieri & Cucca, 2018). The case of influencers also illustrates the shift from status professionalism, based on social position, to heterogeneous occupational professionalisms that are based on the appearance of specialised knowledge and tasks (Klegon, 1978) and that have an essentially discursive dimension (Evetts, 2006).

Influencers can claim professional status by meeting ethics and quality standards in producing and referencing content, showing their expertise in the use of digital platforms, and formalising their collaborations with marketing agencies and other economic actors. However, in this specific case, mastering a substantial body of theoretical knowledge is not systematically considered essential. In order to understand the professionalisation dynamic of SMIs, we thus need an external approach, one that is able to look at the role of occupational resources and their links to the wider social structure and new forms of building collective action and expertise on digital platforms. By challenging the classical notion of "professionalism", in which standards and quality are assessed by peers through the mediation of intermediate bodies, influencers rely on reputational mechanisms, market success, and personal relationships. Professionalism is carried out in the framework of communities of practices where members recognise each other, share values, and develop knowledge and skills in social media. In this context, formal professionalisation would be more of a hindrance than a resource.

Influencers thus constitute a specific case of "hybrid professionalism" (Noordegraaf, 2007), in which quantitative performance criteria prescribed by platforms (number of subscribers, likes, comments, etc.) are combined with creative production that responds to the registers of visibility, proximity, and authenticity. Although they claim expertise and develop and share professional practices in the communications and marketing fields, these actors do not necessarily engage in a real process of institutionalisation (reflecting forms of ethics, skills, knowledge, and experience assessed and supervised by associations and jurisdiction) as this could paradoxically discredit them. Indeed, the influence they exert amongst their communities derives mainly from the way they differ from institutional actors. In order to go beyond traditional approaches, our perspective looks at professionals both as "institutional agents" (Chap. 1: 12) who influence and reaffirm the project and the social role of complex market organisations (as shown by the discourse on "professionalism" deployed by marketing and communications professionals) and as individual actors directly engaged in a struggle for visibility (as shown by the study on health influencers).

The promotion of social and political causes on Instagram leads to a professionalising practice, rooted in a legitimate desire for social change, but resulting in the formation of community interests capable of anticipating or generating demand. By producing a visual and symbolic continuity with communications and marketing contents, influencers co-write a discourse that delivers an ethos and ideals with which to project themselves to online communities. The two different approaches to activism, a connective one that is individualised and centred on personal development, and the collective one, acting through conventional organisations, seem to mirror the distinction between "social critique" and "artistic critique", one referring to claims based on social justice and the fight against inequalities and the other centred on the promotion of authenticity, autonomy, and individual fulfilment (Boltanski & Chiapello, 2011).

In accordance with the new spirit of capitalism, the social influence exerted online by these emerging hybrid professionalisms often relies on the market and favours self-interest and individual motivations and strategies over collective ones.

References

Abdelnour, S., & Méda, D. (2019). *Les nouveaux travailleurs des applis*. Presses universitaires de France.

Bellini, A., & Maestripieri, L. (2018). Professions within, between and beyond. Varieties of professionalism in a globalising world. *Cambio. Rivista sulle trasformazioni sociali, 8*(16), 5–14. https://doi.org/10.13128/cambio-24947

Benford, R. D., & Snow, D. A. (2000). Framing processes and social movements. An overview and assessment. *Annual Review of Sociology, 26*, 611–639. https://doi.org/10.1146/annurev.soc.26.1.611

Bennett, W. L., & Segerberg, A. (2012). The logic of connective action. *Information, Communication & Society, 15*(5), 739–768. https://doi.org/10.1080/1369118X.2012.670661

Boltanski, L. & Chiapello, E. (2011). *Le nouvel esprit du capitalisme.* Paris, Gallimard. (First Edition 1999).

Butler, N., Chillas, S., & Muhr, S. L. (2012). Professions at the margins. *Ephemera, 12*(3), 259–272.

Campbell, C., & Farrell, J. (2020). More than meets the eye: The functional components underlying influencer marketing. *Business Horizons, 63*(4), 469–479. https://doi.org/10.1016/j.bushor.2020.03.003

Casilli, A. (2019). *En attendant les robots.* Seuil.

Cheney, G., & Ashcraft, K. L. (2007). Considering "the professional" in communication studies: Implications for theory and research within and beyond the boundaries of organizational communication. *Communication Theory, 17*(2), 146–175. https://doi.org/10.1111/j.1468-2885.2007.00290.x

Coavoux, S., & Roques, N. (2020). Une profession de l'authenticité: Le régime de proximité des intermédiaires du jeu vidéo sur Twitch et YouTube. *Réseaux, 6*(224), 169–196. https://doi.org/10.3917/res.224.0169

Conley, D. (2010). *Elsewhere.* Vintage Books.

Coutant, A., & Millette, J. (2021). Les métiers de l'influence en contexte numérique : une approche sociotechnique des pratiques professionnelles. *Communication et organisation, 2*(60), 61–75. https://doi.org/10.4000/communicationorganisation.10445

Dorigatti, L., Bellini, A., & Manzo, C. (2019). Interest representation in graphic design and video game development in Italy: Demand, supply and influence on working conditions. In V. Pulignano & F. Hendrickx (Eds.), *Employment relations in the 21st century: Challenges for theory and research in a changing world of work* (pp. 1–21). Kluwer Law International.

Driessens, O. (2013). Celebrity capital: Redefining celebrity using field theory. *Theory and Society, 42*(5), 543–560. https://doi.org/10.1007/s11186-013-9202-3

Evetts, J. (2006). Introduction: Trust and Professionalism: Challenges and Occupational Changes. *Current Sociology, 54*(4), 515–531. https://doi.org/10.1177/0011392106065083.

Echeverri, P. (2022). Professional reflexivity in customer involvement: Tensions and ambiguities in between identities. *Marketing Theory, 0*(0), 1–24. https://doi.org/10.1177/1470593122108771

Frau-Meigs, D. (2017). Les youtubeurs: les nouveaux influenceurs! *Nectart, 5*, 126–136. https://doi.org/10.3917/nect.005.0126

Freberg, K., Graham, K., McGaughey, K., & Freberg, L. (2011). Who are the social media influencers? A study of public perceptions of personality. *Public Relations Review., 37*(1), 90–92. https://doi.org/10.1016/j.pubrev.2010.11.001

Gherardi, S. (2018). Teoria e Prática em Administração. *Practices and Knowledges, 8*(2), 33–59. https://doi.org/10.21714/2238-104X2018v8i2S-38857

Katz, E., & Lazarsfeld, P. (1955). Personal Influence. The Part Played by People in the Flow of Mass Communication. New York. Free Press

Klegon, D. (1978). The sociology of professions, an emerging perspective. *Sociology of work and Occupations*. Sages Publications, *5*(3), 259–283. https://doi.org/10.1177/073088847800500301

Maestripieri, L. (2016). Professionalization at work: The case of Italian management consultants. *Ephemera, 16*(2), 33–54. ISSN 1473-2866.

Maestripieri, L., & Cucca, R. (2018). Small is beautiful? Emerging organizational strategies among Italian professionals. *Canadian Review of Sociology, 55*(3), 362–384. https://doi.org/10.1111/cars.12208

Moeglin, P. (2007). Des modèles socio-économiques en mutation. In P. Bouquillion & Y. Combès (Eds.), *Les Industries de la culture et de la communication en mutation* (pp. 151–162). L'Harmattan.

Noordegraaf, M. (2007). From 'pure' to 'hybrid' professionalism. Present-day professionalism in ambiguous public domains. *Administration and Society, 39*(6), 761–781. https://doi.org/10.1177/0095399707304434

Ricoeur, P. (1978). *L'idéologie et l'utopie*. Seuil.

Sedda, P. (2022). The digital mobilisation: Between emancipation and rationalisation. *Approches Théoriques en Information-Communication (ATIC), 3*(2), 53–74. https://doi.org/10.3917/atic.003.0053

Sedda, P., & Botero, N. (2022). La voix inaudible de la différence. Présence numérique des personnes porteuses d'anomalies dermatologiques. In B. Ferron, E. Née, & C. Oger (Eds.), *Donner la parole aux "sans-voix"? Construction sociale et mise en discours d'un problème public* (pp. 127–142). PUR.

Siguier, M. (2020). Donner à voir le lecteur sur les réseaux sociaux numériques: Bookstagram, entre nouveaux régimes de visibilité et iconographies standardisées. *Études de communication., 1*(54), 113–134. https://doi.org/10.4000/edc.10203

Tarrow, S., & Tilly, C. (2008). *Politique(s) du conflit, de la grève à la révolution*. Les Presses de Sciences Po.

Terranova, T. (2000). Free labor: Producing culture for the digital economy. *Social Text, 18*(2), 33–58. https://www.muse.jhu.edu/article/31873
Vercellone, C. (2011). De l'ouvrier-masse au travail cognitif. Valeur, travail et répartition dans le capitalisme cognitif. *European Journal of Economic and Social Systems, 24*(1–2), 15–43. https://doi.org/10.3166/EJESS.24
Voirol, O. (2005). Struggles for visibility: Outline of an issue. *Réseaux, 129–130*, 89–121. https://www.cairn.info/revue-2005-1-page-89.htm

Practitioner Handbooks

Kuhlmann, T. (2021). A guide to Instagram influencer marketing: Instagram marketing tools to achieve your goals. Jerome Rehagen.
Sammis, K., Ng, J., Lincoln, C., Pomponi, S., & Zhou, J. (2016). *Influencer marketing for dummies*. John Wiley & Sons, Inc.
Wood, B. (2022). *Working with influencers: How to promote your business with the help of social media influencers*. Bill Wood.

14

Conclusions: Making Sense of Professionalism and Social Change

Lara Maestripieri and Andrea Bellini

1 Back to the Idea behind the Book

This book takes its inspiration from an ambitious theoretical challenge: to study professionalism in its interaction with social change over the last 50 years. To do so, we put together a simple but heuristically effective analytical framework based on three "irreducible"—that is, mutually interrelated—dimensions: the "within" dimension, concerning the internal dynamics of a professional group; the "between" dimension, pertaining to the relationships between professions or professional groups; the "beyond" dimension, focusing on the reciprocal influence between

L. Maestripieri (✉)
IGOP/Department of Political Science and Public Law, Universitat Autònoma de Barcelona Campus de la UAB, Bellaterra, Spain
e-mail: lara.maestripieri@uab.cat

A. Bellini
Department of Social and Economic Sciences (DiSSE), Sapienza University of Rome, Rome, Italy
e-mail: andrea.bellini@uniroma1.it

© The Author(s), under exclusive license to Springer Nature Switzerland AG 2023

L. Maestripieri, A. Bellini (eds.), *Professionalism and Social Change*,
https://doi.org/10.1007/978-3-031-31278-6_14

professions and society. From now on, we shall refer to this analytical framework of within-between-beyond as the WBB model.

The aim of these conclusions is to put together the pieces of the puzzle presented in the Introduction (Chap. 1). To do so, we need to remind our readers of our starting point and to emphasise why we need new analytical tools.

A key occurrence in the recent history of Western societies has been the rise of the post-industrial society and the subsequent tertiarisation of the economy (see Touraine, 1969; Bell, 1973). These changes, along with the growing importance of knowledge as a production factor and the related increase in the number of expert occupations (see Machlup, 1962; Drucker, 1968; Bell, 1973), make up our initial focus. We identify the post-industrial transition as the main engine of the processes of change that are considered in this book; this includes the de-standardisation of employment and the feminisation of labour markets. We also consider the effects of globalisation and increasing international mobility, as well as technological change in the specific form of digitalisation (Chap. 1). However, a careful reading of the findings of the selected studies reveals the extent to which the transformation of professions and professional groups is not only a matter of *quantity* of expert labour but also of *quality* in terms of differential integration into society.

That said, these changes are not fully comprehensible if we do not take into account *neo-liberalisation* as the process through which *neo-liberalism* has transformed the economy and has pervaded society. As a matter of fact, neo-liberalisation has become intertwined with other macro-processes and has thus permeated and redirected social change by redesigning institutions. As such, it has promoted the rise of a new model of professionalism.

2 Neo-Liberalism: The Missing Piece

Neo-liberalism is here intended in its most common-sense meaning: the progressive market deregulation and state withdrawal that took place in Western societies during the 1980s and 1990s as an expression of neo-liberalism as an ideology.

The neo-liberal ideology—which quickly spread across the entire Western world—makes the moral and ethical assumptions that the market is the most efficient and effective way of organising human actions and that public regulation should be limited to instead favour a free market (Mudge, 2008). Its dominance in Western culture implies that economic actors (public and private) operate to minimise regulation in economic relationships—even including those that affect the regulation of professions. Neo-liberal agents share a fundamental cultural trait: trust in the power of the market.

As we have already mentioned in the introduction to this volume (Chap. 1), the erosion of barriers to access professions has implied the consolidation of several processes of change that are directly connected to neo-liberalism.

Despite the authors not explicitly mentioning neo-liberalism or neo-liberalisation among their key analytical elements, a cross-cutting analysis of the results of the 12 chapters reveals that most of the contributions refer to their main components: managerialism and marketisation. *Managerialism* assumes that the market provides a more effective and cost-efficient allocation of resources than the state. Its variant as new managerialism or new public management has introduced "business-like" methods and market mechanisms into the public administration (see Hood, 1991; Osborne & Gaebler, 1992; Pollitt, 1993). The diffusion of managerialism in the public sector and protected domains such as professions implies *marketisation*, which involves privatising some services, increasing competition among service providers (either public or private), and focusing on "customers".

Theoretically, it is possible to establish a parallelism between the neo-liberalisation process (specifically, managerialism and marketisation) and the de-standardisation of employment. These two developments have combined to produce increasingly deregulated labour markets, bringing with them a continued increase in temporary employment and self-employment. Neo-liberalisation is also linked to digitalisation and, more significantly, to the rise of new technologies and work platforms. As a matter of fact, digitalisation has brought the idea of marketisation to a higher level, allowing the principles of managerialism to be applied to create new business models such as work platforms. In addition, it has introduced new forms of controlling workers' activities, eroding the autonomy of professionals. Both processes are linked to feminisation:

while neo-liberalisation and digitalisation have created new job opportunities for women, they have also given rise to new forms of gendered inequalities. Neo-liberalisation is also linked to globalisation. Indeed, country-based neo-liberal policies that pursue the retrenchment of public spending and the deregulation of professional labour markets have created labour shortages in some countries and have facilitated the international mobility of professional workers—mainly from the Global South to the Global North, but also across countries where the same language is spoken. Combined, these processes outline the essential traits of what we call *neo-liberal professionalism*, which originated in deregulation policies, leading to its members becoming increasingly exposed to market risks, heterogeneous working conditions, and precarious jobs.

The cultural turn imposed by neo-liberalism thus challenged how professions had been studied up to the 1980s—that is, as occupational groups whose boundaries are determined through mechanisms of social closure that rely on self-regulation and peer control (Abbott, 1988; Freidson, 2001). This model of professionalism, labelled as "collegiate" professionalism, which is an expression of "guild-like" professionalisation (Reed, 2018), has progressively lost its capacity to explain the way occupational groups have been developing and consolidating their professional status. In fact, the rhetoric of neo-liberalism opposes any regulations or limitations being imposed on the market: the organisation of peers that is behind professional groups is at odds with the neo-liberal ideology and as such is something that is becoming progressively questioned.

Making this affirmation does not mean refuting the value of professionalism as a heuristic concept; on the contrary, it encourages us to widen our perspective as sociologists of professions and look at what lies beyond the collegiate model. Professionalism per se is not disappearing but is reconfiguring itself (Noordegraaf, 2020). That is, all the processes of differentiation analysed in this book can be understood along the lines of their impact in terms of reducing barriers to accessing professional work and increasing professionals' connections with the various actors that participate in their markets. Collegiate professionalism continues to retain its importance for traditional professions (e.g. law and medicine), but a new model of professionalism is gaining ground in emerging professions (Maestripieri & Cucca, 2018). This is a model in which professionalism is created in relation to and in connection with the actors that surround professionals, such as clients, stakeholders, and society at large. Noordegraaf (2020) has called this "connective" professionalism as opposed to "protective" professionalism.

3 Using the WBB Model to Study Neo-Liberal Professionalism

As we have seen, the success of neo-liberalism has somewhat eroded the heuristic capacity of collegiate professionalism. Yet the debate in the sociology of professions continues to revolve around theoretical and analytical frameworks that were developed during the twentieth century and can thus only partially intercept current trends. The toolbox to study professions needs to be renewed in order to guide the analysis of changing professionalism and to shed light on ongoing processes of differentiation. Specifically, we need new analytical tools to interpret neo-liberal professionalism. The WBB model takes up this challenge and tries to look beyond the way that professions have been studied up to now.

After this brief definition of the scope of our book, we now need to remind our readers of its main implications. As explained in the Introduction (Chap. 1), the barriers to accessing professions are being eroded, leading to the consolidation of several processes of differentiation. Analysing the findings in the chapters demonstrates the importance of two (interrelated) processes: for private-sector professions, the increasing deregulation of their activities; for public-sector professions, the pervasiveness of new public management, where managerialist principles are transferred to the context of the public administration.

More differentiation implies more heterogeneity among professions and professionals (Parding et al., 2021). By *heterogeneity*, we mean professionals growing increasingly different from each other. There is plenty of evidence of heterogeneity illustrated in the chapters: first, the number of people who define themselves as professionals today is higher than ever; second, an increasing number of expert occupations now fall outside traditional models of professionalism and professional practice; third, the composition of the professional labour force has become progressively diversified in terms of employer organisations and employment conditions, as well as social groups and geographies. In Fig. 14.1, a graphic representation is offered to explain how the WBB model works to interpret professional change in its interaction with social change, with *processes* of differentiation operating along three ideal *dimensions*—within, between, and beyond—to produce heterogeneity as an *outcome*.

In our view, professionalism is a "discourse" that encompasses the social norms, values, and worldviews that define what is necessary for individuals to be considered competent and valuable members of a professional community (Chap. 1). When there is a change in the membership base, work content, workplace, and regulating institutions, this means that professionalism changes. If we merely adopted conceptions of professionalism as relying on the idea of social closure as a set of mechanisms that "detaches" professions from the rest of the world, this would not be possible. In turn, new conceptual tools are needed to understand changing professionalism.

In fact, there is nothing new about highlighting the need for a redefinition of concepts. In the recent past, several theoretical constructs have been proposed to interpret these changes, such as organisational, hybrid, and connective professionalism. Independently from the term we might choose to use, we argue that the WBB model is flexible enough to make sense of the changes brought about by neo-liberalism, which implies differentiation and increasing heterogeneity among professions and professionals.

In our work as editors, we see ourselves as artisans of empirical research into the professions: our toolbox consists of simple concepts that identify the direction and outcome of change—that is, differentiation and heterogeneity—and the ideal dimensions along which change occurs: within, between, and beyond (see again Fig. 14.1). That said, the novelty of the WBB model does not lie in the concepts themselves but in how they are combined. In the following section, we present an overall interpretation of our results.

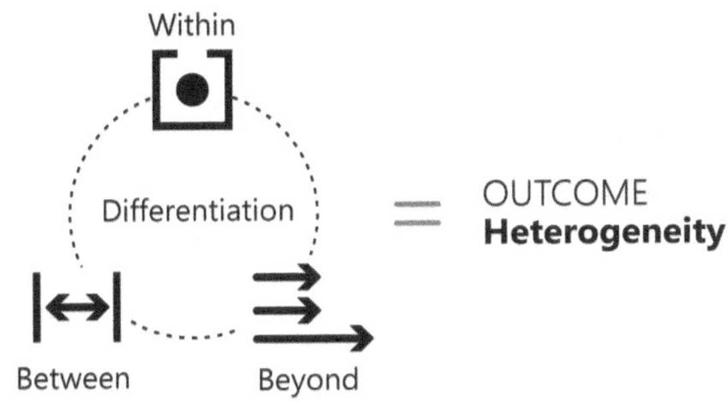

Fig. 14.1 A graphic representation of the WBB model. (*Source*: authors. Design: Jaume Badosa (http://www.jaumebadosa.cat/))

4 Key Findings by Analytical Dimension

In the chapters collected here, the authors have taken up the challenge of studying professionalism in the context of social change, and they have applied the WBB model to their specific cases, which involve various professions in different countries (see Table 14.1).

In this section, we will summarise the key findings along the three dimensions of the WBB model which emerged from the analysis of the 12 cases collected in this edited book. We will proceed dimension by dimension, without focusing on each specific case but trying to reveal the connections within each dimension of the WBB model.

4.1 The "within" Dimension

The first analytical dimension under scrutiny is the "within" dimension. This dimension focuses on the differentiation that is occurring inside professions. From this perspective, the most important driver of change appears to be the proliferation of different work settings. This is directly connected with the easier access to professions caused by the relaxation of the regulations that govern professional labour markets. By work setting, we refer to "the combination of type of organization in which the professionals perform their work and their employment status" (Maestripieri,

Table 14.1 Descriptive features of the 12 chapters

Chapter	Analytical dimension	Professions studied	Countries
Bataille et al.	Within	Academics	Switzerland
Bonnin	Within	Textile designers	South Africa
Insarauto et al.	Within	Lawyers	France, Switzerland
Arcidiacono et al.	Within	Architects, lawyers, journalists, psychologists	Italy
Parding and Jansson	Within	Nurses, teachers	Sweden
Bédard et al.	Between	Doctors, engineers	French Canada
Choroszewicz	Between	Lawyers	French Canada, Finland, Poland
Parcerisa et al.	Between	Teachers	World
Lucciarini and Pulignano	Between	Photographers, video makers, lighting and sound technicians	Italy
Adams	Beyond	Self-regulating professions	British Canada
Gjata et al.	Beyond	Architects	United States
Sedda and Husson	Beyond	Social media influencers	France

2019: 358). Indeed, the story of professions in contemporary society is a story of changing organisational logics and deregulation—in line with the cultural change introduced by neo-liberal ideologies taking root.

The sociology of professions, since Evetts (2006, 2011) and Noordegraaf (2007), has stressed the importance of organisational logics, while it has paid little attention to changing employment conditions—with only a few exceptions (see Maestripieri, 2016; Maestripieri & Cucca, 2018; Collins & Butler, 2020; Cross & Swart, 2021). That said, the chapters collected in the "within" section (but not only in that section) testify that the types of employment status held by professionals are becoming more varied. Temporary employment, economically dependent self-employment, and other hybrid models are on the rise among professionals, who had previously not had to tolerate precarious jobs and poor working conditions. In detail, Chap. 2 by Bataille et al. shows that this phenomenon is due to the de-standardisation of employment in the academic field; Chap. 3 by Bonnin draws attention to the precarious situation of textile designers, once employed as salaried workers, and now exposed to global competition; and Chap. 6 by Parding and Jansson unveils the role of temporary agency work in public welfare professions (nurses and teachers). These chapters show that non-standard employment contracts are gaining ground in professional fields. While extensive research has been dedicated to examining corporate professionalism (see Muzio et al., 2011), more research is needed to explore the diverse work settings where various ways of performing professional work take place.

However, our findings go beyond how the debate over organisational logic has been developed in the field. It is not just a question of traditional partnerships versus professional service firms. Several of the chapters highlight the role of new actors that are entering the field in ways that have nothing to do with professional bodies (e.g. work platforms in Chap. 5; collaboration practices among professionals in Chap. 8; multi-professional mutual aid organisations in Chap. 10). Intermediate bodies in professions are growing in number and changing, opening new research directions beyond the traditional model of guild-like professions. The rise in new forms of working with one's peers, such as those in Chaps. 8 and 10, proves that professionals often form different types of partnerships to protect themselves from market risks, and not necessarily to protect a specific jurisdiction or pursue a professional project. Multi-professional organisations and plural intermediate bodies are realities that are rapidly taking root—confirming what has already been seen in the field (see Maestripieri & Cucca, 2018; Fleischmann et al., 2022).

The way that work settings are becoming differentiated has practical consequences for workers. There are growing inequalities among professionals who do the same job but have different employment conditions. Furthermore, inequalities are distributed along the traditional social fractures in intersectional ways: in the chapters here, young professionals (Chap. 2), women (Chap. 4), and migrant workers (Chap. 7) are those who experience the worst working conditions. The intersectional perspective—derived from gender studies (Crenshaw, 1991; Anthias, 2001)—helps us read what happens in conditions of multiple disadvantages and examine the consequences of diversity among professions and professionals (Choroszewicz & Adams, 2019). Even though professions are, in theory, more accessible than before, thanks to neo-liberal deregulation, poor working conditions are now reproduced for groups—such as women—that had previously been denied access. The worst conditions are experienced when multiple lines of disadvantage *intersect* in an individual, such as being young and being a woman. Chap. 4 by Insarauto et al. shows how young women give up on the male-centred organisational model because they find it impossible to reconcile work and family life. Chaps. 2 and 4 also show how forms of segregation within professions are reproduced based on gender (e.g. in Chap. 4, women specialising in family law) or by a contractual divide (e.g. in Chap. 2, young academics with precarious working conditions adapt themselves to whatever the academic market offers, without achieving a specialisation in teaching, research, or administration).

There is more. In Chaps. 3 and 5, for instance, technological change is the main driver behind the destabilisation of professional work settings. In the case of South African textile designers, the transformation of how they perform their work, with tasks that have shifted from crafting handmade designs to using computer-assisted techniques, has eroded the credentials previously requested in the sector, favouring practitioners that have IT skills. In the case of Chap. 5 by Arcidiacono et al., work platforms have replaced professional bodies and associations as the intermediate actors that clients address to hire the experts they need. In both cases, digitalisation creates a fracture between professionals who have the competencies to ride technological change (e.g. self-employed designers who sell their products on Etsy or Instagram) and those who see their working conditions worsening without being able to protect their status (e.g. professionals dealing with low-paid "gig" work on platforms).

In conclusion, the heterogeneity that emerges empirically *within* professions can be understood as the combined effect of two processes: the de-standardisation of employment (and, specifically, the deregulation of professional labour markets) and technological change in the form of digitalisation. These changes allow new social groups to enter the professions, which leads to the exclusionary processes triggered by social closure mechanisms now being replicated within professions.

4.2 The "between" Dimension

The second dimension is the "between" dimension. The analysis of this dimension looks at the multiple "geographies" of professions and professional groups, focusing on the institutional factors that influence their configurations in different contexts. What emerges is that professional systems are increasingly becoming "connective" systems (Noordegraaf, 2020), which are no longer governed by a triadic configuration of actors—state, university, and professional bodies (see Burrage & Torstendhal, 1990)—but involve multiple actors who play a regulatory role at different levels: local, national, and international.

Chapter 7 by Bédard et al. examines the case of foreign-trained professionals (doctors and engineers) and reveals that recognising their qualifications and competencies is not a prerogative of professional bodies but involves a chain of actors. Similarly, Chap. 9 by Parcerisa et al. shows how educational reforms are carried out by a variable geometry of institutional actors, depending on the specific configuration of professional systems. In addition, Chap. 10 by Lucciarini and Pulignano testifies that professionals—especially those working in flexible organisational domains, such as creatives—can become partners in a way that does not follow traditional patterns within given jurisdictions, but following their own contingent interests—based, for instance, on a shared work setting.

Clients also play a key role in determining how a profession operates. In this regard, the concept of "client professionalisation" was coined to mean that the needs of client organisations contribute to shaping professionalism (Salman, 2019). Following this line of reasoning, Chap. 8 by Choroszewicz demonstrates that clients influence professionalism even in an influential self-regulating profession such as law. Indeed, two of the five strategies the author identifies are developed by looking at the client's characteristics.

As highlighted by Chaps. 7 and 9, there is nevertheless a contradiction between systems of professions that are country-based and the globalised market of professional services. Multinational corporations, transnational projects, and boundaryless careers go beyond a state's regulation capacity and the reach of professional bodies, giving rise to new challenges that imply further regulation efforts at the international level as professional mobility increases. This calls into question professional power and the related capacity to put pressure on regulatory systems that had once been presided over by professional bodies, and which continue to be organised at the national or even the local level (Chap. 11).

Chapter 9 in particular shows how professionalism depends on the institutional system in which professionals are embedded, suggesting that organisational and market logics play different roles in different systems. The authors argue that processes of de-professionalisation and loss of professional autonomy might be at stake in professions and depend on the capacity of professionals to govern the deregulation process. Here, a new line of research emerges that calls attention to how the actors involved manage to translate the new public management into practice and sees this as a critical variable in understanding the possible negative outcomes of this process.

In brief, the empirical evidence provided in this section questions the centrality of the professional project, which is now challenged by neoliberal professionalism. Professions are now increasingly relying on the market and organisations as the loci of professional dominance. Hybridisation is key to interpreting these changes, and it is no longer possible to view professionalism as something separate from the influence exerted on it that comes from outside professional groups (Noordegraaf, 2020).

4.3 The "beyond" Dimension

The third dimension is the "beyond" dimension. Using this lens, we focus on the relationship between professions and society. Doing so allows us to understand how social change influences professions and, in turn, how professions contribute to shaping social change. As has been pointed out in the introduction (Chap. 1), two alternative approaches can be identified here. The first consists of looking at professionals as "institutional agents"—Scott's (2008) "lords of the dance"—who are committed to reproducing or changing institutions. The second implies looking at the role played by professionals in society at large, when they bend their professionalism to "higher" purposes such as engaging in activism or advocating for causes of public interest. In both cases, nevertheless, the discourse of professionalism is—more or less explicitly—laid out as a basis for claiming public recognition.

Falling into the first category, Chap. 11 by Adams shows how the regulation of professions, even self-regulating professions, has been redefined over the years as a result of the interaction of various stakeholders, including consumers, state actors, employers, and other experts—influenced in turn by social change. This contribution brings to light how rising distrust in professions, combined with the neo-liberal rhetoric, has facilitated the introduction of managerialist principles such as accountability, efficiency, and standardisation in professional domains. On the other hand, it provides evidence of the persisting power of professions which, in the long run, have proven capable of reshaping their relationship with the state to preserve and even extend their self-regulating role.

Chapters 12 and 13 have both adopted the second approach, although they focus on different professions and look at the phenomenon—professionals serving the public—from different perspectives. As a matter of fact, Chap. 12 by Gjata et al. attests that professionals (architects) organise around social problems in different ways, either expanding their professional work into other professional ecologies or translating social justice issues into their own profession. When addressing social problems, they develop relationships across institutional boundaries, which contribute to shaping their professionalism. On the other hand, Chap. 13 by Sedda and Husson, which examines the paradigmatic case of social media influencers—who engender a notion of professionalism that is based on reputation, market success, and personal relationships—shows how promoting social and political causes can itself be a path towards professionalisation. In this sense, professionals' social influence may favour self-interest over the public interest.

These cases suggest that professionals do not act in a vacuum but are subjected to external influences, which seem to support Noordegraaf's (2020) main argument about connective professionalism. However, if Chap. 11 and in part Chap. 12 bring evidence to confirm the objection made by Alvehus et al. (2021) that connective professionalism is mostly about strengthening professionalism's protective shields, Chap. 13 proves that, when driven by the market, professionalisation follows less constrictive paths, leading to the formation of communities of interest rather than communities of practice (as professional communities tend to be seen). Accordingly, emerging professions may be regarded as neo-liberal agents, understood as an *epistemic community*—namely "a network of professionals with recognised expertise and competence in a particular domain and an authoritative claim to policy-relevant knowledge within that domain or issue-area" (Haas, 1992: 3)—that promotes the neo-liberal project.

5 Moving Towards a Fuller Picture: Concluding Remarks and Future Directions

Coming to the end of this book, we are satisfied that we have met our challenge to prove the heuristic capacity of the WBB model as a flexible analytical framework that allows us to take advantage of theoretical pluralism and look at a complex phenomenon—professional change in its interaction with social change—from multiple angles. The collected chapters have examined many professions, either established or emerging ones, in different countries and regions of the world, adopting either case-study or comparative approaches. To do so, they have taken up different theoretical perspectives and used various notions of professionalism. Moreover, they have studied different processes of change and forms of professional change. This concluding chapter has tackled the job of putting the pieces together to identify thematic patterns and theoretical links: a challenge within a challenge.

Based on the empirical evidence provided in the 12 chapters, and the overall interpretation of it made in this final contribution, we can affirm that professionalism remains an essential conceptual tool in the study of professions in contemporary society. The flexibility of the term enables scholars to crystallise complex aspects of changing professional work in evocative synthetic definitions that are easy to use for interpretive purposes.

However, caution is required when using this concept, as it maintains an implicit normative value. In particular, when it is used to interpret the rise of emerging professions as the professionalisation of occupations at the margins of the professional field, based on market regulation, it may pose a twofold risk: on the one hand, it might have the paradoxical effect of providing new grounds for legitimising an established system of inequality that relies on the distinction between professions and occupations, implicitly admitting the superiority of the former over the latter; on the other hand, it might feed neo-liberal rhetoric and provide justifications for ever-increasing openness to the market, in turn bringing with it new forms of inequality.

The term neo-liberal professionalism that is used in this chapter might suffer from the same contradiction. The adjective "neo-liberal" makes the normative value of the notion of professionalism explicit. Indeed, neo-liberalism has assumed an ideological connotation over the years, suggesting that its possible uses in research mostly have critical purposes (see Boas & Gans-More, 2009; Venugopal, 2015). In our opinion, nevertheless, the benefits of using the term outweigh the risks, although we do need to clarify some points.

When we introduced this term, we did not intend to propose an alternative model of professionalism. As a matter of fact, this concept is compatible with the most well-known theoretical formulations that aim to interpret professional change, from Hanlon's (1996) commercialised professionalism to Noordegraaf's (2020) connective professionalism. Its added value is that it puts emphasis on the underlying regulatory model as the variable that determines the direction of change. Precisely, it assumes *deregulation* as the key to making professional labour markets more accessible, open, and diverse, at the cost of rising inequalities within and between professional groups, and with the risk of establishing an ambiguous relationship between professions and society. In other words, it indicates that professions are becoming increasingly differentiated in terms of employment and working conditions due to a decline in self-regulation and the growing role of market regulation. On the one hand, collegiate professions seem capable of defending their self-regulating power to a certain extent, but can no longer ensure their members prerogatives such as high earnings, autonomy, or job security, due to profound changes in their social composition (Alacevich et al., 2017; Maestripieri & Cucca, 2018). On the other hand, emerging professions follow atypical professionalisation paths and even embrace the ethos of counter-professionalisation (Avnoon & Sela-Sheffy, 2021), which means becoming exposed to market risks with no safety nets. Generally, professions today are less monadic. They are more open to the outside world but are more heterogeneous and unequal.

That said, referring to contemporary professionalism as *neo-liberal* professionalism forces us to reflect on a fundamental question. Collegiate professions are *institutionalised* systems of inequality based on exclusionary closure (professions versus occupations), while emerging professions are *market-driven* systems of inequality that rely primarily on reputational and relational mechanisms ("good" versus "bad" professionals). Both are systems that propagate inequality. Moreover, they intersect with other systems of inequality, such as age, gender, ethnicity, class, and many others. As such, they give rise to complex social structures. In light of this, it is not possible to say that one model is fairer than the other. A fruitful way of addressing the problem of inequalities in professions might be to go back to how they originate in regulatory processes.

References

Abbott, A. (1988). *The system of professions: An essay on the division of expert labour*. University of Chicago Press.

Alacevich, F., Bellini, A., & Tonarelli, A. (2017). *Una professione plurale. Il caso dell'avvocatura fiorentina*. Firenze University press.

Alvehus, J., Avnoon, N., & Oliver, A. L. (2021). "It's complicated": Professional opacity, duality, and ambiguity—A response to Noordegraaf (2020). *Journal of Professions and Organization, 8*(2), 200–213. https://doi.org/10.1093/jpo/joab006

Anthias, F. (2001). The material and the symbolic in theorizing social stratification: Issues of gender, ethnicity and class. *The British Journal of Sociology, 52*(3), 367–390. https://doi.org/10.1080/00071310120071106

Avnoon, N., & Sela-Sheffy, R. (2021). Counter-professionalization as an occupational status strategy: The production of professionalism in Israeli child-care

workers' identity work. *Journal of Professions and Organization, 8*(3), 311–328. https://doi.org/10.1093/jpo/joab014
Bell, D. (1973). *The coming of the post-industrial society: A venture in social forecasting*. Basic Books.
Boas, T. C., & Gans-More, J. (2009). Neoliberalism: From new liberal philosophy to anti-liberal slogan. *Studies in Comparative International Development, 44*(2), 137–161. https://doi.org/10.1007/s12116-009-9040-5
Burrage, M., & Torstendhal, R. (Eds.). (1990). *Professions in theory and history. Rethinking the study of the professions*. Sage.
Choroszewicz, M., & Adams, T. L. (2019). *Gender, age and inequality in the professions*. Routledge.
Collins, D., & Butler, N. (2020). Success and failure in professional projects: The nature, contours and limits of consulting professionalism. *British Journal of Management, 31*(3), 457–469. https://doi.org/10.1111/1467-8551.12331
Crenshaw, K. (1991). Mapping the margins: Intersectionality, identity politics, and violence against women of color. *Stanford Law Review, 43*(6), 1241–1299. https://doi.org/10.2307/1229039
Cross, D., & Swart, J. (2021). Professional fluidity: Reconceptualising the professional status of self-employed neo-professionals. *Organization Studies, 42*(11), 1699–1720. Artn0170840620964985.
Drucker, P. F. (1968). *The age of discontinuity: Guidelines to our changing society*. Heinemann.
Evetts, J. (2006). Short note: The sociology of professional groups: New directions. *Current Sociology, 54*(1), 133–143. https://doi.org/10.1177/0011392106057161
Evetts, J. (2011). A new professionalism? Challenges and opportunities. *Current Sociology, 59*(4), 406–422. https://doi.org/10.1177/0011392111402585
Fleischmann, A., Holck, L., Liu, H., Muhr, S. L., & Murgia, A. (2022). Organizing solidarity in difference: Challenges, achievements, and emerging imaginaries. *Organization, 29*(2), 233–246. https://doi.org/10.1177/13505084221083907
Freidson, E. (2001). *Professionalism, the third logic: On the practice of knowledge*. Polity.
Haas, P. M. (1992). Introduction: Epistemic communities and international policy coordination. *International Organization, 46*(1), 1–35. https://doi.org/10.1017/S0020818300001442

Hanlon, G. (1996). "Casino capitalism" and the rise of the "commercialised" service class—An examination of the accountant. *Critical Perspectives on Accounting, 7*(3), 339–363. https://doi.org/10.1006/cpac.1996.0038

Hood, C. (1991). A public management for all seasons? *Public Administration, 69*(1), 3–19. https://doi.org/10.1111/j.1467-9299.1991.tb00779.x

Machlup, F. (1962). *The production and distribution of knowledge in United States*. Princeton University Press.

Maestripieri, L. (2016). Professionalization at work: The case of Italian management consultants. *Ephemera. Theory & Politics in Organization, 16*(2), 33–54.

Maestripieri, L. (2019). Fragmented fields: Professionalisms and work settings in Italian management consultancy. *Journal of Professions and Organization, 6*(3), 357–376. https://doi.org/10.1093/jpo/joz011

Maestripieri, L., & Cucca, R. (2018). Small is beautiful? Emerging organizational strategies among Italian professionals. *Canadian Review of Sociology, 55*(33), 362–384. https://doi.org/10.1111/cars.12208

Mudge, S. L. (2008). What is neo-liberalism? *Socio-Economic Review, 6*(4), 703–731. https://doi.org/10.1093/ser/mwn016

Muzio, D., Hodgson, D., Faulconbridge, J. R., Beaverstock, J., & Hall, S. (2011). Towards corporate professionalization: The case of project management, management consultancy and executive search. *Current Sociology, 59*(4), 443–464. https://doi.org/10.1177/0011392111402587

Noordegraaf, M. (2007). From "pure" to "hybrid" professionalism: Present-day professionalism in ambiguous public domains. *Administration & Society, 39*(6), 761–785. https://doi.org/10.1177/0095399707304434

Noordegraaf, M. (2020). Protective or connective professionalism? How connected professionals can (still) act as autonomous and authoritative experts. *Journal of Professions and Organization, 7*(2), 205–223. https://doi.org/10.1093/jpo/joaa011

Osborne, D., & Gaebler, T. (1992). *Reinventing government: How the entrepreneurial Spirit is transforming the public sector*. Addison Wesley.

Parding, K., Bellini, A., & Maestripieri, L. (2021). Heterogeneity among professions and professionals. *Professions and Professionalism, 11*(1), e4398. https://doi.org/10.7577/pp.4398

Pollitt, C. (1993). *Managerialism and the public services: Cuts or cultural change in the 1990s?* Blackwell.

Reed, M. I. (2018). Elites, professions, and the neoliberal state: Critical points of intersection and contention. *Journal of Professions and Organization, 5*(3), 297–312. https://doi.org/10.1093/jpo/joy010

Salman, S. (2019). Towards a "client professionalization" process? The case of the institutionalization of executive coaching in France. *Journal of Professions and Organization, 6*(3), 286–303. https://doi.org/10.1093/jpo/joz012
Scott, W. R. (2008). Lords of the dance: Professionals as institutional agents. *Organization Studies, 29*(2), 219–238. https://doi.org/10.1177/0170840607088151
Touraine, A. (1969). *La société post-industrielle.* Denoël-Gonthier.
Venugopal, R. (2015). Neoliberalism as concept. *Economy and Society, 44*(2), 165–187. https://doi.org/10.1080/03085147.2015.1013356

Correction to: Professionalism and Social Change

Lara Maestripieri and Andrea Bellini

Correction to:

Chapters 1 and 10 in: L. Maestripieri, A. Bellini (eds.), *Professionalism and Social Change*, https://doi.org/10.1007/978-3-031-31278-6

Chapter 1 Introduction: Within, Between, Beyond—A Multi-dimensional Approach to the Study of Professionalism and Social Change, written by Andrea Bellini and Lara Maestripieri, and Chapter 10 Inequalities in Neo-mutualistic Professional Organisations: The Boundary Work of Creative Workers in Italy, written by Silvia Lucciarini and Valeria Pulignano, were previously published non-open access. They have been changed to open access under a CC BY 4.0 license and the copyright holder updated to 'The Author(s)' and and the chapter is forthwith distributed under a Creative Commons Attribution 4.0 International

The updated version of these chapters can be found at
https://doi.org/10.1007/978-3-031-31278-6_1
https://doi.org/10.1007/978-3-031-31278-6_10

© The Author(s) 2024

L. Maestripieri, A. Bellini (eds.), *Professionalism and Social Change*,
https://doi.org/10.1007/978-3-031-31278-6_15

License (http://creativecommons.org/licenses/by/4.0/), which permits use, sharing, adaptation, distribution and reproduction in any medium or format, as long as you give appropriate credit to the original author(s) and the source, provide a link to the Creative Commons licence and indicate if changes were made. The images or other third-party material in this chapters are included in the chapter's Creative Commons licence, unless indicated otherwise in a credit line to the material. If material is not included in the chapter's Creative Commons licence and your intended use is not permitted by statutory regulation or exceeds the permitted use, you will need to obtain permission directly from the copyright holder.

Open Access This chapter is licensed under the terms of the Creative Commons Attribution 4.0 International License (http://creativecommons.org/licenses/by/4.0/), which permits use, sharing, adaptation, distribution and reproduction in any medium or format, as long as you give appropriate credit to the original author(s) and the source, provide a link to the Creative Commons license and indicate if changes were made.

The images or other third party material in this chapter are included in the chapter's Creative Commons license, unless indicated otherwise in a credit line to the material. If material is not included in the chapter's Creative Commons license and your intended use is not permitted by statutory regulation or exceeds the permitted use, you will need to obtain permission directly from the copyright holder.

FSC
www.fsc.org
MIX
Papier | Fördert
gute Waldnutzung
FSC® C083411

Kolibri 360 GmbH
Ferdinand-Jühlke-Straße 7
99095 Erfurt, Deutschland
produktsicherheit@kolibri360.de